Provincial
I N C A

Provincial

INCA

ARCHAEOLOGICAL

AND ETHNOHISTORICAL

ASSESSMENT OF THE

IMPACT OF THE INCA STATE

EDITED BY MICHAEL A. MALPASS

University of Iowa Press Iowa City

University of Iowa Press, Iowa City 52242

Copyright © 1993 by the University of Iowa Press

Printed on acid-free paper

Library of Congress Cataloging-in-Publication Data

Provincial Inca: archaeological and ethnohistorical assessment of the impact of the
    Inca state / edited by Michael A. Malpass.

p.   cm.

Includes bibliographical references and index.

ISBN 0-87745-426-4 (pbk.)

1. Incas—Politics and government.   2. Peru—Antiquities.   3. Andes Region—
    Antiquities.   I. Malpass, Michael A.

F3429.3.P67   1993

985'.01—dc20   93-30296

                                                                          CIP

97 96 95 94 93 P 5 4 3 2 1

Dedicated to Susanne and to

the memory of our firstborn

CONTENTS

ix   Preface

1   Chapter 1
Provincial Inca Archaeology and Ethnohistory:
An Introduction
MICHAEL A. MALPASS

I. Studies in Provincial Inca Archaeology

17   Chapter 2
A Summary of the Inca Occupation of Huamachuco
JOHN R. TOPIC AND THERESA LANGE TOPIC

44   Chapter 3
. . . And He Said in the Time of the Ynga,
They Paid Tribute and Served the Ynga
SUE GROSBOLL

77   Chapter 4
The Inca Occupation of the Province of
Andamarca Lucanas, Peru
KATHARINA J. SCHREIBER

117   Chapter 5
The Identification of Inca Posts and Roads
from Catarpe to Río Frío, Chile
THOMAS F. LYNCH

II. Toward an Archaeological and Ethnohistorical Synthesis

145   Chapter 6
The Provinces in the Heartland: Stylistic Variation
and Architectural Innovation near Inca Cuzco
SUSAN A. NILES

177 Chapter 7
Finding a Fit: Archaeology and Ethnohistory
of the Incas
CATHERINE J. JULIEN

234 Chapter 8
Variability in the Inca State: Embracing a
Wider Perspective
MICHAEL A. MALPASS

245 Bibliography

269 Index

PREFACE

This book began as a symposium at the Society for American Archaeology meetings held in Toronto in 1987. The focus of that symposium was to evaluate how accurate the ethnohistorical documents are concerning the nature of Inca control in provincial areas, using archaeological data as an independent means of verification. Each of the original participants, most of whom have contributed to this volume, was an archaeologist who had worked in a particular part of the Andes and had a regional perspective to bring to this question.

What came out of the symposium was the consensus that there was more variability in the nature of Inca control than was generally believed. There was sufficient enthusiasm about publishing the results that I agreed to act as editor. Catherine Julien's essay was the only one solicited that was not part of the original symposium, and hers was included to provide a larger framework for interpretation. In what I feel is a typical gesture of collegiality for Andeanists, each of the authors agreed to allow her to use his or her essay for this purpose.

The result of this collaboration has been well worth the effort of bringing the book together. Not only has a significant amount of original data concerning the Incas been brought together in a single volume, but a much larger vision of the Inca empire has been achieved, a vision that begins to address some of the larger questions about Inca control that have developed in recent years: How accurate are the ethnohistorical accounts of the Inca empire? How variable was Inca control in the provinces they conquered? What actual effects did this conquest have on indigenous people? How did existing sociopolitical factors influence the nature of the Incas' presence in the provinces?

The effort of bringing this volume to fruition involved various kinds of decisions and compromises regarding orthography. Both Spanish and Quechua terms are common in any study of the Incas, and it is necessary to explain the rationale for the spellings presented. I have used the hispanicized versions of most Quechua terms because they are more generally recognized by lay readers. The notable exceptions to this rule are the terms *kancha* and *kallanka*, which are more gener-

ally spelled in the Quechua form. I have also used the Spanish render-
ings of the names of the Inca royal families.

Following Niles (1987), I have used the Spanish spelling for place
names and archaeological site names when these are the most commonly used versions on Peruvian maps or in the literature. The exception to the use of Spanish orthography is if a site name is in Quechua.
Thus, for example, we will speak of Inca tambos, but in the Andamarca Lucanas region, Katharina J. Schreiber talks about the site of
Inka Tampu. While this double usage may seem somewhat inconsistent, it does have the effect of minimizing the variations in spelling in
the literature while allowing the reader to identify sites discussed in
other scholarly reports.

Regarding the area around the modern city of Huánuco, which is
discussed by both Sue Grosboll and Catherine Julien, the use of the
word "Chupachos" refers to the Inca province of that name; the word
"Chupachu" refers to the specific ethnic group that lived within that
province along with others, such as the Quero.

A final comment on the orthography: All problems with the spellings
are ultimately mine. I decided which of alternative spellings should be
used (for example, Tahuantinsuyo instead of Tahuantinsuyu), and I am
sure my contributors will be unhappy at times with the choices I made.
However, the volume achieves a uniformity in word usage that I hope
makes up for whatever unhappiness this may cause.

As editor of this volume, I owe a large debt of gratitude to many
people. To the contributors, I extend my gratitude for the (generally!)
timely fashion in which they met deadlines for revisions, and I appreciate the patience which all exhibited in the completion of the book.
To the two anonymous reviewers who read and commented on early
versions, I offer my appreciation and the evidence here that their comments were taken into account in the final product. To Tom Lynch,
Catherine Julien, and Dan Sandweiss, I also extend my heartfelt thanks
for their comments on early drafts of my chapters. Catherine Julien
suffered through many changes in her chapter resulting both from
changes in the clientele of the book and in the revisions of the individual authors.

Several individuals and organizations at Ithaca College should also
be recognized. The Department of Anthropology provided logistical
and personal support for the completion of this book, and Lars Fogelin
drafted the final versions of the figure for my introductory chapter and

the map facing page 1. Fred Estabrook of the Instructional Resources Center provided his expertise and materials in the completion of the final illustrations for my essay and Julien's.

I owe the most to my wife, Susanne Kessemeier, for her unflagging support in this undertaking. She has been helpful in various ways, but mostly in providing a constant source of encouragement in the completion of this book.

Lastly, our deep gratitude goes to the anonymous donors who allowed for the publication of the four color plates.

Provincial
INCA

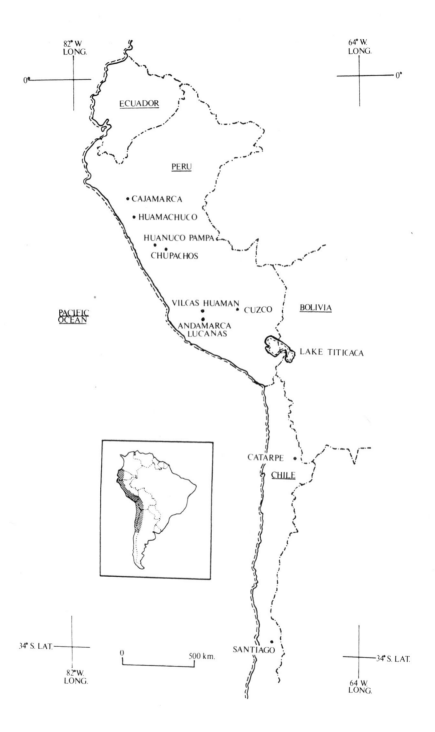

MICHAEL A. MALPASS

PROVINCIAL INCA ARCHAEOLOGY

AND ETHNOHISTORY: AN INTRODUCTION

INTRODUCTION

The nature of Tahuantinsuyo, the Inca empire, has been a subject of
interest since the arrival of the Spanish conquistadores in 1532. One
reason for this interest is its sheer size: the empire extended from
northern Ecuador to central Chile. At its largest, the Inca empire
spanned more than 3,000 kilometers (32 degrees of latitude) and en-
compassed an enormous variety of environments, from coastal deserts
to high-altitude grasslands. Perhaps most impressive, the conquest of
this territory was achieved in less than a century by people who had
neither wheeled vehicles nor animals that could be ridden.

The cultural diversity of the peoples conquered by the Incas was
also impressive. The Incas were able to overcome cultures that varied
tremendously, from agriculture-based polities with an elaborate material foundation, like the Chimu of the North Coast of Peru, to socially
and culturally marginal communities of fisher folk, like the Uru of the
southern Lake Titicaca region. All were incorporated into a strongly
hierarchical sociopolitical system that developed as the empire spread
during the Late Horizon (A.D. 1438–1532).

The nature of the Inca presence in the conquered areas is the subject
of this book, which has two distinct but related focuses. The first is
analytical, aimed at evaluating the ways in which we understand the

Inca empire and its relationships with conquered peoples. The two principal sources of information on the Incas and provincial peoples are ethnohistorical documents and archaeology. Each uses a different data base and provides different kinds of information, yet they are linked both by the common subject matter and by a common means of analysis (Netherly 1988a: 257–262). The essays in this book look at the kinds of information available through each source for different areas. The results indicate that the two sources used together can provide a much more thorough description of the structure and organization of the Inca empire than either one taken by itself. While this is certainly not a new idea, it gains considerable support through the specific ways in which the authors use the two sets of data.

The second focus of the book is empirical and derives from the first. This focus provides specific archaeological means for identifying the presence of the Incas in provincial areas. The authors draw on several distinct kinds of evidence in order to indicate the changes that occurred as a result of the Inca expansion. An important result of the discussions concerning these two focuses is the presentation of new data on how the Inca state incorporated ethnic groups into its empire. The evidence supports an emerging picture of the Inca polity as flexible and heterogeneous, responding to the challenges of integrating groups that varied tremendously in size and sociopolitical complexity (Morris 1988a: 245).

HISTORY OF RESEARCH

Until the middle part of the twentieth century, virtually all our information concerning the Incas and the peoples of the provinces of the Inca empire came from the early Spanish chroniclers' accounts, with archaeology more focused on pre–Late Horizon occupations (Morris 1988a: 233). This dominance of the ethnohistorical record over archaeology has continued to this day, although the archaeology of the Incas and contemporaneous groups has contributed increasingly over the past five decades. Still, information on Late Horizon developments from archaeological research falls far short of the knowledge obtained from ethnohistorical records. Both ethnohistorical research and archaeological investigations on the Inca empire have evolved over time, and it is instructive to look at how each has changed in order to understand our present state of knowledge. It is particularly useful to note how developments in ethnohistorical research have influenced subsequent archaeological investigations.

D'Altroy (1987: 2–3) has outlined three major developments in Inca ethnohistory that have influenced our thinking about the nature of the empire. Until the mid-1950s, our views were generally dominated by the descriptions of the Inca state given by post-Conquest writers such as Cieza de León, Cobo, Polo de Ondegardo, and Guaman Poma. These general descriptions accentuated the idea of a uniform, centrally controlled polity of remarkable homogeneity. While the nature of the empire varied with the author, from feudal to socialist to totalitarian, the emphasis was on the uniformity (D'Altroy 1987: 2–3). Even Rowe's now classic "Inca Culture at the Time of the Spanish Conquest" (1946) implies a relative uniformity in Inca culture across the empire.

Early archaeological research on the Incas was often focused on particular sites, notably Machu Picchu and Cuzco (Bingham 1930; Valcárcel 1934–35). A more regional approach to Inca archaeology became evident with the work of Rowe (1944) around Cuzco and Tschopik (1946) near Lake Titicaca. These reports provided the first thorough descriptions of material culture in the Inca provinces. The latter study was also important for its descriptions of remains from an area outside of the Inca heartland.

A shift in ethnohistorical research occurred with the completion of Murra's (1980 [1956]) dissertation on the Inca economy, which indicated that the Incas used preexisting local political and economic structures in their governance (D'Altroy 1987: 3), although they reoriented the structures to their own purposes (Julien 1988a). Murra suggested that the relationship between the Inca bureaucracy and the conquered peoples was modeled on the relationships that already existed between local rulers and their subjects. At the same time that Murra's research was beginning to have an impact on Inca studies, Zuidema (1964) undertook another approach, focusing on the relationships among Inca cosmology, religion, and sociopolitical structure (D'Altroy 1987: 4).

Archaeology, too, during this period began to identify variability within the Inca empire, both as a result of Murra's work (Morris 1966, 1967) and independently (Menzel 1959). Menzel's study was the first to emphasize the utility of combining both ethnohistorical and archaeological work, as well as showing that archaeology alone could provide important data (Morris 1988a: 235). Investigators began to be concerned more with identifying the systemic nature of Inca culture than with identifying only specific aspects.

A final development in Inca ethnohistory began in the 1970s with a shift to the use of regional documents, such as the *visitas* (administrative surveys) for Chupachos and Chucuito (Ortíz de Zúñiga 1967, 1972; Diez de San Miguel 1964) or the documents pertaining to central Peruvian coastal societies identified by Rostworowski de Diez Canseco (1970, 1977, 1981). These documents, discussed in more detail below, indicated a greater variability in Inca provincial economic organization than had been suggested previously. Additional regional studies expanding this view have come from Hidalgo (1972), Netherly (1978), and Salomon (1986), to name just a few.

During the 1970s and continuing to the present, archaeologists have exhibited a greater tendency to use such regional documents to inform their research. Part of the reason for the shift has to do with the more explicit scientific approach to hypothesis testing that resulted from the development of the New Archaeology (Binford and Binford 1968; Watson, LeBlanc, and Redman 1971). The more detailed information from documents could be used to phrase hypotheses about the expansion of the Inca empire that could then be tested with archaeological data. Nonetheless, archaeological research incorporating these ethnohistorical documents necessarily has been restricted to the areas covered by them, notably Huánuco (Morris and Thompson 1985), the altiplano (Julien 1978), and the central and northern coasts of Peru (Dillehay 1976, 1977; Morris 1988b; Netherly 1978; Sandweiss 1989).

Additional archaeology of the Inca empire, whether the heartland or the provinces, is surprisingly scant. After Rowe's pioneering efforts in the Cuzco area, relatively little was done until the 1970s and 1980s, when Dwyer (1971), Niles (1987), and others provided additional information on that region, with work by Kendall (1974a, 1976, 1978) and Bauer (1990) in nearby areas.

Outside the Inca heartland, projects contributing to our understanding of Inca archaeology have been few as well. One of the most extensive research efforts involving a region before and during the Inca empire is the Upper Mantaro Archaeological Research Project (UMARP) of Earle et al. (1980, 1987; see also D'Altroy and Earle 1985). Through detailed survey, excavations, and analyses, this project has been able to identify the political and social changes effected by the Incas, elaborating on the more scanty information from the ethnohistory of the region. Hyslop's research on the Inca road system and settlement planning (1984, 1990) are other notable studies that have provided new insights into the archaeology of Tahuantinsuyo.

Thus we see that research on the Inca expansion has moved toward greater and greater synthesis of archaeological and ethnohistorical information and that projects employing both sources have given us a more thorough understanding of the nature of the Inca empire. What has not yet occurred is a broad analysis of such projects over an area wider than a single region, with the intent of evaluating the impact of the Inca empire as a whole. Such an analysis is the principal goal of this volume.

ANALYTICAL FOCUS

A wide variety of written documents discuss the Inca empire or the Spanish colonial policies pertaining to the conquered Inca state. Certainly the most important to our general understanding of the history and organization of the empire are the chronicles, historical narratives, and administrative documents written by the earliest Spaniards to come to South America. These documents were until recently the exclusive sources of information and thus have greatly influenced all thought about the Incas. For an excellent review of these sources, see Rowe (1946).

The chronicles (e.g., Anonymous Conqueror 1929; Estete 1918; Xérez 1917) chiefly describe the Incas, whose political hegemony had reached a crisis just before the appearance of the Spaniards. The authors of the chronicles had actually witnessed Inca institutions in operation or talked with people who knew them. Historical narratives, like those of Cieza de León and Sarmiento de Gamboa, often give accounts of earlier times that draw on Inca historical tradition. The reports of particular administrators shed light on some of the differences between Inca and Spanish organization. They often describe the basic organization of the empire, how particular provinces were annexed, and whether the local populations actively resisted being incorporated into the empire. Administrative documentation—visitas, for example—provides details about the political and economic relationships of specific areas, such as Chupachos and Chucuito, to the Inca empire (Ortíz de Zúñiga 1967; Diez de San Miguel 1964). Litigation from the early

Colonial Period gives clues to the Incas' movement of people around the empire, and what people provided to the Incas (AHC AR 1540, AR 1570 [cited in Wachtel 1982]; AGN, PRyU, L2, C25 [cited in Espinoza 1973]; AGN, TP, L13, C348, 1590 [1571–1590] [cited in La Lone and La Lone 1987]).

How can we evaluate the accuracy of the ethnohistorical records of the Inca empire? All of these documents have limitations. First, with the chronicles and historical narratives we are at the mercy of individuals' accounts of behaviors and institutions that were no doubt very foreign to them and thus may not be accurately described. It is certainly the case that an individual's background influenced his or her perceptions of what was seen (e.g., Barnes and Fleming 1989). In addition, as Rowe (1946: 193) pointed out, many early Spanish writers copied from each other, with distortions introduced both by carelessness and by deliberate prejudice. Although cross-checking different sources can clarify ambiguities and identify inaccuracies, we are still left with a degree of uncertainty concerning the true nature of described behaviors and institutions. The situation is exacerbated when a particular piece of information is mentioned in only one source.

The same problems exist for other colonial documents, such as the visitas, and for litigation in which the individuals involved, both Spaniards and natives, might have had ulterior motives that influenced the information they gave. Local informants might have attempted to minimize tribute burdens to the Spaniards by giving incorrect census data and productivity figures. Local leaders might have attempted to grab power over rivals by claiming greater prestige under the ruling Inca than they really had (Murra 1982: 250). Finally, the Spanish officials themselves could have manipulated information for their own benefit. For example, Juan de Ulloa Mogollón (1965), *corregidor* (Spanish magistrate) of the Collaguas province in the department of Arequipa, provided a good description of this province and its resources in 1586, suggesting that little agriculture was evident, but much herding. Yet five years later, we see him accused of illegally selling maize grown by the natives of the valley (Crespo 1977).

Another problem with the historical documents is a certain vagueness with regard to details of place or person. For example, early writers discussed places along the Inca road in different areas, and often different chroniclers recorded different locations or names. A more fundamental problem involves the exact locations of the settlements mentioned in the texts. Because of the large-scale displacements of people that have occurred since the Conquest, the positions of the settlements are often difficult to determine today.

Litigation is frequently very specific about the people and the place involved, and one wonders if the system that is read between the lines of such documents is particular to that place or more general in nature (Pease 1982). Sometimes the information presented is very general; other times it is very specific. Usually, if there are many documents or very specific documents for an area, such as for the Chupachos region, we can have greater confidence in the information provided.

Given the above-mentioned problems, it is fortunate that other means exist to expand on the information provided by the ethnohistorical documents. One option is through archaeological research. With regard to the Incas, this method of gathering information has always been very important. Archaeology provides data of a fundamentally different nature from those of ethnohistory; in addition, it can often provide information about aspects of culture seldom or never mentioned by early writers, such as site layouts, subsistence, and technology.

The essays presented in this collection attempt to evaluate the ethnohistorical record using archaeological data. In all cases, the archaeology provides information additional to that included in the documents, thus allowing more insight into the administration of the Inca empire. For example, in the Huamachuco area, ethnohistorical sources indicate that the main Inca road passed through the province and that the provincial capital and several *tambos* (way stations) were located along it. Yet nowhere is a precise position for the capital or the tambos given. John R. Topic and Theresa Lange Topic determined through archaeological research that the present town of Huamachuco is located on top of the Inca capital, and they identified several probable tambos as well. Thomas F. Lynch identified Catarpe as a probable Inca center, not just a tambo, along the Inca road in Chile, elaborating on the sparse historical records for this area. Katharina J. Schreiber identified a considerable range of goods and services that the Andamarca Lucanas provided to the Incas, although the ethnohistorical accounts state that they supplied only litter bearers for the Inca emperor.

The data provided by archaeology alone are also incomplete. Early documents from Huamachuco indicate the presence of lowland colonists in the area, but that fact has not been documented archaeologically. And there is little chance of our discovering evidence of the emperor's litter bearers in the archaeological record.

What these essays do is provide more detailed pictures for several provinces that were previously either not known or poorly known. In so doing, they allow us to evaluate the ethnohistorical sources using the archaeological record and thereby reach a greater understanding than either source could provide independently. This better understanding comes at the regional level, where the studies give a broader view of Inca control as it was manifest in several different regions, and also at the imperial level, where they allow a better view of the administrative variability in the empire than do the historical documents alone.

EMPIRICAL FOCUS

Despite the detailed studies that have been undertaken, exactly how the Incas incorporated such a diversity of sociopolitical units into a single empire is still poorly understood (Julien 1988a: 257; Le Vine 1987: 14; Murra 1982: 238; Pease 1982). Were large polities such as the Chimu incorporated in the same fashion and according to the same rules as small ones like the Uru? Were there distinctions among different areas with respect to imperial administration? Was the core area around the Inca capital of Cuzco organized differently than conquered areas at a distance from Cuzco? While recent archaeological and ethnohistorical research has begun to answer some of these questions, much remains to be learned about the specific ways that the Incas incorporated conquered peoples into their empire.

One of the major problems confronting archaeologists who are interested in discerning the nature of Inca influence on local cultures is differentiating the two. An important part of this problem is identifying exactly what is Inca culture. How can we recognize it archaeologically?

As mentioned, the classic summary of Inca culture was presented by Rowe in 1946, drawing both on ethnohistorical sources and on his earlier archaeological work in the Cuzco area (Rowe 1944, 1946). In these articles, Rowe identified a series of characteristics of Inca culture, as it is found in both Cuzco and the provinces. Some of these characteristics have been elaborated by subsequent researchers (e.g., Bauer 1990; Gasparini and Margolies 1980; Hyslop 1990; Kendall 1974a,

1974b, 1985). Several distinctive features of Inca material culture may be useful for archaeological identification of the Incas in other areas. These features include architecture, settlement planning, engineering works, ceramics, and, to a lesser extent, other artifacts. It is instructive to review briefly the descriptions of these aspects of Inca culture so as to provide an archaeological baseline for the articles that follow.

Concerning architecture in the Cuzco area, most houses were rectangular, single-roomed, and made of fieldstone or adobe with gables and thatched roofs. The majority had only one story, although two- and even three-story buildings are known. Doors, windows, and interior wall niches were often included and were usually of a trapezoidal shape. The better-class houses were plastered to conceal the rough stone construction. Typically, the houses were built in groups enclosed by a high wall with a single entrance. The houses, which could vary in number, were arranged around a central courtyard. This compound constituted the *kancha,* and appears to have been used for both residential purposes and special activities by both lower and upper classes (Hyslop 1990: 17).

Another basic Inca architectural form was the *kallanka,* a long rectangular hall of one room. Rowe's discussions do not include this form, perhaps because the best examples are found outside of Cuzco (Hyslop 1990: 18). These structures probably served multiple purposes, but what those purposes were is not well known.

The best-known Inca architecture is the public variety, constructed for state-related purposes according to careful plans. Many, but not all, of these structures were built with the finely worked stones that give Inca architecture its fame and distinction. State buildings of worked stone are common in the Cuzco area, reflecting its importance as the Inca capital and center of government, but they are often rare in provincial areas and restricted to special buildings (Hyslop 1990: 12; Lynch, this volume). Finely worked stone was also used in the construction of private residences and structures belonging to the highest nobility in Inca society (Niles 1987).

Regarding settlement planning, Rowe (1946: 228) indicated that the Incas practiced a policy of relocating conquered peoples to towns laid out by imperial architects. The ideal town was arranged in blocks containing kancha-type enclosures. Where public buildings were needed, they were constructed in the Inca style, as just discussed. Other new settlements were constructed to serve Inca administrative needs, such

Figure 1.1. Inca ceramic forms (adapted from Rowe 1944: fig. 8).

as Huánuco Pampa. Hyslop (1990) has discussed in detail the nature and variability of Inca settlements, and little can be added to his excellent study. Worth emphasizing are his comments that often it is difficult to identify an Inca presence from site plans alone, since the Incas accommodated their needs to local political, technological, and social situations. Thus, though sometimes Inca settlements can be readily identified by architectural forms (kanchas, kallankas, buildings made of finely cut stone, etc.), at other times it is necessary to rely on different aspects of material culture. The essays in this volume give ample support to this statement.

Certainly another of the hallmarks of Inca culture is pottery, one of the most durable materials recovered at any archaeological site. Inca pottery is highly distinctive in both form and decoration. The two most common forms are a shallow plate with one or two handles and a long-necked jar with pointed base and two handles located low on the body (the so-called *aryballos* form). The former was used for eating and the latter for storage and transport of liquids (Rowe 1946: 243). Other forms include pitchers, cooking or serving vessels, goblets, footed vessels, and braziers (fig. 1.1).

Inca pottery is most commonly decorated with repetitive geometric designs, such as triangles and diamonds, done in lustrous black, red, and white mineral pigments. Other decorative elements include straight and wavy lines, zigzags, and stylized fern patterns (Rowe 1944).

Other artifacts made and used by the Incas are less useful for identification purposes, typically because so few examples exist. Cloth artifacts and metal objects fall in this category.

The Incas are duly famous for their engineering works, including roads, bridges, agricultural terraces, and irrigation canals. The extensive Inca road system formed the infrastructural support of the empire and as such is one potential means of identifying an Inca presence. As Hyslop (1984: 3) noted in his study of the road system, however, it is not always easy to identify a road as Incaic without associated structures and/or settlements built or used by the Incas. Thus, using the road as an indicator of an Inca presence requires other forms of evidence, either archaeological or, in special circumstances, ethnohistorical. The same problem exists for the identification of Inca bridges. While few, if any, bridges built by the Incas remain today (cf. Thompson and Murra 1966), it is sometimes possible to identify the foundations for such structures at river crossings by distinctive stonework or artifacts.

Finally, the Incas considerably expanded agricultural systems in many parts of the Andes in order to maximize productivity, especially of maize. In the highlands, they often constructed large terrace systems that were fed by sophisticated irrigation networks. While the use of such constructions for identifying the Incas has not been widespread, in some instances it has been possible to differentiate terraces associated with Inca activities from earlier ones (Malpass 1987; Schreiber 1987). Again, however, it is often necessary to identify the cultural affiliation of the terraces by other means, such as associated ceramics or architecture.

At a fundamental level, then, Inca influence can be identified by the appearance of distinctive architectural forms (kanchas or kallankas), stonework, and ceramics. When these aspects are associated with other kinds of material culture (such as roads, terraces, and canals), then the latter can also be identified as Inca-authorized. The essays in this volume address the ways that these various characteristics can be used to identify the signs of Inca control or influence in the provinces.

An important contribution of this book is the case presented for variability in the Inca administration of provinces. The evidence, carefully gleaned from both archaeological research and ethnohistorical sources, indicates that the interaction between the Incas and subject peoples was often diverse and complex.

The empirical evidence discussed falls into two categories. The first is the specific evidence for an Inca influence in provincial regions. The essays in this volume indicate that Inca material culture varied widely in the different areas of their influence: In some places, Inca pottery and architecture, including entirely new sites built by the state, are both widespread and prominent. Such is the case, for example, in northern Chile, as discussed in the chapter by Lynch. In other areas, evidence for Inca influence is concentrated in a single center, such as Huánuco Pampa, with evidence outside the center sparse and more difficult to find, for example, in the Chupachos region discussed by Sue Grosboll.

Another aspect of identifying Inca culture deals with the ways that material remains of local people during the Inca empire can be differentiated from the remains of the same groups before the Inca expansion. The authors' explicit statements of how one can differentiate the cultural remains of the two time periods will be very helpful to researchers elsewhere. This problem has hampered the delineation of a cultural chronology for the period before the Inca expansion in several areas of the Andes, for example, the Colca Valley (Malpass 1987). The articles by Grosboll, Schreiber, and the Topics address this issue specifically.

A final contribution of this volume, which is an incidental by-product of the analytical and empirical focuses discussed above, is a significant amount of new information concerning the Incas and the nature of their expansion. By evaluating the ethnohistorical sources using archaeological data, the authors have identified new ideas about the Incas in their respective study areas. We now have an expanded data base on which to develop further research which will enable us to understand more clearly the nature of the Inca empire.

ORGANIZATION OF THE BOOK

The book is divided into two parts. Part I provides basic comparisons of the archaeology and ethnohistory of several of the Inca provinces. The organization follows geography (see map facing page 1), beginning with the Topics' discussions of the Huamachuco region of northern Peru and progressing through Grosboll's evaluation of the Chupachos. The essays continue with Schreiber's analysis of the Inca occupation of Andamarca Lucanas in the central Andes and end with Lynch's discussion of the evidence from his research at Catarpe and other installations in northern Chile.

Part II consists of two essays and a concluding chapter. The essays, one by Susan A. Niles, the other by Catherine J. Julien, provide more detailed analyses of ethnohistorical documents and less specific archaeological data than the previous studies. Niles's essay focuses on the royal estates around Cuzco and thereby provides data from the Inca heartland for comparison with data recovered in the provincial areas. She uses this information to suggest several new means of interpreting Inca remains in other regions. Julien presents a new, geographical approach for the study of the Incas and demonstrates its utility with examples drawn from the other essays in the volume. Her essay also presents productive new lines of research for the future. In the final chapter, I summarize the salient conclusions to be drawn from the volume as a whole.

Part I

STUDIES IN PROVINCIAL

INCA ARCHAEOLOGY

Part I provides archaeological and ethnohistorical information on several areas of the Andes that came under Inca control. These discussions highlight how the use of both kinds of information leads to a greater understanding of the past. They also constitute basic archaeological contributions concerning the nature of Inca control in the provinces.

The regions represented here cover a wide range of geographic conditions and cultural variability. The Huamachuco region, discussed by John R. Topic and Theresa Lange Topic, was much more densely settled by a group at a higher level of complexity than were the arid northern deserts of Chile, discussed by Thomas F. Lynch, which were sparsely populated by groups of no great cultural complexity. The Andamarca Lucanas and Chupachos regions, discussed by Katharina J. Schreiber and Sue Grosboll, respectively, lay somewhere between Huamachuco and the Chilean deserts in terms of population demographics and complexity. This variation allows useful comparisons for understanding the nature of the Incas' incorporation of different regions.

2

JOHN R. TOPIC AND

THERESA LANGE TOPIC

A SUMMARY OF THE INCA

OCCUPATION OF HUAMACHUCO

EDITOR'S INTRODUCTION

The Topics found that while archaeology could have identified the overall historical developments concerning the Inca conquest of this area, subtle political and administrative nuances were provided by the documents, such as the addition of a section of *chaupi yunga* (middle-altitude lowland) territory to the province, and the places of origin of *mitima* (individuals living outside of their place of origin) settlements. Thus, in a sense, the ethnohistorical information elaborates on the basic archaeological data for the region, rather than the reverse.

Archaeologically, Inca control can be discerned from new settlement types that appear, such as domestic sites, tambos, and mitima settlements, and the main Inca road, which passed through this province and along which these occupations are located. It is hard to differentiate Late Horizon ceramics from Late Intermediate Period ones, reflecting strong continuities in the traditions through time. As in the Huánuco region (to be discussed by Grosboll), the discovery of aryballoid shapes indicates the Inca presence, along with animal head lugs and sometimes distinctive pastes. The discussion of pre-Inca remains is useful for identifying the nature of the Inca impact on the region.

INTRODUCTION

The Incaic province of Huamachuco was located in the northern sierra of Peru, north of Conchucos and Huaylas and south of Cajamarca. It extended from the chaupi yunga zone of the Chicama, Moche, Virú, Chao, and Santa valleys in the west to the Río Marañon in the east and from the Río Crisnejas in the north to Corongo in the south (fig. 2.1). It is not one of the best-known provinces of the Inca empire: although archaeological and ethnohistorical data are available, both are limited in scope.

The archaeological information from Huamachuco is relatively recent and focuses on the area immediately around the modern town. The Huamachuco Archaeological Project has been working in the Huamachuco area since 1981 and has recovered useful information on the Inca presence, though that was not one of the major goals of the project. Previous work by Max Uhle (1900), Theodore D. McCown (1945), and John P. Thatcher (1972) had emphasized earlier time periods and had not in fact been able to identify remains related to Inca control of the province. The archaeological perspective is broadened somewhat by a surface survey of fortified sites that we conducted in the western part of the province from 1977 to 1979. That survey, however, was done before we had acquired much familiarity with the ethnohistorical information. Although Inca-influenced sites exist in that area, we will limit our discussion here largely to comments on the road system.

The ethnohistorical information is rarely very detailed, but it does give an overview of the province. Chronicles frequently mention both the town and the province of Huamachuco, but usually only in passing; these references lead one to expect a fairly substantial Inca presence in the Huamachuco area. Cieza de León (1986: 235–236) reported that the province was large and thickly settled, with great lords and large flocks. He commented also on the presence in the town itself, among the tambos, of two large buildings 22 feet wide and a horse's gallop long. Miguel de Estete (1947: 338) described Huamachuco as a large town in a valley surrounded by mountains, with a good view and good lodgings. Huamachuco was located along the main north-south road, and at a crossroads providing access toward the west to the Moche Valley and eastward to the Río Chusgón, a tributary of the Marañon. Some of the tambos along the main highway are listed by Guaman Poma (1980a: 1003). Garcilaso de la Vega (1966: 342) provides a certain amount of information about Huamachuco, most of it erroneous: "This tribe indeed was extremely barbarous and cruel in its habits. . . . They had no settled towns, but lived dispersed about the countryside in scattered huts, lacking any form of social organization or order. They lived like beasts." In Garcilaso de la Vega's account, the lord of Huamachuco was delighted to accept the gifts of civilization from the Inca.

Two other useful documents provide a different kind of information. Their broader, provincial-scale information helps to balance the more local nature of the archaeological data. Juan de San Pedro (1992) discusses a number of shrines scattered throughout the province and indicates that there was an oracle in Huamachuco which was worshiped from Cuzco to Quito. Betanzos (1987) provides the fullest description of the destruction of this oracle by Atahuallpa. For the most part, Juan de San Pedro (1992 [1560]) emphasizes the local nature of the religious shrines and practices.

The other document is the *Orden sobre el servicio de los tambos del Repartimiento de Guamachuco*, written by Gregorio González de Cuenca in 1567. This document, published in Rostworowski de Diez Canseco (1989) and cited here as the González de Cuenca *Ordenanza*, provides the names of seven towns occupied by *mitimas serranos* (individuals originally from the highlands but living outside of their place of origin), eight towns occupied by *mitimas yungas* (individuals originally from the lowlands but living outside of their place of origin), twenty-five towns occupied by the local population, and nine tambos. The local population was divided into four ranked *huarangas* (an Inca administrative unit of a thousand households), of which the two western huarangas were much larger, and also ranked higher, than the two eastern ones. (This is an interesting point of departure from the Inca ideal, in that clearly the huarangas were not equal in size.) Espinoza (1974: 22, 35) feels that the third-ranked huaranga, Lluicho, was split off from the first-ranked huaranga, Llampa, by Huayna Capac, the eleventh Inca king (died ca. 1527). If this is so, it would be reasonable to assume that fourth-ranked Andamarca was split from second-ranked Huacapongo at the same time. Two other huarangas were formed by the

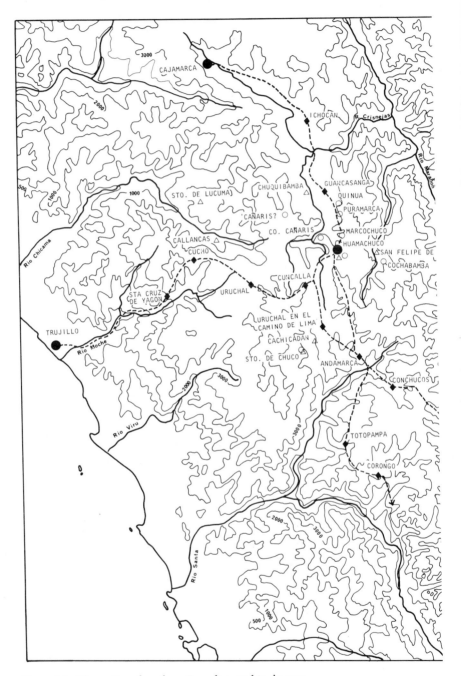

Figure 2.1. The section of northern Peru discussed in the text.

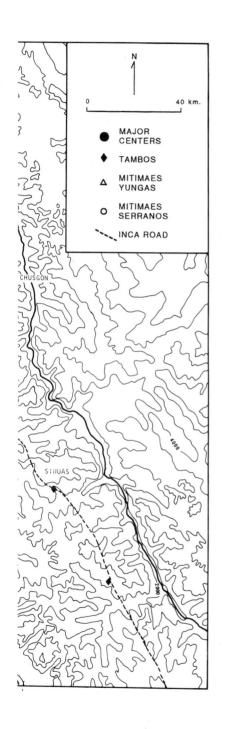

mitimas serranos and mitimas yungas. Finally, although they formed a distinct group, the chaupi yungas populations of at least the Moche Valley, and perhaps the Virú and other adjacent valleys as well, owed allegiance to the *curaca* (local lord) of Huamachuco.

In this chapter we will discuss the recent archaeological evidence available for Huamachuco and then consider the ways in which this information relates to the ethnohistorical data.

THE PROVINCIAL CAPITAL

The location of Incaic Huamachuco has been the subject of some controversy among those who have worked or visited in the area over the past century. The largest site in the region, Marcahuamachuco, lacks Inca architecture and artifacts and has never been a serious candidate for the Inca center. Two other locales have been championed by various writers: the modern town of Huamachuco and Viracochapampa, a site lying 2 kilometers north of town.

Charles Wiener (1880: 141–142), one of the earliest travelers with "scientific" interests to make his way through Huamachuco, considered Viracochapampa to be the main Inca center. He also noted the presence of an artificial platform in Huamachuco, under the chapel San José on the north side of the plaza (fig. 2.2). He concluded that the platform was ancient, though not necessarily Inca (Wiener 1880: 145). Somewhat later, E. M. Middendorf (1974: 227) considered Viracochapampa to be an early Spanish town whose construction was never completed; he did not specifically address the question of where the Inca center was located. Uhle spent three months in the Huamachuco area in 1900. He reacted very strongly to the numerous inaccuracies in Wiener's work and went out of his way to show Wiener wrong whenever possible (Uhle 1900: 110–111). He insisted that Huamachuco was essentially a modern town, that San José itself and the platform on which it stood were early Spanish constructions, and that occasional finds of Inca pottery in the town indicated only that a small settlement had existed there. Uhle felt that Viracochapampa must have been the main Inca settlement, citing the lack of Spanish-style streets there, architectural similarities to Inca sites, and similarities in plan to Pachacamac to back up this view (Uhle 1900: 110, 134–138). Julio C. Tello (in Mejía 1955: 336) visited Huamachuco briefly in 1937 and pronounced the

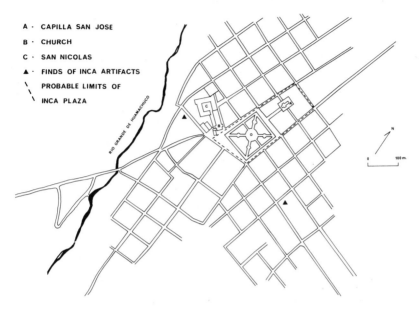

A - CAPILLA SAN JOSE
B - CHURCH
C - SAN NICOLAS
▲ - FINDS OF INCA ARTIFACTS
PROBABLE LIMITS OF
INCA PLAZA

Figure 2.2. The modern town of Huamachuco.

platform under San José to be ancient, though he, like Wiener, did not specify that it was Incaic.

McCown was aware of all these opinions and carefully examined the platform. He noted that there were two very thick rubble walls incorporated into the platform that suggested pre-Hispanic workmanship, whereas the chapel itself dated from the early Spanish occupation (McCown 1945: 256–257). He assumed, erroneously, that this chapel was the original convent built in the 1550s by the Augustinians, in the same plaza where the Incas had large buildings (Juan de San Pedro 1992 [1560]: 157). Despite these observations, he considered Huamachuco to be largely a Spanish town with no evidence of a major Inca occupation (McCown 1945: 256, 330). Largely because of similarities to Pikillacta, McCown identified Viracochapampa as the main Inca center (McCown 1945: 273, 330–331, 343).

Thatcher (1972: 94–95) dated eleven sites to the Late Horizon, but he did not consider any of these to be the Inca capital. Viracochapampa was, of course, eliminated as a candidate since he was able to date it to Middle Horizon 1B (Thatcher 1972: 87–88). Although he never discusses the modern town in any detail, he clearly did not think that Huamachuco was the Inca center, suggesting instead that the Inca site should be sought some 10 kilometers to the south, in the Pampa de Yamobamba (Thatcher 1972: 95).

We have decided that the most likely locale for the provincial capital is Huamachuco itself, on the following grounds:

1. The town has an atypically large trapezoidal plaza.

2. We agree with McCown that the Capilla de San José rests on an ancient artificial mound.

3. The statements by the Augustinians clearly indicate that they founded their convent within the Inca center.

4. The town is located on an ancient road junction.

5. There are frequent finds of Inca pottery in corrals and patios around the plaza.

6. Worked-stone blocks are occasionally incorporated into building foundations.

7. Inca storerooms are found on three hills overlooking Huamachuco.

Huamachuco has been heavily settled for several centuries, and nowhere in town is any original Inca construction visible. Occasionally pieces of worked stone are pointed out as Incaic, but many of these could well be colonial. For example, shaped and drilled pieces of trachyte served as the original pipes for the fountain in the plaza and are probably Spanish in date. Other blocks of trachyte, however, are shaped like ashlars, with their largest dimension varying between about 30 and 80 centimeters. These are not very common but do occur occasionally in wall foundations, curbs, borders of patios, and as post bases. An informal survey consisting only of walking around the streets of Huamachuco and visiting in a few houses suggests that these worked stones are most common in the blocks surrounding the southern half of the plaza.

The Huamachuco plaza is exceptionally large for a town of this size, and unusual in its shape. The plaza is trapezoidal, narrower in the north and wider in the south, and its southwest corner forms a very acute angle. The Augustinians probably established their convent at the southwest corner, not where San José now stands. Their statement on this point is worth quoting in full: "And here they placed another house in the very pampa or plaza of Huamachuco itself where there were large buildings of the Inca, and now the monastery is in the same building that they call there 'tambo' where the order has been and is now" (Juan de San Pedro 1992 [1560]: 157, our translation). It is clear that the Augustinians did not just build in the general area of the plaza, but rather that they occupied existing Inca buildings. The principal church was located on this corner in 1785 when Martinez Compañon (1978) made his inspection and founded a school alongside the church. Although both the school, now called San Nicolás, and the church have undergone complete rebuilding since then, they are still oriented at an angle to the plaza.

The streets extending south, or uphill, fan out from the corners of the plaza, while those extending to the north tend to converge slightly. Probably the orientation of these streets was at least partially determined by the layout of the Inca plaza and buildings. We suspect that the platform under San José at the north end of the modern plaza was the Inca *ushnu* (ritual complex consisting of a platform, basin, and drainage system [Hyslop 1990: 69ff.]) and that the Inca plaza may actually have extended much farther to the north. While no diagnostic Inca masonry is preserved on the exposed faces of the platform, local tradition considers it the Inca ushnu. It now has three stairways, on the south, the east, and the west. Wiener (1880: 145) notes that there were originally four stairways and that these served as the points of departure for the layout of the Spanish streets. As just discussed, this last statement does not seem to be true of the north-south streets in the center of the town, but it may be true of the east-west streets on the northwest, north, east, and southeast sides of the plaza.

Like the worked-stone blocks, finds of Inca-style artifacts are most common in the area to the south, southeast, and southwest of the plaza. Examples include:

1. a cache of four aryballoids, a long-necked jar, half of a double-chambered whistling jar, and a gold pin with a llama head, 20 centimeters long, shown to us by townspeople;

2. a wooden *quero* (drinking goblet) inlaid with stone and shell from a patio 200 meters east of the plaza;

3. probably the two aryballoid jars collected by Uhle in 1900, one of which was illustrated by McCown (1945: pl. 20d). They were found in graves located in the court of a house 250 meters east of the plaza.

We think it unlikely that any intact Inca architecture will be found in Huamachuco or that the size and layout of the city can be determined without an intensive program of excavation. The information just presented, however, suggests that Huamachuco was at least a medium-sized Inca center which had a large plaza, complete with ushnu, probably two kallanka-type buildings, and perhaps a royal enclosure. The layout of streets and the distribution of artifactual material suggest that the majority of Inca buildings were located around the southern half of the plaza. The scarcity of worked stones suggests that much of this architecture might have been built of adobe or unworked stone set in mud mortar.

STOREROOMS AND TERRACES

On the hills to the south and southwest of Huamachuco are Inca structures in varying states of preservation (fig. 2.3); for a more complete discussion, see Topic and Chiswell (1992). Rows of *colcas* (storerooms) were first recognized by the project in 1981 and test excavations were conducted in 1982 and 1983. The greatest number are on Cerro Santa Barbara, where the fragmentary remains of five parallel terraces are arranged along the contours of the hill. Four of the terraces have some preserved colcas on them. The uppermost terrace has 26 to 27 colcas on it, but preservation of the lower terraces is worse. The second terrace has at least 18 colcas, the third has about 12 poorly preserved colcas, the fourth has only parts of 6 recognizable colcas, and the fifth terrace now has no preserved buildings. We estimate that there originally may have been about 125 colcas on this hill. Cerro Mamorco has three sets of colcas, totaling about 60 rooms; all three sets are at about the same elevation, extending along the side of the hill for a kilometer. On Cerro Cacañan there is one row of 23 to 26 structures. Two radiocarbon assays were run on samples from Santa Barbara, with results of A.D. 1475 ± 65 and A.D. 1550 ± 75.

Just to the west of the storerooms on Cerro Santa Barbara is a set of agricultural terraces, which have been only briefly surveyed as yet. Air photos from 1952 indicated the presence of stone facings, but these have since been largely dismantled. As usual, it is very difficult to date these agricultural terraces, but their location near storerooms and the town of Huamachuco suggests a Late Horizon date.

The exterior dimensions of the colcas range from about 4 by 5 meters to 4 by 8 meters. The preserved walls are constructed of pirca masonry, but the upper parts of walls may also have incorporated adobe. Three structures on Cerro Mamorco have small trapezoidal doors preserved, facing downslope. These structures, unlike other known Inca colcas, are never conjoined; instead, each is separated from the others by 1 to 5 meters of open space. Also unusual is the fact that no sherds of large storage vessels are associated with the buildings. Test excavations were carried out at selected colcas on all three hills, and two distinct types were noted:

1. Elevated colcas. This type of storeroom was raised off the ground on a foundation consisting of three parallel walls. The two outer walls served as both the short end walls of the structure and supports for the floor joists. The middle wall was the central support for the floor joists. The construction allowed air to circulate beneath the structure; these colcas must have been designed to provide a low-humidity environment for storing such materials as seed crops, textiles, and leather. All four of the excavated examples on Cerro Santa Barbara were of this type.

2. Nonelevated colcas. The other class of colcas was constructed on bedrock, with channels cut into the bedrock 40 centimeters deep and 45 centimeters wide, running downslope. A flooring of wood and cane topped with packed dirt probably overlay the canals, allowing for drainage of water out of the structures as well as the introduction of water into the subfloor layer. We suspect that these structures were designed to provide a controlled higher-humidity environment for tuber storage. Both of the excavated examples on Cerro Cacañan and two of the three examples from Cerro Mamorco were of this type; the third example from Cerro Mamorco was similar in most respects, but lacked the subfloor canals.

Analysis of macro- and microbotanical remains seems to confirm this functional typology (Chiswell 1984). Carbonized maize kernels were found in the Cerro Santa Barbara colcas and in the one colca on Cerro Mamorco that lacked drains. Since sherds of large storage jars were not found in these colcas, we can conclude that the maize was probably stored in bags. All the excavated colcas on Cerro Mamorco also had higher than normal quantities of *ichu* (a high-altitude bunch grass) phytoliths, suggesting that tubers, packed in the ichu, might have been stored there. Botanical remains from the Cerro Cacañan colcas were not sufficient to allow determination of the crops stored there.

Larger administrative structures were also found in association with the colcas on Cerro Cacañan. Here six to eight larger structures (18 by 6 meters) were grouped together but 250 meters distant from the colcas themselves. These pirca structures are arranged in linear fashion along the hill. Some have two doorways, while others have one, always

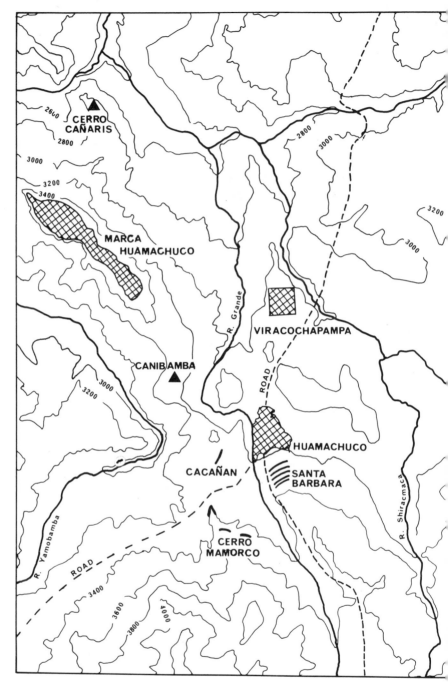

Figure 2.3. The Huamachuco area. Cross-hatched sites have all been proposed as the Inca provincial center, solid lines represent storage complexes, and triangles denote smaller Inca sites.

in the long wall facing downslope. The structures lack the subfloor features that characterize colcas. Only one example was excavated. There were low benches along the interior of the wall and a small room set on a low platform in one corner. Two circular pits filled with small river-rolled stones served as the bases for internal posts to help support the roof. The structures produced almost no artifacts and lacked domestic debris. They probably served an administrative function relating to control of stored goods.

We estimate that there were once about 215 colcas on these hillsides. The total storage capacity of the colcas was relatively low in comparison to that of larger centers like Huánuco Pampa and Jauja, which may indicate that these colcas were used for imperial services performed primarily on a local scale.

ROADS AND TAMBOS

Both archaeological and ethnohistorical information is available on the road system around Huamachuco. It is clear from this information that, while Huamachuco persisted as an important node on the road throughout the Late Horizon and Colonial periods, the road system around Huamachuco underwent considerable change.

Many fragments of roads are still preserved in the province of Huamachuco, and these have received some scrutiny from archaeologists. John Hyslop (1984: 59–67) surveyed the Inca road from Cajamarca south to Huamachuco. After crossing the Río Crisnejas (fig. 2.1), the road runs along the eastern side of the Río Condebamba, as does the modern road. On nearing Huamachuco, though, the pre-Hispanic road took a more direct route toward the city, passing only a few hundred meters to the east of Viracochapampa. This road undoubtedly predates the Inca expansion by a considerable margin. The road south from Huamachuco had two branches, although only the western branch is ever mentioned in colonial documents. The western branch leaves Huamachuco and climbs gently up the Pampa de Yamobamba to the *jalca* (high-altitude zone above the limits of vegetation); Betanzos (1987) refers to this area as Ñamoc Pampa. The road skirts the steep flanks of Cerro Huaylillas, the highest peak in the area, at 4,733 meters above sea level. We have found a few poorly preserved segments of this branch of the road in the Pampa de Yamobamba. The other branch climbs almost directly over the top of the peak itself and traverses a scenically more spectacular route. A small shrine on this route marks the first view of Marcahuamachuco. We have surveyed about 22 kilometers of this branch; because of a long flight of steps on Cerro Escalaría it is impassable to wheeled transport and difficult for horses. It clearly was of no importance to the Spanish in colonial times, and is not mentioned in contemporary documents. We see no reason to assume that it was not in use during the Late Horizon but expect that it was built well before then. The two branches of the road come together around modern Mollebamba, 40 kilometers to the south.

Both Estete (1947: 338) and Guaman Poma (1980a: 1094–1103) provide lists of tambos along this north-south road. [Editor's note: The place names are spelled as they appear in the documents and maps cited.] The tambos which Estete mentions within the province of Huamachuco are Guancasanga, Huamachuco, Tambo, Andamarca, Totopamba, and Coronga. In 1702, the toponym "Huancasanga" referred to land owned by the community of Lluicho (Espinoza 1974: 214), apparently located between Cauday and Cajabamba. Estete's "Tambo" is probably near the modern hamlet of Tambillo, 12 kilometers northeast of Santiago de Chuco, Andamarca is near modern Mollebamba, Totopamba is probably identified by the toponym "Cerro Tambillo" above the Pampa de Tuctubamba 12 kilometers east of Tauca, and Coronga is Corongo in the Santa drainage. Guaman Poma's list for the same area is less extensive and suggests that changes in the road system were already pronounced. In place of Guancasanga, Guaman Poma gives Caxa Pamba (Cajabamba), a *reducción* (settlement of local people founded by the Spanish). Guaman Poma's "Guamachuco" and "tanbillo" correspond to Huamachuco and Tambo in Estete's list. In place of Andamarca, Guaman Poma lists "Tanbo Nuebo," which may indicate that the tambo had been moved since Inca times. South of Andamarca there were again two branches to the north-south road; while Estete followed the western branch, which continued south through the province of Huamachuco, Guaman Poma lists only the tambos on the eastern branch, which runs through the province of Conchucos. Again, this may be an indication that the Andamarca-Corongo branch had fallen out of general use by the late 1500s.

Cabello Balboa (1951: cap. 16) states that after the conquest of Cajamarca the Inca army descended to the coast through the territory of Huamachuco. This road west from Huamachuco to the coast can be reconstructed, in part, by examining the González de Cuenca *Ordenanza*. Moving inland from the coast, the first tambo listed is Santa Cruz de Yagón, which was probably located near modern Challuacocha above the north bank of the middle Moche Valley, where the toponyms "Santa Cruz" and "Santagón" still occur. Near here there are still fragments of preserved roads which climb steeply up from the chaupi yunga to the highlands (Coupland 1979), passing sites dating to the Late Intermediate Period and the Late Horizon. The next two tambos, Cucho and Uruchal, have no modern toponymic equivalents but probably were located in the area around the modern hamlet of Tambillo, 10 kilometers north of Otuzco, and Laguna Tambo, 24 kilometers east of Otuzco, respectively. There is still a well-preserved road from Laguna Tambo to Santa Ana Cruz on the jalca near the Continental Divide; this road not only connects Otuzco to Huamachuco, but a branch from Santa Cruz also provides the most direct route to Santiago de Chuco. Mogrovejo (1920: 250) notes that, traveling from Santiago de Chuco to Otuzco, he spent the night at a tambo called Guarargual; we suspect that "Guarargual," "Uruchal," and the modern toponym "Huadalgual," located near Laguna Tambo, all refer to the same place. The next tambo, Cangayo, can be identified as modern Cuncalla, located east of the Continental Divide on the descent to the Pampa de Yamobamba. On reaching the Pampa de Yamobamba the road joined the north-south trunk route.

The *Ordenanza* lists five other tambos. One of these, Uruchal en el camino de Lima, corresponds to the modern toponym "Urucchalda" and probably is the proper name of Estete's Tambo and Guaman Poma's "tanbillo." Andamarca and Huamachuco are also listed. The document is internally inconsistent in the case of two tambos, Yanabamba and Lluicho; we feel that these names refer to a single tambo that either corresponds to or replaces Estete's Guancasanga. The final tambo listed, Collambay, is located in the chaupi yunga zone of the Río Sinsicap, a tributary of the Río Moche, and seems to be of only local importance.

The González de Cuenca *Ordenanza* provides two interesting insights into changes in the province's road system with the strengthening of Spanish control after the conquest. First, we see the increasing importance of the road from Trujillo to Huamachuco, a road which served to link the coast with the highlands. For the Inca, travel and communication along the length of the mountains had always been

more important than connections to the coast, and this relative signifi-
cance is shown clearly by the greater number of administrative centers,
storage complexes, and tambos along the highland routes. The colonial
Spanish were economically and politically oriented toward Spain, and
Pacific ports provided the most direct links to that country. The
Trujillo-Huamachuco transverse link in the road system became more
important after the conquest, achieving equivalent status to the highland road segment within the province; each had sixty taxpayers assigned to a center (Yagón and Huamachuco, respectively) and three
tambos.

The second point of interest is that no route to the east of Huamachuco is mentioned; in fact, only Martinez Compañon (1978), on his
map of Huamachuco, mentions a road to the east, referring to it as the
"camino para Chusgón" (road to Chusgón). His map indicates that the
road to Chusgón leaves Huamachuco along what is now the route to
Cajabamba and Cajamarca; in his day, the "calzada [paved road] para
Caxabamba" was still the Inca road, which leaves town in the direction of Viracochapampa. The street leading to Viracochapampa is still
referred to by the older residents of Huamachuco as "Calle de los
Calzados."

OTHER LATE HORIZON OCCUPATION

Late Horizon occupations have proved difficult to distinguish cerami-
cally from Late Intermediate Period occupations.[1] Known Late Horizon
assemblages are small and nondescript, and there is considerable continuity in paste, form, and decoration from ceramics of the preceding
Tuscan phase. Thatcher (1972: 94) dated eleven sites to the Late Horizon by seriating a local style found in mixed surface collections to
this phase; none of the sites actually exhibited Inca sherds. Our resur-
vey of the eleven sites also failed to find any Inca sherds, and excavations at the site which provided the phase name produced evidence of
a significant Early Intermediate Period and Middle Horizon occupation, but no Late Horizon. We considered it preferable to rename the
phase "Santa Barbara," after a site with demonstrated Inca presence.
While acknowledging that many Late Intermediate Period sites probably continued to be occupied into the Late Horizon, we have taken a
conservative approach to dating Late Horizon sites and include here

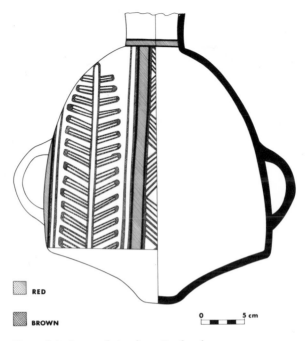

RED

BROWN

0   5 cm

Figure 2.4. Inca-style jar from Canibamba.

only those which have either diagnostic ceramics or architectural evidence of Late Horizon occupation. Inca provincial ceramics are relatively rare in the Huamachuco area but are, of course, useful indicators of site date where they occur. The aryballoid jar is the most frequently encountered form, as it appears through much of the territory controlled by the Inca (fig. 2.4). The animal head lugs often found on aryballoid shoulders (called "rope nubbins" by Bingham 1930: 123–133) also occur with some frequency. A light, hard paste with crushed-rock temper is usually associated with Inca forms; this paste can sometimes be recognized at suspected Late Horizon sites in the area and is considered diagnostic when it occurs on tall jars with sharply everted lips that are *not* decorated in the Tuscan Phase, Huamachuco-on-White style. Also suggestive are certain gridlike geometric designs painted in dark red or brown on orange paste.

In addition to the storeroom complexes and Huamachuco itself, which have already been discussed, we date seven sites to the Late Horizon. These seven sites seem to represent three types, mainly local occupations, a possible tambo, and possible mitima occupations.

Late Horizon remains have been found at Canibamba, on the same ridge as Marcahuamachuco but at a much lower elevation. Here a rather large aryballoid jar in good Inca provincial style and an *olla* (cooking pot) with everted painted lip and horizontal handles were turned up by farmers plowing a field. Subsequent excavation cleared a room that had been covered by a mudslide, but the only other artifact of Inca inspiration was a face-neck jar of distinctly nonlocal appearance (see Bingham 1930: fig. 118-f for a very similar specimen). No other Late Horizon structures could be found in the vicinity, but the area is much affected by slump and by farming. Canibamba controls the access to Marcahuamachuco but also overlooks some prime lower-elevation fields. The site is also located just at the foot of Cerro Amaru, which was a major shrine during the Middle Horizon and continued to have some occupation in the Late Intermediate Period. Uhle (1900: 133) mentions that he saw an Inca bottle which had been found at Cerro Amaru, but it is possible that this bottle actually came from the area we would call Canibamba.

Two other sites are located on the ridge between Laguna Sausagocha and Laguna Collasgón. One of them (site 40), on Cerro Negro, had been occupied in both the Early Intermediate Period and the Late Intermediate Period. There is virtually no preserved architecture, but sherds extend over an area of approximately 300 by 50 meters. The Late Horizon occupation is inferred from ceramic paste characteristics and the diagnostic tall neck jar form. The other site (site 69), on Cerro Pan de Azucar, does have preserved architecture and seems to date only to the Late Horizon. The architecture is constructed with low, unchinked, double-faced stone walls. The rooms, about 3 meters on a side, are arranged in conjoined rows, and the rows of rooms often bound one or two sides of an open space; this is a common arrangement for rooms in the Huamachuco area. Some of the rooms have rounded interior corners. There are also a few larger rooms and walled, but probably unroofed, enclosures which might be corrals. The ceramics include no diagnostic features, but share paste and shape characteristics with other Late Horizon collections.

An interesting, though enigmatic, site (site 36) is located on the very peak of Cerro El Toro, a steep-sided hill which dominates the whole area from Laguna Sausagocha to Huamachuco. The site covers an area of only 48 by 60 meters and is very poorly preserved. We estimated that there might have been about 18 small (2 by 2 meters) rooms, and there are indications of slate paving stones. The site is distinguished by an unexpectedly high sherd density for such a small and isolated site and a high proportion of kaolin and decorated sherds from a number of different time periods. The Late Horizon ceramics include an animal head rope nubbin, tall-neck jars, and an example of the gridlike geometric painting.

The possible tambo (site 157) is very poorly preserved. It is located on the road which leads directly south from Huamachuco at an elevation of 4,050 meters. The road probably ran directly past the site, but was destroyed by bulldozers when a dam was built nearby. Now only a few double-faced wall foundations can be seen. These seem to form a rectangular plaza surrounded by rectangular rooms. Overall, the site is about 25 by 10 meters. Ceramics were scarce, generally very small and eroded but consistent with Late Horizon dating by paste and the presence of strap handles.

One possible mitima site (site 165) is located on a small hill below and north of Marcahuamachuco. The hill is called Cerro Cañaris, and the name obviously influences our interpretation. It is quite clear from the González de Cuenca *Ordenanza* and other sources (Espinoza 1974: 89) that there were mitimas of Cañaris in Huamachuco from the Cañar province in Ecuador. It is not as clear, however, where these mitimas were located. The *Ordenanza* suggests that at least some Cañaris were located in San Marcos de Chuco (in other documents also referred to as San Marcos de Cañar, de Cucho, and de Corchop), where they were mixed together with another, unspecified, group of mitimas serranos. San Marcos de Chuco may be modern Marcochuco, located seven kilometers east of Cerro Cañaris, although this identification is not at all certain. San Marcos, however, was a reducción founded in 1565 (Espinoza 1974: 89), and the Cañaris may have been located elsewhere earlier. Espinoza (1974: map following p. 12) places them some 23 kilometers northwest of Huamachuco, where there is a modern hamlet called Cañaris.

The site of Cerro Cañaris is located in good maize-growing land, and there are agricultural terraces which probably date to the main occupation of Marcahuamachuco (A.D. 400–1,000), about 1.5 kilometers away. It is covered by dense brush that obscures most of the architecture. There are two partly artificial and partly natural terraced platforms separated by 60 to 80 meters. One of these platforms has on it a circular building 6 meters in diameter and other rooms, patios, and possible corridors on the lower terraces. The ceramics include pastes characteristic of the Late Horizon, tall-neck jars, and strap handles.

The other possible mitima site, Alto Corazón (site 179), is located on a hill just south of and overlooking Marcochuco. Though it probably covers at least 1.5 hectares, it has been only partially surveyed. A typical complex has an unroofed enclosure or patio measuring 6 by 12 meters, with rows of small (2 by 4 meters) rooms flanking one or two sides. Many of the animal head rope nubbins were observed on the surface during survey in 1986. If Alto Corazón is in fact a mitima settlement, the original homeland of the settlers is not known; if Marcochuco is the colonial reducción of San Marcos de Chuco, the people from Alto Corazón may have been resettled there, together with those from Cerro Cañaris.

OTHER ETHNOHISTORICAL INFORMATION

The number of mitima settlements in the Huamachuco area can be clarified somewhat more by examining the ethnohistorical information. Espinoza (1974: 25) lists seven groups of mitimas serranos, four groups of mitimas yungas, and five groups of mitimas from the coast, highlands, and Chachapoyas that he classifies as ecological enclaves. Unfortunately, this list is based on seventeenth-century documentation and is not ideal for our purposes.

The González de Cuenca *Ordenanza* specifies that there were two huarangas of mitimas, one composed of serranos and the other of yungas. According to that document, in 1567 the serranos were located in Santiago de Chuco, Quinua, Puramarca, Lochababamba (Cochabamba?), San Marcos de Chuco, and Huamachuco. The yungas were located in Callancas, Santiago de Lúcuma, Santiago de Chuco, Cachicadán, San Felipe de Chusgón, Chuquibamba, and Huamachuco. The *Ordenanza*, however, gives no information about the derivation of the mitimas. Moreover, many of the towns named in the *Ordenanza* were reducciones founded in 1565, resulting in the conflation of different mitima groups. For example, it is clear that both mitimas yungas and mitimas serranos were mixed together with the local population in Santiago de Chuco and Huamachuco. Less clear is the mixing of different groups of either serranos or yungas, as in the case of San Marcos de Chuco discussed above. Finally, Lúcuma and Cachicadán were populated by mitimas yungas as well as representatives of the indigenous population. On the other hand, the mixing of these groups by 1567 was probably not as extensive as Espinoza (1974: 86) has inferred, based on a misinterpretation[2] of the González de Cuenca *tasa* (tax assessment), part of which he excerpts (Espinoza 1974: 291–295).

While it is still difficult to locate all mitima groups precisely, a detailed analysis of just the *Ordenanza* and the tasa provides the general pattern of their distribution. The mitimas yungas were scattered in several settlements throughout the upper Chicama, as well as in settlements in the Condebamba, Chusgón, Tablachaca, upper Virú (Río de la Vega), and upper Moche valleys. As well as being dispersed, these settlements were small. Calculations based on data in the *Ordenanza* indicate an average of only 26.5 taxpayers (married and single) per town in a sample of eight towns. A similar calculation based on the tasa, where the mitimas yungas cannot be separated from the chaupi yunga groups and only the number of married taxpayers can be determined, indicates that the average number of married taxpayers in ten chaupi yunga and mitima yunga towns is thirty-three. The small size and dispersed nature of the mitima yunga groups is probably not coincidental, most likely reflecting an Inca policy of dividing and isolating these groups as part of a strategy of controlling the remnants of the Chimu kingdom. Netherly (1988a) makes the same point when she notes that the assignment of the chaupi yunga, with its important coca fields, to Huamachuco was designed to sever lands from the coastal polities.

In contrast to figures from lower elevations, the *Ordenanza* indicates an average of 55.3 taxpayers in each of six mitima serrano towns; since the tasa does not differentiate mitimas serranos, it is impossible to arrive at any estimate based on that source. The mitimas serranos were concentrated in the center of the province: three of their six towns were located on the Inca road between Cajabamba and Huamachuco; one was located somewhat to the east of the main road, in the upper Chusgón drainage; and Huamachuco and Santiago de Chuco each had mitimas serranos resident in them. The concentration of highlanders would, again, seem to reflect an Inca strategy of controlling the heart of the province by controlling the major roads.

While Espinoza's (1974: 25) list of *mitima* groups is based on seventeenth-century sources, at least some of the groups are referred to in earlier documents. Espinoza himself (1970) provides further documentation for one group, the Huayacuntus, who were moved south to

Huamachuco from the area around Huancabamba and Ayabaca by Topa Inca; they were weavers and were apparently located in two locations, to the north and south of Huamachuco. We have not had the opportunity to examine the documents relating to the *Residencia* of González de Cuenca ourselves, but Eric Deeds, while working as a research assistant for the Huamachuco Project, prepared a brief report; only mitimas from Chachapoyas and Incas from Cuzco are clearly identified. The Incas may have been brought to Huamachuco from Canco in the valley of Jaquijahuana (cf. Rowe 1946: 189); Juan de San Pedro (1992: 186) states that the mitimas Incas Orejones from Cuzco brought a *huaca* (idol) with them, a small, black plumb-bob-shaped stone called Topallimillay; Cristóbal de Albornoz (Duviols 1967: 27) states that the Indians of Canco had a huaca called Llimillay, which consisted of several stones. The presence of Cañaris in Huamachuco is confirmed by the González de Cuenca *Ordenanza* as already discussed. The only yunga group whose derivation is securely known to us is a group from Paiján in the Chicama Valley, which was resettled in Chuquibamba, apparently to serve some colcas located there.[3]

Our field surveys are not sufficiently extensive to allow us to say whether the local population was always removed to other provinces in order to make room for these mitimas or whether in some cases the mitimas were settled on lands which had been underpopulated. The only reference we have located regarding the resettlement of the Huamachuco population is in the *Relaciones Geográficas de Indias (Perú)* (Jiménez de la Espada 1965: tomo 184: 255) which identifies mitimas from Huamachuco in the province of Chimbo, Ecuador. This account, written in 1581, indicates that there were 301 mitimas ("souls") from Huamachuco in the town of Azancoto, where they were mixed with mitimas from Cajamarca, Huambos, and "many other places." The association of mitimas from Huambos, Cajamarca, and Huamachuco is interesting because it suggests that the Incas may have considered these three provinces as one large administrative unit (*huaman*), as the Spanish later did.

CONCLUSIONS

The Inca expansion clearly had a major impact on the province of Huamachuco. It is interesting to consider how well we would understand the changes introduced by the Inca if we had to rely only on the archaeological record, unaided by ethnohistorical information. We suspect that in such a scenario the overall historical picture would emerge, but the political and administrative nuances would be lost.

Traditional archaeological methods would verify Inca presence in the area. Artifact distributions would not suggest heavy influence, but the major settlement shift after the Late Intermediate Period would draw attention. The regional center was abandoned and a new town built; a loss of local autonomy might well be inferred from the diminished grandeur of the new center compared to the old. Late Intermediate Period Huamachuco elites had not undertaken any new construction at Marcahuamachuco, but had lived and worked in very impressive surroundings. An archaeologist studying Late Horizon Huamachuco without benefit of ethnohistory would certainly note that Huamachuco lacked embellishments seen at other centers and would conclude that Huamachuco was less important and less powerful than Huánuco Pampa or Cajamarca.

The storerooms on the hills around Huamachuco would document Inca involvement in the local economy, but again, comparison to other areas would suggest that this involvement was less intensive than elsewhere; the total storage capacity is relatively low, and the virtual absence of terracing suggests that the Inca invested less heavily in the Huamachuco area. The location on the road system would be eloquent witness to the overwhelming importance of communication to the Inca, but survey would show that the road predated the Inca presence in Huamachuco.

Many of the organizational changes that are revealed by the ethnohistorical sources would be archaeologically invisible. The division of the two original huarangas into four may have no material correlates, and the assignment of chaupi yungas territory to the province might well escape notice, even with extensive survey. With luck it might be possible to document the presence of mitima enclaves in the province, but it is most unlikely that their number, roles, and home territories could be identified.

Moreover, the tantalizing suggestions of political maneuvering that appear in the documentary sources would be entirely lost. These include, on the one hand, the efforts to break up the Chimu kingdom and disperse the population. On the other hand, the Garcilaso de la Vega account may be erroneous in fact, but not in its reflection of political ideology. There is definite archaeological evidence that the

Late Intermediate Period saw the decline of Marcahuamachuco as the dominant provincial center. This decline corresponded to the rise of several major sites on the western slopes overlooking the coast. Certainly, from the point of view of the Good Prince Huamachucu, this reflected political disintegration to conditions of "*behetría*," a state of anarchistic chaos preceding the development of kingship. He would have welcomed the recentralization of his position under the Inca and direct access to coca and other resources of distant areas of "his" province. The fact of the Inca conquest would be demonstrable in Huamachuco on solely archaeological grounds, and its role as a tertiary Inca center, perhaps largely administered through Cajamarca, could be correctly interpreted. The ethnohistorical sources allow these bare bones to be fleshed out considerably, greatly increasing our understanding of Huamachuco at the end of prehistory.

ACKNOWLEDGMENTS

The fieldwork on which this article is based was made possible by generous grants from the Social Sciences and Humanities Research Council of Canada and the Trent University Research Committee. Permission for the fieldwork was granted by the Instituto Nacional de Cultura of Peru. We wish to express our thanks to the many colleagues and students who have collaborated with the project during its lifetime. Special thanks are due to John H. Rowe and Maria Rostworowski de Diez Canseco, who provided transcriptions and a copy of the *Ordenanza*, and to Eric Deeds, whose notes on a number of documents were extremely useful. Susan Niles suggested that we look at the size of blocks in Huamachuco. Conversations with Geoff Spurling have broadened our perspective on the ethnohistorical literature.

NOTES

1. Our phase designations for the latter part of the Middle Horizon, the Late Intermediate Period, and the Late Horizon differ from those proposed by Thatcher (1972). Thatcher brought considerable order to the Huamachuco sequence, but worked primarily from surface collections, with some reference to pieces purchased by Uhle in 1900 and excavated by

McCown in 1942. Thatcher defined a Tuscan Phase for the latter half of the Middle Horizon, a Toro Phase for the Late Intermediate Period, and a Sazón Phase for the Late Horizon. We have made the following changes (Topic and Topic 1987: 22–25): (1) Because of considerable continuity in the Huamachuco ceramic tradition as expressed at Marcahuamachuco, we have defined an Early Huamachuco Phase (A.D. 400–600) and a Late Huamachuco Phase (A.D. 700–1000), separated by the Amaru Phase (A.D. 600–700), during which Huari influence was felt in the area. The Tuscan ceramic phase definition remains unchanged but is moved into the Late Intermediate Period. The dominant style in this phase, characterized by geometric designs painted in red and/or brown on a light slip (illustrated by McCown 1945: pl. 22c–e, h–k, r, v), has been named Huamachuco-on-White by Andrzej Krzanowski (1986). (2) The ceramic assemblage characteristic of Thatcher's Toro Phase is now recognized as intrusive from the Upper Chicama Valley, and represents the presence of a different ethnic group in the Huamachuco area. (3) The Sazón Phase of the Late Horizon has been renamed Santa Barbara, for reasons given in the text.

2. In the tasa, the total tribute which was to be paid by the population of the province was divided into three parts, as follows: (1) Married highland taxpayers (indigenous and mitima) and married mitima yunga taxpayers from San Agustín de Huamachuco, San Felipe de Chusgón, San Cristóbal de Cochulla, San Mateo de Cachicadán, Santiago de Chuco, San Salvador de Guaso, Santa Cruz de Yagón, and Santiago de Lúcuma paid three pesos, two *tomines* in silver, one bird, and one-half *hanega* of maize each. (2) Married mitima yunga and chaupi yunga taxpayers from Cormoc (Cormot?), Guataca, Callanca, Chiquibamba, Churucpampa, Colcapampal, Poqueda, Muchar (Mochal?), Mayachua, and Catin paid one piece of cotton cloth, nine tomines in silver, one-half hanega of maize, and one bird. (3) All unmarried taxpayers paid one peso, six tomines in silver, and one-half hanega of maize.

Espinoza (1974: 86) takes these figures to mean that mitimas yungas were mixed with serranos in each of the reducciones named in (1), and that mitimas yungas were present in each of the reducciones named in (2). Since the eighteen towns listed in (1) and (2) above are only about half the number of towns listed in other places in the González de Cuenca *Residencia* and *Ordenanza*, it is clear that residents of the towns listed in the tasa are being singled out in some way. It is also clear from the total number of taxpayers listed and the total tribute owed that married taxpayers living in the towns not mentioned paid the same tribute as those in (1) above. It is also clear that all the cloth was provided by the towns mentioned in (2). Thus, it seems that the tasa is simply defining which mitimas yungas were assigned part of the tribute in clothing and which were assigned a larger portion of the monetary tribute. This interpretation implies that there were indeed mitimas yungas in each of the towns mentioned in (1), but not necessarily that each town had a mixed population of yungas and serranos. Similarly, on the basis of the *Ordenanza* it seems that some of the towns listed in (2) were occupied by mitimas yungas while others were occupied by chaupi yunga groups, but that the two populations were not necessarily mixed in any of these towns.

3. This information has been provided by Eric Deeds, who cites a document in the Archivo Departmental de La Libertad, Sección Judicias, Corregimiento, Causas Ordinarias 168: 336.

3

—

SUE GROSBOLL

. . . AND HE SAID IN THE TIME OF

THE YNGA, THEY PAID TRIBUTE

AND SERVED THE YNGA

EDITOR'S INTRODUCTION

Grosboll's essay is a direct comparison of the rich ethnohistorical sources for the Huánuco region with archaeological data. This study focuses on looking for evidence of Inca control in the indigenous settlements, and as such it is a good contrast to Craig Morris and Donald E. Thompson's research at the Inca administrative center at Huánuco Pampa. Because her study was based on a more extensive survey, Grosboll (1987, 1988) was also able to expand on and reinterpret the results of earlier studies, especially Thompson's (1967). As with Katharina J. Schreiber's study in this volume, the results generally corroborate the ethnohistorical documents, which indicated that there was no strong local penetration by Inca personnel, that the decimal system was implemented, and that the Incas moved people around for economic reasons. However, the strict ethnic boundaries implied by the documents were not confirmed archaeologically.

Inca artifacts and architecture were scarce, except in the far northeastern sector and especially at the site of Ichu, where a local huaranga official lived. Outside of this sector, no Inca architecture was found, although single rectangular structures at three sites suggested local imitations of Inca houses, perhaps by other local lords in service to the Incas. Inca control at most sites was indicated solely by the appearance of aryballoid shapes in small percentages, probably associated with tribute payments.

This essay also provides information on the pre-Inca archaeology of the region. Local ceramics and architecture appear to be relatively similar across the ethnic boundaries described by the historical documents. While differences can be discerned that might be useful for identifying pre-Inca groups, the general conclusion is that movement between these groups occurred with a great deal of fluidity. Thus, the strict boundaries implied by the colonial documents were probably an Inca construct.

INTRODUCTION

Archaeological investigations in the hinterlands of the Inca empire are providing a more comprehensive view of the basic framework of Inca rule as well as illustrating the adaptability of that administration to local circumstances. But deciphering the prehistory of the Late Horizon outside of the Cuzco heartland is made complicated by the necessity of distinguishing between the material remains of Inca subjugation and that of the local peoples. We must peel away the broad overlay of Inca introductions in order to comprehend the ethnic and sociopolitical differences of the indigenous groups at the regional and subregional level.

The strength and character of Inca influence at the local level can be evaluated only with firm knowledge of the preexisting cultures of the region. The variability in the reproduction of Inca state symbolism is a reflection of differential Incaic interest in particular regions or communities as well as local interest in such symbols. In the material record, the appearance of Inca characteristics in smaller Andean communities can be interpreted as a direct, forced intervention of Inca administration in local affairs, the willingness by the local groups to adopt new traits and technologies from the Incas, or a combination of these two extremes. But even within one small region, the character of Inca administration and its subsequent impact on local structures can be complex. The separate analysis of archaeological and documentary evidence for one such region highlights the complexity of deciphering the Late Horizon developments and demonstrates that a synthesis of these

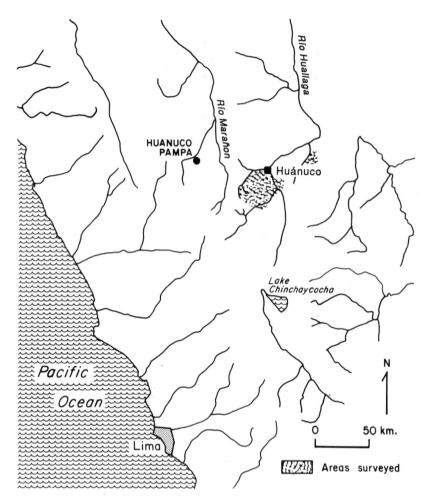

Figure 3.1. The central Peruvian Andes showing the area of study around the modern city of Huánuco and its relationship to the Inca regional center of Huánuco Pampa.

sources is essential for interpretation. The results of an investigation in the southeastern portion of the department of Huánuco, Peru, illustrate these points.

A SUBREGION OF THE INCA EMPIRE

An area physiographically and politically on the margin of the major Andean powers (fig. 3.1), the study zone in southeastern Huánuco provides striking evidence of the regional and subregional variability in Inca administration. The study of this region was facilitated by two factors. The proximity of Huánuco Pampa, a major Inca administrative center, allowed direct comparison between ceramics and architecture of the surrounding local communities and those of Inca state culture as represented at Huánuco Pampa. The region also has available ample early colonial documentation (Ortíz de Zúñiga 1967, 1972) describing the pre-Hispanic economic and political structure of these Inca-dominated communities. By interweaving and reinterpreting the archaeological and documentary sources of evidence, it was possible to delineate Inca and pre-Inca characteristics. This dual analysis gave greater insight into questions of Late Intermediate Period indigenous culture, Incaic regional policies specific to the region, and the impact of those policies.

Both archaeological and documentary evidence provides separate as well as corroborating data on aspects of the Incaic administration of the southeastern Huánuco region. In general, the two forms of evidence support one another with regard to the Incaic presence in the region, but neither source should be assumed to be more reliable than the other in all cases. The discussion which follows evaluates the documentary evidence first, as a predictor of the pattern to be found archaeologically. After summarizing the actual archaeological evidence, we shall compare the results of both analyses and integrate the information to present a more comprehensive view of provincial Inca rule.

EVIDENCE FROM THE COLONIAL VISITAS

The Spanish visitas of 1549 and 1562 (Ortíz de Zúñiga 1967, 1972) provide a wealth of information on nonmaterial cultural traits before and during the early Spanish colonial era. The focus of testimony by local leaders (*caciques, principales,* and *mandones*) in these documents was on answering questions of colonial and Inca tribute requirements. Visitations were made of villages throughout the region, villages that were occupied before the Spanish conquest and, most likely, before the Inca conquest (fig. 3.2). Information was compiled concerning the demography of the communities, their present level of tribute to the Spanish, the previous Inca control and taxation, and their political and economic ties to one another and to the Inca.

Specific questions on procedures in "the time of the Ynga" were

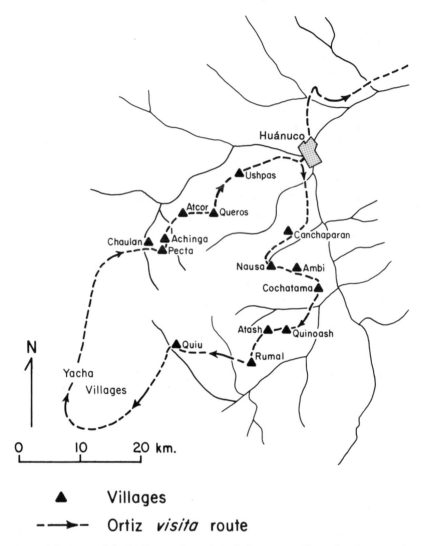

▲   Villages

--▶-- Ortiz *visita* route

Figure 3.2. Route of the 1562 visitadores through the western Chupachu, Quero, and Yacha territories. These villages were targeted in this study because of the availability of both 1549 and 1562 census data about the communities.

asked of the local leaders regarding the character of Inca government, the system for the naming of local leaders, the quantity and type of tribute paid to the Incas, the means of ascertaining the level and payment of tribute, and the construction and maintenance of government facilities such as administrative centers, way stations along the royal highway, temples, mines, and storehouses. The interest of Spanish officials in asking such questions was in utilizing the Inca governmental framework for their own purposes, rather than in reestablishing the pre-Inca sociopolitical structure.

Testimony on the Pre-Inca Period

Though explicit descriptions of pre-Inca social, political, and economic systems were not given within the testimony, the documents provide intriguing hints as to the nature of these systems, the character of the Inca takeover, and the amount of disruption of the systems by that takeover. A variety of what may have been separate ethnic groups is listed in the 1562 census of Ortíz de Zúñiga (1967: 22–94). The testimonies of the leaders refer to peoples of the region as Chupachu, Quero, Yacha, Wamali, or Yaros. Though the criteria for these group distinctions are not specifically stated in the visita, Murra (1967) assumed them to be separate ethnic groups.

The spatial distribution of villages referred to by these ethnic names, as determined through visita testimony and limited archaeological survey in the 1960s, shows them to have had some physiographic integrity (fig. 3.3), but the clarity or strength of spatial boundaries between the groups before the Inca conquest is not discernible from the visitas. Whether the groups were smaller entities within a larger regional sociopolitical unit or separate small polities is not certain. Their level of interaction or cooperation is also not apparent, but the 1562 visita describes a practice of resource utilization that involved the spatial intermixing of the various peoples rather than the maintenance of distinct geographic boundaries between them. For instance, several high-elevation Quero villages, lacking sufficient middle-elevation cropland in Quero territory, cultivated some of their crops in a valley to the southeast, within Chupachu territory (Ortíz de Zúñiga 1967: 160, 171, 188).

". . . In the Time of the Ynga"

With the Inca takeover of the region, these economic and political structures were altered—to what degree is not clear from the documentation alone. The Inca administration restructured political boundaries between several ethnic groups in order to create demographic units of decimal proportions. The local ethnic groups or polities were

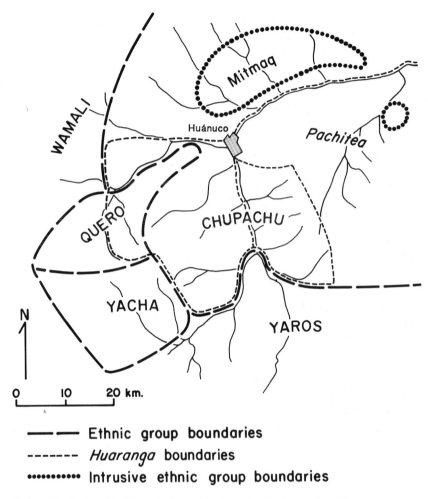

Figure 3.3. Sociopolitical boundaries within the region during the Late Horizon as described in the 1562 visita of Ortíz de Zúñiga. Mitmaq is an alternative term for mitima.

physiographically divided into hierarchical units based on ten, one hundred, and one thousand households. The four Chupachu huarangas, each of one thousand tribute households, were subdivided into ten *pachacas* of one hundred tributaries each. To conform to this Inca decimal model, it was necessary for the Inca administrators to include three pachacas of the Quero area with the western Chupachu huaranga for an even one thousand tribute households. This matter of bureaucratic bookkeeping would have greatly altered the chain of command among local leaders. The most obvious example of the political impact of such restructuring is the placement of the Quero leaders of the appended pachacas as subject to the Chupachu leader of the encompassing huaranga.

While each Inca-constructed huaranga had a cacique, it is not certain from the visita whether these were four equally powerful leaders or one acted as the overall leader. Though Don Diego Xagua testified in 1562 that he was the leader of all four huarangas, as well as of the Pachitea huaranga, other leaders did not agree (Ortíz de Zúñiga 1967: 70, 78, 81, 85). Their disagreement can be interpreted in various ways. The political hierarchy of the Incas may have included one cacique principal, a chain of command that had begun to disintegrate with the Spanish conquest, as evidenced by the leaders' rejection of Xagua's position. It is equally possible that this was a post-Conquest tactic by Xagua to establish greater power for himself under Spanish rule.

Ortíz de Zúñiga reported that even after the Spanish conquest of the region, local leaders retained their positions as community caciques, principales, or mandones. However, there does not appear to have been an ordered hierarchy of these positions. Principales may have led one or several villages, and secondary villages may or may not have had the subordinate leader called a mandon. Murra (1967), in his analysis of the Ortíz de Zúñiga documents, points out that there was a great deal of variability in the leaders' power and responsibility. In all likelihood, a preexisting political hierarchy was not present or was only loosely structured in the Chupachu and Quero communities and the Inca takeover of the region imposed a more rigorous hierarchy of control, particularly through the role of huaranga cacique.

Under Inca control, the succession of leadership passed from father to son, or to a relative of the father if the son was too young to lead. But these transitions were not carried out independently at the local level. The new officeholder was required to personally seek permission from the Inca king, either by going to Cuzco for an audience or through the king's representative at the regional center of Huánuco Pampa. The Inca king's stamp of approval was probably a mere formality in the case of smaller or less important communities. But for the position of huaranga cacique, the succession would have been more tightly controlled. Because of his power, the regional cacique, if one did exist in the Late Horizon, would have had to be either sympathetic to or controllable by the Inca administration in order to maintain peace in the region.

As well as overseeing or sanctioning the naming and succession of local leaders, the Inca official was responsible for the administration of justice in the area. This aspect of the position included the settlement of grievances and the review of cacique and principal governance of local affairs. Again, the degree of influence probably depended on the level of the village or official in the political hierarchy. The local leaders settled disputes and dispensed justice in their own communities, but their actions could be reviewed by the Inca administration if their decisions were called into question.

Of greater importance to the Inca administration was the care of Inca projects and the collection of tribute. The emphasis of control was on the maintenance of Inca lands, particularly those used for maize cultivation. In the testimonies within the 1562 visita, the Incas were most concerned with the cultivation and harvesting of state field crops. But they also kept watch on the administration or completion of tribute in the form of labor on the highways or at the shrines, way stations, or mines. The terms of the tribute required from each huaranga or community were reassessed each year (Ortíz de Zúñiga 1967: 17), according to the needs of the empire at that time. The level of involvement by the Inca administration again seems to have been in the pronouncement of the amount of tribute, but the means of payment of that tribute was left in the hands of the local leaders.

While Inca administration in matters of tribute and succession may have been direct or indirect, depending upon the circumstance, even indirect actions would have forced changes in local political traditions. The pre-Incaic rule of succession as described in the visitas was based not on inheritance but on community selection. Under the Inca administration, the right of nomination was removed from community control. Such a revision would have eliminated the need to reindoctrinate each newly elected community leader, since the acceptance of Inca state principles would presumably be handed down from father to son.

A more important change in the local political structure was the placement of a leader in two reciprocal relationships: one with his community and one with the Inca administrators. New demands were placed on the local leader by the state bureaucracy, but the state also gave a leader new power within his community and set his household apart, politically, socially, and economically.

The mitima program as described in the Ortíz de Zúñiga visita was a physical intrusion of foreigners into Chupachu territory. Two hundred Cuzco households were settled among the villages of the northern Chupachu huaranga, particularly toward the east, ostensibly to prevent rebellion and to maintain the eastern forts and temples of the Inca state. But Ortíz de Zúñiga (1967: 179, 1972: 38) also mentions that the mitimas were involved in economic pursuits, such as the trade of lowland and highland produce. The positioning of Inca settlements at the edge of the lowlands would certainly have ensured the control of valuable resources from this zone.

Some state tribute demands were accomplished by the Incas through the establishment of trade-specific communities, where residents were assigned specializations such as pottery making or leather working. The extent of forced resettlement with local people is not known, and yet that might have been the factor that had the greatest impact on local polities. The Ortíz de Zúñiga document tells of the importation of foreign mitimas into the Chupachu/Quero territory, but there are only scattered references to resettlement of the Chupachu and the Quero themselves. Such references are not clear as to whether the assignment of a household or person outside the home community was made in response to Inca needs ("placed here in the time of the Inca") or a local leader's economic needs ("here to serve his cacique"). I suspect that both types of tribute resettlements were occurring regionally during the Late Horizon.

We can only assume from the scarcity of references in the visita that movement of locals did not occur on a large scale. (However, such community disruption did occur in the Chaupihuaranga/Yacha area, where villages contained many mitimas; see Mayer 1984 and Bird 1970.) Though the presence of foreign households or villages is readily detected within the Chupachu territory, the forced movement of Chupachu people within the region would be much more difficult to discover, since variability in their material record from that of the transplanted local residents would not be easily discerned.

ARCHAEOLOGICAL IMPLICATIONS

Examination of the colonial documentation on matters "in the time of the Inca" leads us to several expectations as to what might be found archaeologically. Material evidence that would confirm the 1562 testimonies would take various forms. From the visitas, one can surmise that though the Inca administration held control over local leaders, Inca overlords were not actually installed at the community level. The Inca administrator's influence in decisions and tribute assessments would be difficult to verify, particularly if he remained most of the time at Huánuco Pampa or Cuzco and/or if the local leaders normally were called to him. The rarity of his physical presence within the communities themselves suggests that little or no archaeological evidence reflecting such visits would be expected.

However, the establishment of a political hierarchy and its consequent increase in power for certain community leaders might be manifested in a disproportionate distribution of material remains within and between communities. If the village was large or politically prominent, then some material symbols of the empire might be present, perhaps as state architecture or gifts of pottery to the local lord. Because of the Inca penchant for uniformity and structure, the archaeological presence of Cuzco polychrome pottery or the architectural forms of rectangular structures with trapezoidal niches and doorways would be expected to appear without variation. The resistance of the Chupachu and the Quero to the Inca takeover and the lack of direct Inca intervention at the local level would result in minimal material evidence of Inca dominance in those communities. Conversely, when such material evidence does present itself, one would assume that the Incas had a strong desire to use or regulate that community or subregion directly.

Based upon the use of specific terms for the groups in the region, spatial boundaries, which reflect ethnic boundaries, should be seen within the material remains. If so, ceramic and architectural differences might be expected between the western Chupachu and their neighbors the Yacha and the Quero. Internally, the various huarangas of the Chupachu should show little cultural variability. This should also be true for the Yacha and the Quero who, according to the Ortíz de Zúñiga document, had formed a single ethnic group before Inca reorganization.

In sum, several pre-Hispanic features described within the documentary evidence could be apparent archaeologically if they in fact existed. If the pre-Inca groups of the region were discrete polities or ethnic groups, the distinctiveness of their ceramic and architectural remains might be expected to follow the spatial pattern drawn along the physiographic lines indicated in the visita village list (fig. 3.2).

Second, there should be little evidence of intrusion of nonlocal administrative personnel at the community level. We would not expect, for example, to see an annex to each site with fine Inca ceramics and architecture that could have housed a resident representative of the government. The movement of goods went in the opposite direction, with the delivery of tribute goods from the villages to Huánuco Pampa. Some tribute wares should be found at each site, since almost all villages were required to pay tribute in ceramics to the Incas.

Third, the Ortíz de Zúñiga document refers to the Inca-directed influx of mitimas but makes little mention of local resettlement. We would therefore expect to see little or no change in the local settlement pattern subsequent to the Inca entrance to the area. In general, the sites of the Late Intermediate Period and those of the Late Horizon should be the same. A third line of investigation is the Inca system of administration through existing local leaders while Inca officials remained at Huánuco Pampa.

ARCHAEOLOGICAL EVIDENCE

Archaeological evidence is available for the southeastern sector of the department of Huánuco as a result of various investigations. The research team led by John Murra in the 1960s laid the groundwork for further study by establishing the potential for combined archaeological and documentary analysis. However, he and his colleagues were unable to physically locate and survey many of the sites mentioned in the visitas. The Pachitea zone has been investigated in greater depth by Thompson (1967). My own work (Grosboll 1988) concentrated on discovering those villages described in some detail in both the 1549 and the 1562 visitas (fig. 3.2). I was able to locate numerous visita villages (fig. 3.4) which had not been previously studied. The following discussion, though concentrating on the Quero and the western and eastern Chupachu huarangas, will also incorporate archaeological data from throughout the region.

Chupachu/Quero Ceramics and Architecture

In summarizing the general characteristics of local architecture and ceramics I will first address the eastern and western Chupachu hua-

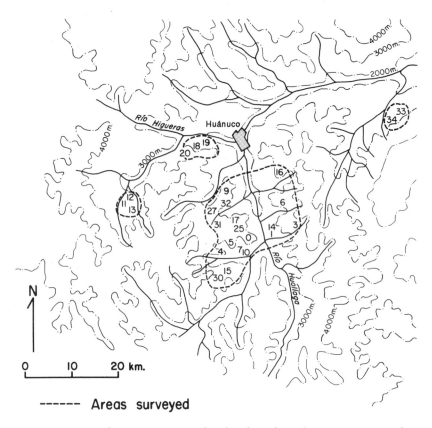

------ Areas surveyed

Figure 3.4. Areas of intensive survey within the Chupachu and Quero territories. The numbers refer to Late Horizon sites recorded during the survey.

rangas, including the Quero. (I will postpone until later the discussion of the northeastern and far eastern Chupachu, where heavy mitima settlement occurred.) The Late Horizon villages of the Chupachu heart-land and the annexed Quero pachacas were generally small in size, with the average village containing three hundred to four hundred people and the largest having several thousand. The sites consisted of tightly packed house/patio units with simple one-story oval or circular houses (fig. 3.5). All architecture fell into the domestic categories of house (fig. 3.6), tomb (fig. 3.7), storage chamber, patio wall, or terrace. Each patio group generally contained one or two houses, though there were rare instances of three to five houses within a patio. These irregu-larly shaped domestic patio units were separated by terrace levels or surrounding walls.

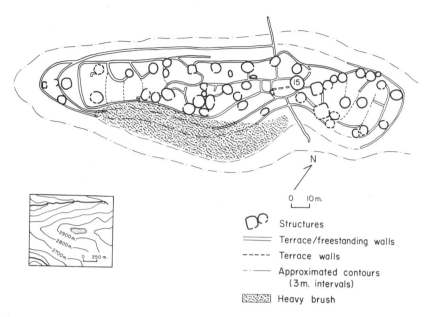

Structures

Terrace/freestanding walls

Terrace walls

Approximated contours
(3 m. intervals)

Heavy brush

2900 m.
2800 m.
2700 m.

0   250 m.

N

0   10 m.

15

Figure 3.5. Plan of the southeastern Chupachu site of Suncho.

Figure 3.6. Chupachu house from the site of Atash. Chupachu houses have distinctive doorways that are bowed toward the top.

Figure 3.7. Chupachu tomb from the site of Atash. Smaller structures such as tombs had domed ceilings, overlapping stone slabs, and flat roofs.

The ceramics of the Chupachu and Quero were extremely simple, consisting of undecorated utilitarian wares of a thick red or brown crude paste. The only notable form of variation between the ceramics of the two groups was in paste constituents and slip color. The latter had a very narrow range, primarily orange-red, red on orange, or burnished brown, though yellow and pinkish slips also exist. The forms of these thick-walled vessels were simple also, consisting primarily of ollas and jars with long, diagonally flared rims (fig. 3.8) and horizontal, indented handles (fig. 3.9).

Beyond their own ceramics, the local villages produced undecorated utilitarian ceramics, primarily storage jars, as tribute for shipment to Huánuco Pampa. The slip color, fineness of paste, hardness, and form of these tribute wares stood out from the local wares. Unlike the Inca tribute wares, which had a consistent wall thickness throughout the vessel, the local ceramics had a much thicker rim than body. In addition, the smoothing of the vessel wall was much more cursory for Chupachu/Quero wares.

Within villages, little variability could be seen in material remains. The overall impression in both ceramics and architecture is one of little

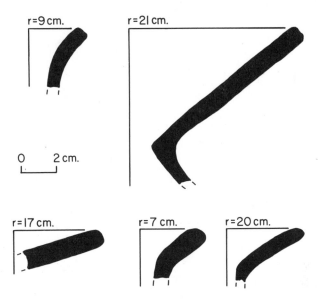

Figure 3.8. Rim profiles of the most common Chupachu and Quero vessel forms.

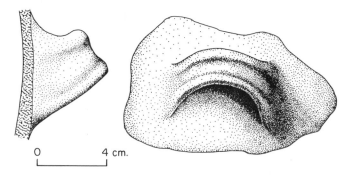

Figure 3.9. Profile and front view of Chupachu/Quero handle forms. Both the orientation and the quality of these handles vary dramatically from the introduced Inca forms.

social distinction between households. Only a greater patio size or perhaps a slightly larger house may have indicated the household of a more influential family within a community.

While a general pattern of consistency in architecture and ceramics existed throughout the Chupachu territory, spatial variation did occur within that pattern. Gradual shifts in both ceramic and architectural style occurred across space. Minor architectural variations were seen moving east-west or north-south within the territory, but particularly where the Huallaga and Higueras rivers divide the territory. Subtle changes in ceramic vessel form and finishing techniques also followed this pattern.

Across the entire Chupachu territory, the greatest variance in ceramic and architectural style was displayed between the Pachitea area of the far eastern huaranga and the remainder of the Chupachu communities. In place of roughly circular structures with flat-roofed rooms, the Pachitea sites consist of rectangular, gabled structures (Morris and Thompson 1985: 119–138). The eastern two-thirds of the northern huaranga appears to be a complex mixture of traditional Chupachu architecture, the style found in the Pachitea area, and styles brought in by state mitimas. In contrast to the lack of Cuzco polychrome pottery at most Chupachu/Quero sites, both the far eastern Pachitea area and the northern huaranga yielded many examples of Inca non-tribute wares.

Incaic Impact at the Local Level

Both the architecture and the ceramics of most Chupachu and Quero villages were distinct from the classic Cuzco styles (Gasparini and Margolies 1980). Only in a few instances (to be discussed later) were there any structures in these small communities that contained architectural elements reminiscent of the Incaic model. The primary evidence for Inca influence at the community level was the small percentage of each site's ceramics which matched those of Huánuco Pampa and were associated with ceramic production for tribute. In contrast to the Cuzco polychrome ceramics, these were the standard utilitarian wares of the empire; they were of a different form (primarily the aryballoid) and were constructed with a finer paste, more regular wall thickness, and a harder finish. It is worth noting that individual elements of the Inca ceramic style do not seem to have been adopted by local potters, and the two products remained separate.

The general pattern for both architectural and ceramic remains shows the continuation of local tradition with minimal forced or adapted inclusion of Inca traits in the local culture. The archaeological evidence speaks for little or no direct Inca impact within the small villages, thereby supporting the picture presented in the colonial documentation of Inca regional control.

Exceptions to this general pattern of course exist, with evidence of

Cuzco or Cuzco-like traits at several sites within the region. One such site is Ichu in the Pachitea area (fig. 3.4, site 33), which has been described by Thompson (1967; Morris and Thompson 1985). The village was known from the colonial visitas to have been the home of the huaranga cacique Paucar Guaman, possibly the highest official of local governance. The site is notable for the abundance of Cuzco polychrome and large rectangular structures with trapezoidal niches, in the style of Inca state architecture. Obviously the village of Ichu was important enough to warrant the greater quantity and higher quality of Inca symbols.

The quality and the style of the masonry and ceramics of these structures at Ichu are distinct from the local forms. Though not as grand or as perfectly rendered as the administrative structures of Huánuco Pampa, these buildings do suggest that Inca craftsmen or overseers participated directly in their construction. Excepting these large structures, the domestic buildings at Ichu are comparable to those of the other Chupachu sites in size and type of masonry. However, the domestic structures of Ichu and other Pachitea sites vary from the Chupachu/Quero standard in being rectangular and gabled like those of the Cuzco area.

Outside the northeastern sector of Pachitea and the mitima zone are three sites which also contain evidence of some Inca influence in architecture or ceramics: Akush, Suncho, and Aukimarka. Akush (fig. 3.4, site 0) is located on the western slope of the Huallaga River, in the huaranga of cacique Chinchao Poma. Suncho and Aukimarka (fig. 3.4, sites 3 and 6, respectively) are on the eastern slope, in the huaranga of cacique Quirin. All three sites have structures which suggest Inca influence but do not fit the ideal Inca architectural model.

At Akush, one small rectangular structure (fig. 3.10) sits among the circular structures common to Chupachu villages. There are no trapezoidal niches or doorways, and the quality of the masonry matches that of the surrounding circular structures. The placement of the doors and the size of the structure negate the possibility of its construction as a colonial church but do suggest the general house style of the Cuzco region (Gasparini and Margolies 1980: 190; Niles 1987: 40–49). One Cuzco polychrome sherd was found at the site, along the outside wall of this rectangular structure.

At Suncho is another rectangular building, of slightly larger dimensions (fig. 3.11). It appears to have been created by the alteration of an

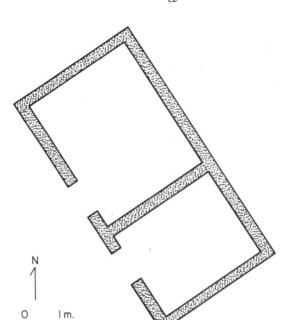

Figure 3.10. Probable Inca structure at the site of Akush. The use of an interior wall, double doorways, and rectangular form is extremely rare in the region.

older structure, incorporating several house and terrace walls to form the new structure. Along one long wall there are two large doorways. Though heavily damaged, they do not appear to have been trapezoidal. Overall, their size, form, and number are more consistent with Inca than Chupachu architecture. Like the intrusive structure at Akush, this Suncho construction is an anomaly among the circular or oval Chupachu structures. No Cuzco polychrome ceramics were found at Suncho.

The final example of nonlocal architecture comes from another southeastern Chupachu site. Within the site of Aukimarka are four structures which look like colcas, standard Inca storehouses (Morris and Thompson 1985: 147). However, this row of Inca-like structures does not strictly follow the dimensions of those at Huánuco Pampa, being smaller than standard colcas and of a slightly different style of masonry. The presence of large, formal storage structures is extremely unusual in this region.

Unlike the standard Inca architecture of Ichu, these special buildings

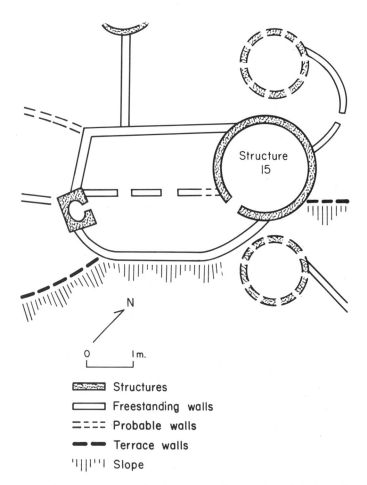

Figure 3.11. Alterations to patio of structure 15 at the site of Suncho. The wall with two doorways which divides the patio appears to be a Late Horizon addition to the compound.

of Akush, Suncho, and Aukimarka are only suggestive of Inca influence. They are unlike local structures in form but similar in masonry style. The proportions are slightly off from the Inca ideal, but the form suggests an Inca model. At Akush, the single polychrome sherd hints that the structure's use may have been connected with state business. It is worth noting that the buildings are located in the centers of their sites, at Suncho next to one of the largest residences at the site. The structures of Akush and Suncho could have been built for the occasional visit by an Inca administrator or to carry out new political or tribute-related responsibilities as mandated by the Inca administration.

These buildings do reflect Inca influence in smaller communities, but the character of that influence is uncertain. The state administration may have regarded these villages as politically less important than Ichu but still requiring some material mark of the empire. The state could have requested the construction of the buildings but allowed local craftsmen to do the job without state guidance. A second interpretation of these sites is that the local leaders of the communities took it upon themselves to build the structures, as symbols not necessarily of the Incas but of the power and prestige bestowed by the Incas upon these leaders.

Independent construction by locals is possible but not probable until after the Spanish conquest, since the Inca administrator controlled or reviewed all actions of the local leaders and was not likely to have allowed activities that were aimed at personal power building. Although not all peoples were hostile to a takeover by the Incas, most groups were rebellious and would have resisted accepting any material symbol of their subjugation.

Two possible conclusions can be drawn regarding these structures. They may mark villages that were important to the empire early in the Inca takeover of the region but were subsequently superseded by Ichu as the focus of Inca activity shifted to the northeastern sector of the region. Alternatively, their presence may indicate that these villages were of lesser stature than Ichu and consequently did not warrant symbols of state that were as elaborate as those at Ichu.

Whatever the reasons, the material record reveals the disproportionate distribution of Incaic influence in the region. Certainly the greatest quantity of archaeological evidence for Inca regional dominance is distributed in the northeastern sector of the Chupachu territory, where Ichu is located. The examples given above are very minor exceptions, pointing out the Incas' lack of either interest or direct involvement in a major portion of the Chupachu/Quero territory.

Evidence for Ethnic Boundaries

From the previous discussion of Quero and Chupachu communities, it should be obvious that no true physiographic boundary was found in the material remains of these two ethnic groups. Likewise, neither the

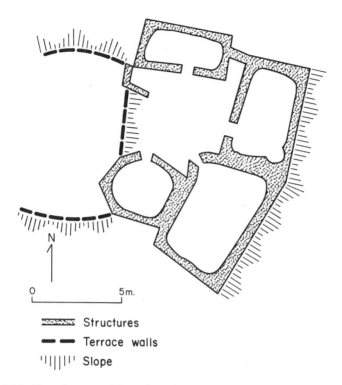

Structures
Terrace walls
Slope

Figure 3.12. Plan of compound from the Yacha site of Wakan. Note that the irregular rectangular form and interior curved corners are in contrast to the probable Inca structure at Akush (fig. 3.10) (from R. Matos 1972).

architectural nor the ceramic remains support the idea of strong ethnic differences among the Chupachu, Quero, Yacha, Wamali, and Yaros, as is suggested by the visitas.

The Chupachu, Quero, and Yacha villages display similarities in the layout of patio groups and overall site plan. But Yacha domestic structures, roughly rectangular in shape (fig. 3.12), are easily distinguished from the more circular Chupachu and Quero structures. However, this architectural variability among ethnic groups is not delineated on the ground by a clean physical boundary line.

Within communities at the Yacha/Chupachu border, rectangular and circular house forms are intermingled. At the Chupachu village of Atash, interspersed among the circular houses which dominate the site, are a few rectangular structures reminiscent of those at Wakan (fig. 3.12). Whether these buildings represent Yacha households liv-

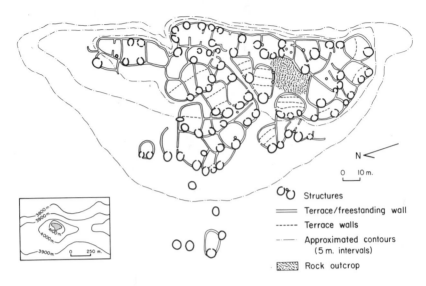

Figure 3.13. Plan of the Quero site of Marcamarqaycoto.

ing among the Chupachu is unclear. Interestingly, the ceramics of the southwestern Chupachu are very similar to those of the Yacha (Bode 1967). Both the architecture and the ceramics imply that ideas and perhaps people were moving across the ethnic border between the Chupachu and the Yacha.

Most surprisingly, there does not seem to be a distinction in material remains between the Quero and the Chupachu. In fact, the Quero architecture and ceramics are more closely related to northwestern Chupachu remains than to those of the Yacha sites. This is particularly apparent when one compares the domestic architecture of the Chupachu, the Yacha, and the Quero (figs. 3.5, 3.12, and 3.13). Both the patio compound and the house form of the Quero site of Marcamarqaycoto show greater similarities to Chupachu architecture (fig. 3.5) than to Yacha architecture (fig. 3.12). Here again the archaeological evidence reflects a pattern different from that anticipated, given the colonial documentation, where it was stated that the Quero had been linked, politically or ethnically, to the Yacha before the Inca takeover.

The strength of an architectural and ceramic boundary between the Chupachu and the Wamali, or the Chupachu and the Yaros, is less clear, since little or no archaeological work has been done on these

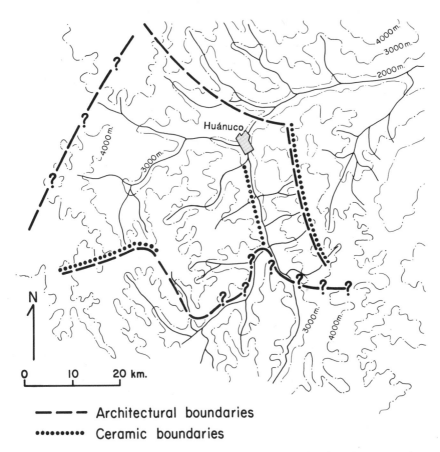

— — — Architectural boundaries

•••••••• Ceramic boundaries

Figure 3.14. Composite of ethnic boundaries based on the archaeological remains. The strongest boundary is represented by the line to the east and north of the city of Huánuco. Scarcity of evidence concerning the Wamali and Yaros suggests variability to the Chupachu pattern, but this is not certain.

other ethnic groups. The greatest variability appears to have occurred with the Wamali, whose sites contained much larger circular structures and multistoried towers (Morris and Thompson 1985: 159–160), in contrast to the Chupachu/Quero sites, where only domestic architecture is present. The Wamali sites are reported to have had larger populations and greater functional complexity.

The pattern of ethnic variability without strict demarcation that is demonstrated in the archaeological evidence (fig. 3.14) is also present

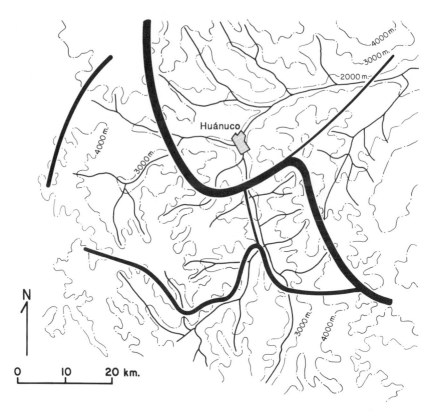

Figure 3.15. Linguistic boundaries in the study area. Line width indicates strength of dialectical variation.

in the modern linguistic patterns for the region (David Weber [1983] and personal communication) (fig. 3.15). A strong Cuzco influence in the northeastern sector of the region separates it from the remainder of the region and creates the strongest linguistic boundary. Differences between the Quero and the Chupachu are minor, since these two groups are more closely related linguistically to one another than to the neighboring Yacha. The linguistic separation of the Chupachu from the Yaros is less certain, although some variability has been noted along the southern Chupachu boundary.

Though it is not certain that variability in ceramic and architectural styles can be used as a marker of the strength of ethnic boundaries (Grosboll 1987), these factors combined with supporting linguistic evidence present a strong case for reinterpreting the picture of ethnic separation presented by the colonial visitas. I would conclude that several related, loosely formed polities existed in the southeastern Huánuco region before the Late Horizon. The Quero were most closely allied to the northeasternmost Chupachu, rather than to the Yacha (as the visita suggests). The Quero, in fact, may have been a separate entity before the Inca incursion and only briefly connected (politically or bureaucratically) to the Yacha before their inclusion in a Chupachu huaranga. This would explain the persistence of a separate ethnic name for this group of villages called the Quero. The unification of the Chupachu as a single polity is not supported by the archaeological evidence, which points instead toward direct Inca involvement for regional unification and the imposition of hierarchical leadership.

Mitima and Local Resettlement

The heavy influence of mitimas in the northeastern sector of the region, the huarangas of Paucar Guaman and Marca Pari, has been confirmed archaeologically in surveys by Donald E. Thompson (1967, 1972), Christine A. Rudecoff (ms.), and Craig Morris and Patrick Carmichael (personal communication). Though the zones of mitima settlement have been confirmed, the separation of mitima and local villages has proved difficult. The various foreign ethnic groups that comprised the settlers of this sector have yet to be spatially delimited (Morris and Carmichael, personal communication). But survey by Daniel Morales of the University of San Marcos, Lima, and air photos of the area northwest of the city of Huánuco show less influence of such settlement. The sites revert to the standard Chupachu model in structural form, settlement pattern, and ceramics, reflecting neither mitima nor Pachitea influence.

The evidence for Pachitea settlement before the Late Horizon is not apparent, and excavated sites seem to be shallow (Thompson, personal communication). These two factors, along with the differences in architectural style between the Pachitea and the rest of the Chupachu region, suggest that the Pachitea settlements may date primarily to the Late Horizon.

Could the Pachitea sites have been resettlements of Chupachu peoples? While the Pachitea domestic architecture reflects a Cuzco model, the ceramics of this area are most like those of the southwest zone of the Chupachu. The largest pre-Inca communities were in the southwest, the villages of Atash (fig. 3.4, site 30) and Rumal. These sites existed into the Colonial Period, but with only a small portion of their once high populations. A 1520 population estimate based on archaeological survey shows Atash to have had more than 1,300 people. By 1549, Atash was reported to have had only thirty-two houses, occupied by a population of perhaps 160 people.

Even taking into account the terrible devastation of these villages because of epidemics, this population decline is far greater than that experienced in other communities of the region. The resettlement of southwestern Chupachu peoples during the Late Horizon by the state could explain the decline in population as well as the unusual nature of the material remains for the Pachitea zone. Such movement would have broken the power of the more populous villages in the region and at the same time helped to expand Incaic dominance into a region chosen for development.

No mention of a resettlement of the southwestern Chupachu appears in the Ortíz de Zúñiga visita, and the scenario discussed above must be taken only as speculation at this point. Further archaeological investigation may reveal that the population of the Pachitea sites was other resettled Cuzco people or that the Chupachu of this far eastern sector were merely materially different from their more westerly brethren.

ARCHAEOLOGICAL VERSUS
DOCUMENTARY EVIDENCE

The correspondence between the archaeological and the documentary evidence concerning the Late Horizon of southeastern Huánuco initially could be interpreted as both conflicting and supportive. Both sources offer information regarding the nature of Inca influence in the region, the preexisting ethnic boundaries of the region, the distinction of Inca and local cultural patterns during the Late Horizon, and the changes to the local social, economic, and political structures during that period.

Though groups in this area distinguished themselves or others through the use of specific ethnic group names, the archaeological evidence portrays a region without strict spatial boundaries between these groups. There is no support for either social or political separations, and movement between the communities occurred regardless of their ethnic affiliation. The Inca empire's imposition of the decimal system of administration on these people produced a firmer definition of boundaries than had ever existed before the Late Horizon.

Both archaeological and documentary evidence confirms the lack of involvement at the local level by Inca officials in most parts of the region. The primary Inca remains at the small Chupachu/Quero villages are ceramics matching those of Huánuco Pampa, and prepared specifically for tribute purposes. The distinctive characteristics of the architectural and ceramic symbols of the empire were not adopted by these communities as individual traits in their pottery or houses. Only in villages of particular leaders are there to be found symbols of the Inca presence and/or of the local political power resulting from the Incaic period.

A demographic analysis (Grosboll 1988) using both lines of evidence lent support to the validity of the visita testimony regarding the Inca political division of the territory into four huarangas based upon decimal quantities of tribute payers. In this study, estimation of the Late Horizon population was based upon architectural evidence and demographic projections from the colonial censuses. The western huaranga population by Inca division should have been approximately 10,000 people (1,000 tribute payers [males between thirty and fifty years of age] times ten [these males represented 10 percent of the total Late Horizon population, based on a study of both modern and colonial censuses; see Grosboll 1988]). Based on the archaeological evidence, the 1520 population estimate for this area is between 9,517 and 11,377 (Grosboll 1988), with the latter figure being the closer approximation. A similar test compared the archaeologically derived population of the three Quero pachacas to the figure expected by Inca reckoning. These pachacas, which should have constituted 30 percent of the western Chupachu huaranga, did in fact contain 33 to 37 percent of the total population. While exact decimal divisions of population probably proved impossible to maintain, the decimal ideal of Inca policy would appear to have some validity, and administrative bookkeeping apparently took precedence over preexisting sociopolitical arrangements.

The disproportionate distribution of Inca-related ceramics and architecture found in the archaeological record can also be explained by returning to the colonial documentation for direct as well as indirect references to Inca interest in the northeastern sector. Though the general policy of the Incas seems to have been to leave existing local institutions intact and to standardize the hierarchy of political units, there were some geographically specific policies.

For instance, the distribution of mitimas was not even across the four huarangas. The heaviest concentration was in the northern portion of the region, the huaranga of Marca Pari, particularly the eastern two-thirds of that sector. There were various governmental goals to mitima settlement, but some of the settlements were specifically placed to prevent rebellion of the local peoples. Murra (1967: 400) has suggested that the numbers of mitimas in this zone may indicate that the pre-Inca Chupachu focus of activity was toward the *selva* (jungle), in the northeastern sector of the region, and therefore mitima garrisons were needed there as a safeguard.

A secondary zone of mitima settlement was in the easternmost Pachitea area, the huaranga of Paucar Guaman and later of Diego Xagua, who was possibly cacique of all four huarangas. Again, this position of an important leader in the northeastern sector of the region implies that the area had or was given a dominant position in the region over other Chupachu areas. It is probable that the prominence of Paucar Guaman's or Xagua's position and of this part of the region was raised as a consequence of the Inca conquest, rather than being a preestablished state of affairs. If this far eastern zone was of particular interest to the Incas, the naming of its leader to the highest position among all the huarangas would have politically focused Inca control into this one zone of development. If Xagua was not in fact cacique principal, after the Spanish takeover he may have used his previous position of more direct contact with Inca officials to subsequently appoint himself cacique principal.

The prominence of the northeastern area is indirectly suggested in other parts of the Ortíz de Zúñiga visita. The final list of those who testified before the Spanish does not reflect equal representation of the huarangas. The visita testimony came primarily from caciques of the northeastern sector, seven of the twelve leaders reporting. This means that three-quarters of the geographic Chupachu area was represented by only five leaders: one from the Quero area, one from the southwestern area of the Chupachu, two from Aukimarka on the eastern slope, and one from the southeastern sector of the Chupachu. The distribution is not even, neither between the huarangas nor across space.

If those testifying were the leaders of greater power in the region, this suggests that the sphere of influence was in the northeastern portion of the region in 1562. Whether such an imbalance of power occurred during pre-Inca times or was the result of Inca administration of the region is not discernible from the Ortíz de Zúñiga document. The archaeological evidence, however, supports the latter view, since the Pachitea sites do not show long occupation, while those outside the northeast, particularly in the southwest, do suggest large populations of long duration.

Several interpretations can possibly explain the presence of nonlocal mitima and Inca architecture and ceramics in this northeastern sector. During the late Late Intermediate Period, the Chupachu may have turned their attention to the northeast, away from the southwest and sites such as Atash and Rumal. Upon conquest of this region, the Incas centered their control in those zones of greatest Chupachu power and development. But it is equally likely that the geographically imbalanced Inca presence is related to Inca economic interests rather than to previous sociopolitical structures.

Inca economic interest in the northeast is not hard to understand when one sees that area's potential for maize cultivation and access to lowland products such as coca. It is highly probable that the Incas merely used preexisting communities or resettled Chupachu from the southwest to cultivate state fields for tribute under direct Inca supervision. Such a resettlement would better explain the rapid depopulation of the southwestern sites of Atash and Rumal. Interestingly, David Weber and other linguists (personal communication) who have worked throughout the Chupachu/Quero territory have described the prehistoric irrigation systems of the northeastern sector (the mitima and Pachitea areas) as far superior to those in other parts of the territory. Bird (1970) found in his study of modern and prehistoric maize of the region that the only area displaying possible Inca influence in the type of maize was the Pachitea area. If the Inca agricultural interest was the factor which increased settlement and political strength in this sector, it offers a dramatic example of direct involvement in local and regional administration and highlights the fact that the spatially disproportionate influence of the Incas can be seen within even a small subregion.

CONCLUSIONS

Two contrasting patterns emerge for the Late Horizon indigenous communities of the southeastern Huánuco region. For the majority of the Chupachu and the Quero, their Late Horizon architectural and ceramic remains continue traditions of the Late Intermediate Period. The presence of Incaic status architecture or pottery is rare in these small villages. This evidence fits well with the image of governance presented in the Ortíz de Zúñiga visita, of Inca administrators working through the top level of local leaders, with little or no contact beyond those leaders. Little within the archaeological record marks the Inca dominance of the region, since few Inca goods and ideas flowed into the local communities and most communities displayed indifference or resistance to the adoption of things Incaic.

The exceptions to this pattern of nonintervention at the local level are notable. They represent either differential Inca involvement within the region, as in the northeastern sector, or the appropriation of Inca symbols by individual leaders. This study supports the assumption that the quantity of Incaic material remains is reflective of the quantity of their political, economic, and social influence on the individual sites. But it is through the combined use of archaeological and documentary evidence that the character of the Inca administration and the fullness of its disproportionate impact on the local southeastern Huánuco ethnic groups were deciphered.

The closer involvement of the Inca administration in specific locales, as marked by the presence of standard state architecture and ceramics, was not distributed evenly throughout the region nor even among the four huarangas. At those communities outside the Inca focus, the small percentage of utilitarian wares made to Inca specification is the primary material evidence of Inca control. Without the documentation and a regional survey approach, it could easily be inferred that these villages were barely within the Inca empire.

While there is archaeological support for an Inca policy of strict hierarchy and minimal local contact, as depicted in the visitas, that overlay of control must be weighed against specific interests and special projects. The political and economic use of the Pachitea area and the mitima settlements constitutes direct involvement, perhaps including the movement of local people into new communities. But even if Chupachu resettlement on a·large scale did not take place under the Incas, the sphere of action moved away from the southwest Chupachu territory to the northeast huarangas of Paucar Guaman and Marca Pari. The large southwestern sites of Rumal and Atash were mere remnants of their former size by the early Colonial Period.

This study has also shown that investigation of an entire region, rather than only a few sites, is necessary if we are to appreciate the complexity of Inca state administration. A survey of only the Pachitea area or of only the southwestern Chupachu sector would have yielded two very different interpretations of the Late Horizon for the region. What Thompson (1967, 1972) saw in Pachitea and what I found in the Chinchao Poma and Quirin huarangas of the western Chupachu were quite different, but both represent the Late Horizon Chupachu. For a true interpretation of the impact of the Incas upon the various ethnic groups, a broad regional perspective was necessary.

Can archaeological results in one region be taken as representative of another region? Southeastern Huánuco did not constitute a regional power of the Andes, comprising instead numerous small polities. The Inca response in administration of these small villages would of course have been different from that applied in more politically and militarily powerful regions and in larger population centers (Earle et al. 1987; Costin and Earle 1989). For the analysis of more complex or larger regions, the task would be more difficult, particularly if the researcher did not have the advantages of the Huánuco project: early detailed colonial documentation, simple sites, and a nearby regional center for comparison of Incaic materials.

The Inca empire responded to the social and political diversity of its subjugated peoples by developing flexibility in the application of Inca policy among the various groups. If Incaic influence and control were not consistently applied throughout a small frontier backwater such as southeastern Huánuco, then it would be more reasonable to look for bureaucratic adaptation rather than consistency among the various localities and regions within the empire.

The standardization and institutionalization of Inca policy are most easily seen in the mass reproduction of architecture and ceramics as symbols of the state. We now recognize the adaptability of Inca administration to local and regional needs and the variability that is found in the archaeological record as a consequence of such localized adaptation. The interpretation of the Late Horizon throughout the Inca empire is made more complex by an additional factor. Those subsumed under that Andean order responded in distinctive ways due to the diversity of their sociopolitical structures as well as the individual motives of their leaders. The reception or interpretation of Inca policy by the conquered local communities created yet more variability in the material record of the Late Horizon.

4
—

KATHARINA J. SCHREIBER

THE INCA OCCUPATION OF

THE PROVINCE OF ANDAMARCA

LUCANAS, PERU

EDITOR'S INTRODUCTION

Schreiber's essay discusses the results of her research in the Carhuarazo
Valley, south of Ayacucho. Using archaeological evidence, she is able
to demonstrate that this region provided more food and other material
to the Inca empire than the ethnohistorical sources indicated. However, the documentary information stating that the area provided only
litter bearers and *yanaconas* (permanent service personnel) was archaeologically unobservable. As did the Topics, Schreiber concluded
that both sources contribute important but complementary kinds of
evidence concerning the region.

Like Grosboll, Schreiber found little clear archaeological evidence
for a large Inca occupation of the valley. Architecturally, there were few
Inca structures, and only one had finely cut stonework. The Inca road
was an obvious focus of settlement in this zone, with a tambo, colcas,
and a mitima settlement located along it. Inca-style pottery was virtually nonexistent, but the mitima settlement was identified by its distinctive, nonlocal ceramics. In general, Inca control was recognized
more through its nonlocal characteristics than through distinctively In-

caic evidence. As does Grosboll's article, this report provides information on the pre-Inca developments in this region which put the Inca data in a broader context.

INTRODUCTION

The archaeological identification of an imperial occupation is not always as obvious as one might hope. In this chapter I discuss the case of the Inca empire and its occupation of the province of Andamarca Lucanas, an occupation known both from archaeological data and from ethnohistorical documents. I shall stress the archaeological approach to understanding this occupation, my major thesis being that much of what is "foreign" must be defined on the basis of differences with the local culture. I shall also identify points at which written documents add to, or differ from, what is visible in the archaeological record.

The Carhuarazo Valley

The province of Andamarca Lucanas was located in a southern affluent of the Río Pampas, a valley that I refer to as the Carhuarazo Valley. Located in the modern province of Lucanas in the department of Ayacucho, this is a rather isolated valley in the high Andes of south-central Peru (fig. 4.1). It is surrounded by *puna*, grass-covered high plains used for grazing, lying at altitudes averaging 4,400 meters above sea level. From occupied valleys to the west, south, and east, it takes at least two days to walk to the Carhuarazo Valley. To the north, downstream, the river enters a deep chasm, effectively cutting the valley off from other occupied areas. To the east lies the snowcapped mountain Qarwarazu, home of the great *wamani* (mountain deity) of the same name.

In the valley itself, there are today located nine villages and numerous tiny hamlets. As in the past, modern subsistence is based largely on herding and agriculture. The adjacent puna lands provide pasturage for alpacas and llamas, as well as vicuñas. Within the valley, major indigenous crops are potatoes and quinoa, grown generally between elevations of 3,300 and 3,600 meters, and maize and *tarwi* (an Andean legume), grown below 3,300 meters. In the lowest parts of the valley, as far down as 2,900 meters, some vegetables (beans, squash) and fruit trees grow. The maize zone is largely terraced, and this valley has some of the most extensive and impressive terraced hillsides in all of the Andes.

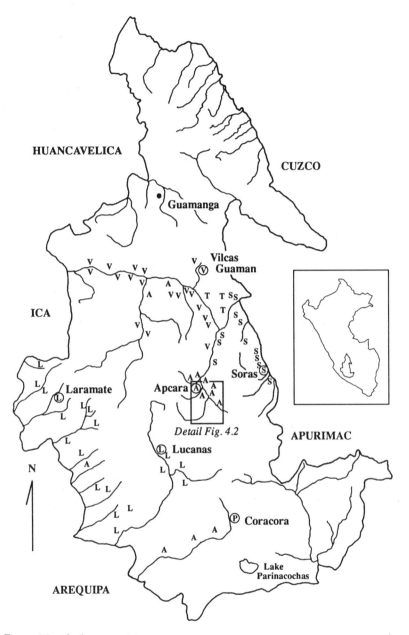

Figure 4.1. The location of the Carhuarazo Valley within the Department of Ayacucho. Indicated are the locations of villages and their ethnic affiliations in 1586 (post-
reducciones). A = Andamarca Lucanas, L = Lucanas/Laramate, S = Soras, V =
Vilcas (mitima), T = Tanquigua.

The Data Base

In 1981, we undertook an archaeological survey of the valley, with the explicit goal of understanding the Huari and Inca imperial occupations there (Schreiber 1987). In the case of the Incas, the data include surface remains of sites and the artifacts found on those sites. We did not undertake excavations at any sites dating to the Late Intermediate Period or the Late Horizon. The relative date of each site was determined on the basis of a chronological sequence of ceramic styles (discussed below). The entire central core of the valley was surveyed up to an elevation of 4,000 meters. We did not survey the two upper tributaries of Andamarca and Chipao but did visit sites in the vicinity of Andamarca.

CHRONOLOGY AND SETTLEMENT PATTERNS

We developed a relative chronology to date sites in the valley from a combination of results of stratigraphic excavations at Jincamocco (Schreiber 1992) and surface collections at each site recorded in the 1981 survey. While the chronology for the period from the end of the Early Horizon through the collapse of the Huari empire was defined primarily from stratigraphic excavations, the sequence for the Late Intermediate and Late Horizon is based solely on surface collections.

The late sequence is defined on the basis of presence or absence of thirteen styles of decorated pottery with discrete but overlapping temporal ranges. The evidence results in a sequence that can be roughly divided into three general phases: Marke, Toqsa, and Jasapata (table 4.1).

The Marke Phase begins at the time of the Huari collapse. Ceramics include black-on-red and white-on-red painted vessels with simple geometric designs. Rim-ticked bowls—small, rounded bowls with a completely red slipped interior and a partially or completely red slipped exterior—are common at this time. On the rim, which is slightly thickened to the interior, are painted ticks—white, black, gray, or an iridescent white-gray. Also occurring in low proportion at all sites is grayware, vessels that have black painted designs on a red-purple slip. The distinctive aspect of these sherds is that they appear to have been fired at an extremely high temperature and are nearly black inside and out. Sand particles in the temper have actually melted, producing black vitrified bubbles on the surface of the sherds. These grayware vessels

Table 4.1. Temporal Distribution of Ceramics from Andamarca Lucanas

Ceramic Styles	Phases		
	Marke	Toqsa	Jasapata
Black/red	|————————————————————|	
Grayware	|————————————————————|	
Rim-ticked bowls	|—————————————————|	
White/red	|———————|		
Black/plain	|——————————|	
Various/orange		|————————|	
Red/plain	|—————————?		
Black-and-white/red		|—————————?	
Brown-slipped		|————————————————|
Multi-slipped		?————————|	
Orange-slipped		?————————|	
Inca polychrome			?———|
Colonial			|—|

are distinctive in shape and design, and so do not represent "wasters," indicative of ceramic production areas. They may be imports from elsewhere. Five sites, all small villages, date to the Marke Phase. Two of these were fortified.

Ceramics of the following Toqsa Phase include black-on-red painted vessels, but the white-on-red style drops out. Other painted designs include black-on-plain, red-on-plain, black-and-white-on-red, and painted designs on an orange slip. Vessels with brown slip, but without painted designs, are also typical of this phase. Rim-ticked bowls continue in high proportion, and the same low-frequency occurrence of grayware continues through this phase.

The Toqsa Phase exhibits an increase in the number of sites, and probably gradual population increase. Twelve (or thirteen) sites were occupied at this time, three of them fortified. This phase probably saw the beginnings of the development of local chiefdoms, centered at Apucara and Queca. One well-fortified site, Toqsa (which gives its name to this period), is located high above the valley on the top of a ridge. Toqsa is as large as all the other sites combined and may have been a hilltop redoubt to which the entire population of the valley could flee in the event of invasion from outside.

The Jasapata Phase sees a continuation of black-on-red and red-on-plain painted vessels, as well as brown slipped ware. Grayware also continues through this period, again in low frequency, as in earlier phases. Vessels with multiple slip colors, usually red on one side and either white or pink on the other, are seen for the first time. And vessels with orange slip, but no other painted decoration, also occur. A handful of Inca-style sherds also is present, and some sites have a few pieces of colonial pottery. Interestingly, rim-ticked bowls occur at some sites (possibly occupied since earlier times) but never at the same sites as Inca sherds.

During the Jasapata Phase, the Incas took control of the valley. The Jasapata Phase continued the local trends of the Toqsa Phase, but with less emphasis on defense. Of the nine or ten local sites occupied at this time, only one was fortified. Two large towns in the valley, Apucara and Queca, dominated the local culture (fig. 4.2). The location of these towns and their size suggest that they might have been small political centers and that there were two small chiefdoms in the valley at the time of the Inca incursion (figs. 4.3 and 4.4). The unsurveyed areas around Andamarca and Chipao each have a single large site as well, suggesting a total of four small chiefdoms in the region. In addition to the local villages and towns, three Inca storage centers (one of which served as a tambo), three Inca buildings, and an Inca bridge were identified. These Inca features will be discussed in detail below.

THE DOCUMENTARY INFORMATION

Before describing the archaeological remains of the Inca occupation of this valley, I will summarize what we know of it from ethnohistorical sources. First of all, the Andamarca Lucanas were often considered

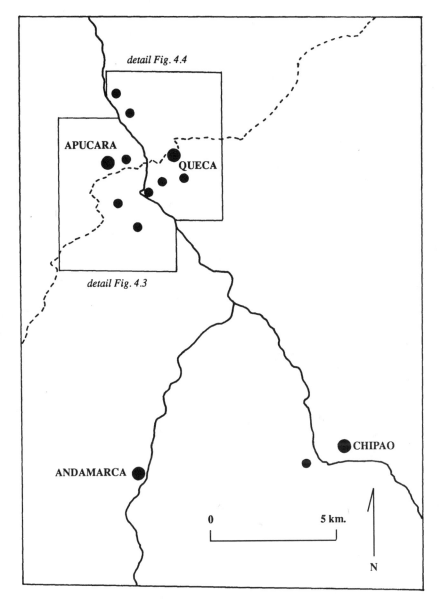

Figure 4.2. The Carhuarazo Valley, with sites of the Jasapata Phase and possible chiefdoms noted. Dashed line indicates Inca road.

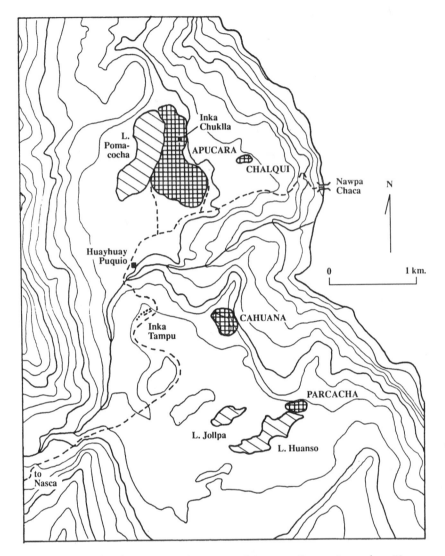

Figure 4.3. Local and Inca sites in the vicinity of Apucara. Contour interval = 50 meters.

together with the Lucanas and the Soras, groups located to the south-west and the northeast, respectively; the Andamarcas are rarely mentioned by name. So, for example, Cieza de León speaks of the conquest of the Soras and Lucanas in one passage (Cieza de León cap. LXXXVIII; 1984: 251), then repeats essentially the same account referring to the

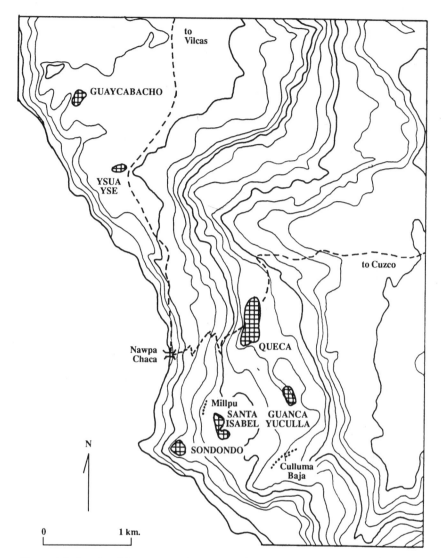

Figure 4.4. Local and Inca sites in the vicinity of Queca. Contour interval = 50 meters.

Soras (Cieza de León cap. XLVII; 1985: 138). Cobo writes that the Vilcas, Soras, and Lucanas were subdued with little effort by Pachacuti (Cobo libro 11, cap. XIII; 1964: 80).

According to Cieza de León, the Soras and Lucanas were defeated by the Incas in a great battle in which both sides lost many people. The surviving Soras then retreated to a high, rocky fortress, where the Incas laid siege for two years until the Soras gave up (Cieza de León cap. LXXXVIII; 1984: 250–251; cap. XLVII; 1985: 137–139). Cobo tells the same story of the retreat to a great fortress and a prolonged siege, but says that the people were from Guamanga (Cobo libro 11, cap. XIII; 1964: 80). Guaman Poma illustrates the battle waged by the Inca captain, Inca Mayta, against the Andamarcas, Lucanas, Soras, and others, who were shown fighting from a high fortress (Guaman Poma 1980a: 134–135 [ff. 155–156]). Cobo also tells us that the people of Lucanas were well suited to being litter bearers because they walked at an even pace and that all litter bearers were from this province (Cobo libro 11, cap. XXXIII; 1964: 133).

Beyond these general accounts, there are several ethnohistorical documents that pertain specifically to this valley in the century after the Spanish conquest and that tell us something of the Inca occupation there. The first document of which I am aware that treats the region in some detail is *Cédula de encomienda*, written in 1540 and discussed by Guillermo Cock (ms.) in his treatment of ethnicity in the case of the Andamarca Lucanas. The document lists all the towns in the valley and the number of tributaries in each. This document is especially important because it was written some decades before the towns and villages were "reduced" to new locations.

The second document is one of several published together in the *Relaciones Geográficas de Indias*. In 1586, the local corregidor, Luis de Monzón, answered a questionnaire about this valley and the human and natural resources there (Monzón 1965b). He also provided the same information for Soras and Lucanas (Monzón 1965a, 1965c). Along with descriptions of the area around Vilcashuamán (Carabajal 1965), these documents give us a broad regional picture of towns occupied after the reducciones, and which ethnic groups, or *ayllus*, occupied each (see fig. 4.1). In the case of the Carhuarazo Valley, Monzón includes many details specifically about the Inca occupation of the region.

And the third document is the famous *Nueva corónica y buen gobierno*, written by Guaman Poma de Ayala (1980a), already mentioned. He was a native of this valley, and his general descriptions of life under the Incas probably pertain largely to the experience of his home territory. He does not offer too many specifics about the region, but there are some exceptions, as will be noted below.

THE SPECIFIC INFORMATION
OF THE DOCUMENTS

First of all, the documents tell us the names of the people and their towns. The group that occupied this valley was known as the Andamarca Lucanas, and they were related to the Lucanas to the southwest and Hatun Soras to the northeast. In 1586, villages of Andamarca Lucanas were located in some other valleys as well (Monzón 1965b: 240). Those in the Río Pampas Valley, Alcamenga and Huamanquiquia, may have been put there by the Incas as mitima settlements. Those in the upland portions of certain coastal valleys may also have been mitima communities or—equally likely—may have predated the Inca occupation, representing satellite communities with access to coastal resources, otherwise unavailable in the Carhuarazo Valley.

The document of 1540 lists the towns occupied in that year. It is possible in nearly every case to identify the archaeological sites that pertain to each name, and hence to identify the villages occupied at the time of the Spanish conquest—and presumably during the Inca occupation.

The document of 1586 provides very specific, and important, data regarding the Inca occupation of the region. As we shall see, these data in some cases confirm the interpretations based on archaeological remains, in some cases amplify those interpretations, and some cases conflict with the archaeological evidence.

Inca Political Organization

The town of Apucara was the provincial capital under the Spanish (Monzón 1965b: 239); it is therefore likely that it was the Inca capital as well, as the Spanish co-opted existing political organization wherever they could. The document of 1586 states very specifically that an Inca (i.e., a member of the royal family) was principal lord of the province (Monzón 1965b: 243), charged with carrying out the orders dispatched by *quipu* (a knotted-string device used in record keeping) from the Sapa Inca (the emperor in Cuzco). He meted out punishment; even slight offenses were punishable by an unpleasant and slow death (Monzón 1965b: 243). He gave women to the *indios* (in this case, native inhabitants), "according to their quality"; in each village there was an enclosure with houses inside in which were collected the women hidden by the Inca—it was from these groups that he chose the women for the indios. These women were allotted lands, but the head of each village was responsible for planting and harvesting them (Monzón 1965b: 243).

Inca Road

The 1586 document states that the royal road of the Incas passed through this valley, via Apucara and Queca, and that it continued on to Soras (and eventually Cuzco) to the northeast (Monzón 1965b: 239). Guaman Poma, in his list of tambos along the Inca highways, also describes the route of this road (Guaman Poma 1980a: 1004 [f. 1089]). In one passage he declares that it was one of the two most important roads in the empire (1980a: 756–758 [ff. 812–813]), but later he says it was one of several major roads in the empire (1980a: 994 [f. 1074]). In either case, he was emphasizing (and perhaps exaggerating) the roads in his home valley.

Tribute

Several documents point out that the Andamarca Lucanas were the litter bearers of the Inca and so were accorded special status. They were nicknamed "the feet of the Inca" and were entitled to wear an elegant red and white *guaraca* (headdress) (Monzón 1965b: 241). Guaman Poma (1980a: 307 [f. 333]) illustrates the Andamarcas (along with the Lucanas, Soras, and Parinacochas) carrying the Inca Huayna Capac into battle (fig. 4.5). In addition to serving as litter bearers, the Andamarca Lucanas also supplied the Incas with yanacona (Monzón 1965b: 241). The people told Monzón that they paid no other tribute besides serving as litter bearers and supplying yanacona (Monzón 1965b: 241).

Pre-Inca Organization

What do the documents tell us of the pre-Inca political organization of the region? Monzón writes that each village had its own lord, or curaca, and that there was much warfare between villages (Monzón 1965b: 241). The document of 1586 describes the ecclesiastical administrative hierarchy present in the valley at that time, but there may be very little correspondence between this and pre-Inca organization. The

Figure 4.5. Drawing by Guaman Poma showing Andamarcas as litter bearers of the Inca.

document does state, however, that there were four ayllus in the region, named Andamarca, Apcara, Omapacha, and Uchucayllu (Monzón 1965b: 237). Guaman Poma lists the same four ayllus (Guaman Poma 1980a: 993 [f. 1073]). As ayllus were one of the organizing principles of the native Andean peoples, this organization probably reflects pre-Spanish patterns, and perhaps pre-Inca ones as well.

The names of the ayllus, corresponding to different locations in the valley, suggest that the ayllus may have had some sort of territorial component. It is tempting to suggest that the Andamarca ayllu may correspond with the simple chiefdom centered around Andamarca, and the Apucara ayllu may represent the Apucara chiefdom, etc. However, this must remain the most tentative of suggestions.

The term "ayllu" is a confusing one, as it seems to range in meaning from "patrilineage" to just generally "group." The Spanish recorders probably had an imperfect understanding of its meaning, and their use of the term can be misleading. The ayllus found in this region today reflect a very different organization: each town has several ayllus that are defined on the basis of patrilineal descent (Palomino 1971: 239–240). So the nature of ayllus has probably changed through the centuries in this valley, and may have been changing in prehistoric times as well.

Inca Occupation of Surrounding Regions

Finally, the documents of 1586 tell us something of the Inca occupation of surrounding regions, which allows us to put the Carhuarazo Valley into a broader regional perspective. There was a major Inca administrative town at Vilcashuamán to the north (Carabajal 1965: 205). The Soras were conquered by the Incas, but no mention is made of any royal Incas residing in this province; the Soras paid tribute by providing litter bearers and chasqui (messengers) (Monzón 1965a: 222). In Lucanas, a local leader named Guancar Illa was put in charge by the Incas and ruled in their name (Monzón 1965c: 231). The Lucanas also paid tribute by providing litter bearers, and stressed that this was their only tribute requirement (Monzón 1965c: 231). And the Río Pampas Valley was largely depopulated by the Incas, who then filled it with mitima settlements (Carabajal 1965: 219). Only one small part of the Vilcas province, around the town of Guanpalpa, was left intact with its original Tanquiqua inhabitants (Carabajal 1965: 219).

THE ARCHAEOLOGICAL DATA

The picture emerging from the historic documents suggests that Apucara was the Inca provincial capital and that a royal Inca resided there. This site and Queca were located along the royal highway connecting the coast and the highland roads. The people paid tribute by providing litter bearers to the Incas, and they stressed to the Spanish *visitador* (census taker) that they paid no other tribute. Little is discernible about the pre-Inca occupation, except that there was much warfare and that there might have been four ayllus present.

Turning to the archaeological data, we find evidence of the Inca occupation that agrees with what is in the documents, but we also find areas of discrepancy. The Inca remains in an area are not always obvious and in many cases are defined on the basis of their distinction from local remains.

Inca Artifacts

In all, more than 8,500 potsherds were collected from sites occupied in the Jasapata Phase, of which only 9 are identifiable as Inca styles; these came from only four of the ten village sites. Three of them came from Apucara, the Inca capital of the province. Five Inca sherds came from two other sites that had no other trace of Inca material culture.

The last Inca sherd came from a site that had no other Inca remains but that was otherwise distinguished from the local culture. This site had local architecture, and Jasapata Phase ceramics, but it also included sherds of an entirely different style, unrelated to either local styles or known Inca styles. As discussed below, this community may have been a mitima settlement, the foreign styles being brought to the site by people who were moved there from some other region by the Incas.

Unlike other parts of the Inca empire where local potters copied Inca styles and incorporated Inca elements into the local style (Menzel 1959), Jasapata ceramics show no clear Inca influence. Not only are Inca ceramics very distinctive from local styles, they are exactly the same as Inca styles known from Cuzco. In fact, these few examples are so different from local styles and technology that it is probable that they were imported rather than made locally.

Local Architecture

All local sites occupied during the Late Horizon were characterized primarily by a single style of architecture: round houses made of broken stone set in mortar. Houses ranged in interior diameter from four to nine meters, and had a single doorway. They were often arranged in groups of two or more within a walled compound. This style of architecture extends at least back to the Early Intermediate Period, so it has a long local tradition. As well, round stone houses were the predominant style of architecture throughout much of the central highlands of Peru at this time. The roofing of the houses is unknown, but the data suggest that they were of corbeled stone topped with stone slabs.

Inca features, on the other hand, are very distinctive from local styles. Not only are they identifiable as Inca constructions by their similarity to Inca remains known elsewhere, but even if we knew nothing of the Incas, these features would stand out as foreign constructions.

Inca Special Function Architecture

Two constructions within the survey area are defined as some sort of special-function architecture: a small stone and adobe building within the site of Apucara, located next to a very large but unworked stone (called collectively Inka Chuklla/Hatun Rumi); and an artificial platform with retaining walls of fitted intermediate-style masonry, located next to a spring (called Huayhuay Puquio). Both sites may represent sacred places, but both probably served additional functions as well. A third Inca building is found at Canichi, near Andamarca, outside the survey area.

Inka Chuklla/Hatun Rumi

Within the site of Apucara, which was the largest town in the province in the Late Horizon, is a single structure of Inca-style architecture. It is a two-story rectangular building, the first story constructed of fieldstone, the second of adobe blocks (fig. 4.6). Centrally located within the site, it stands immediately adjacent to an unworked boulder more than five meters tall (fig. 4.7). The exterior dimensions of the building are 6.1 by 11.2 meters, a width:length ratio of 1:1.84. These proportions lie well within the range of typical Inca buildings, as defined in the region around Cuzco (Niles 1987: 41). The building is oriented nearly exactly to true east-west along its long axis (fig. 4.8).

Figure 4.6. Inka Chuklla showing west end exterior with stone and adobe construction.

Figure 4.7. Inka Chuklla showing location adjacent to Hatun Rumi.

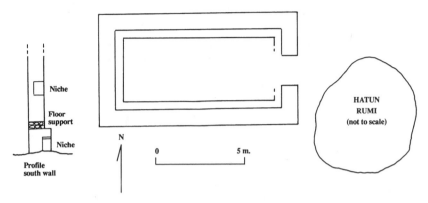

Figure 4.8. Plan of Inka Chuklla.

The fieldstone of the first story is set in mud mortar. There are six niches on the interior of each of the long walls, with possibly a stone projecting from the center of each wall at the level of the lintel of the niches. The niches measure roughly 60 by 80 centimeters and are 50 centimeters deep. Both the wall face and the niches were coated with a layer of mud plaster. The niches here give no evidence of trapezoidal shape, in contrast to typical niches at other Inca sites. The wall at the west end of the building has three niches, measuring 40 by 70 centimeters and 40 centimeters deep; above the center niche is a window measuring 55 by 90 centimeters, with a lintel that is even with the upper edge of the first story. The door to the building was in the east end wall, affording a view across the valley toward Queca. This wall is too poorly preserved to know what the door dimensions were, what its shape was, or if there were niches to either side.

The interior dimensions of this first story are estimated to be 3.5 by 8.6 meters. Exact measurement is difficult because all the facing stones have been pulled off the interior walls, except for those around some niches. The current ground surface inside the building is even with the base of the niches, in contrast to the exterior (at the west end) where the current ground surface is at least a meter lower. The greater amount of fill in the interior was at least partly caused by the collapse of the second floor and the roof. Even so, the amount of fill inside the building is more than one would expect, and may indicate intentional filling at some time. In any case, it is not possible to measure the height of this story above the floor.

At a height of about 80 centimeters above the niches the wall is

Figure 4.9. Inka Chuklla showing detail of interior adobe wall, with niches and projecting stone.

carefully leveled off with small chinking stones and then set back about 40 centimeters, creating a shelf around all four walls of the building; the shelf supported the second floor. Typically, Inca buildings have such setbacks just on the two long walls (Kendall 1974b: 21), rather than on all four walls, as this building has. Beginning at the setback, two courses of stones were laid, and again chinking stones were used to create a level surface, probably even with the top of the flooring placed on the setback.

From this point up, the walls of the second story are of adobe blocks. They average 25 by 58 by 18 centimeters in size, and were laid in alternating rows of endwise and lengthwise placement. As on the first floor, there are six niches on the long south wall. Although we could not reach these to measure them, figure 4.9 shows that they vary in size and shape from nearly square to more rectangular. There is clearly a single projecting stone in the center of this wall, slightly above the level of the niche lintels. The long north wall is preserved only up to the level of the niches, so it is not clear whether they existed there also. The center of the west end wall is not preserved, but there are still preserved two clearly trapezoidal niches there, one on either side. In the center, below the level of the niches and only about 50 centimeters above the floor level, is preserved the base of a window. In the east end wall, as on the first story, there is a doorway; it measures 180 centimeters wide, and may have had a double jamb, similar to other known Inca doors. The interior dimensions of the second story, measuring 4.3 by 9.4 meters, are slightly greater than those of the first story, given the thinner walls above the setback.

The shape of the roofline of this structure is not entirely clear. It likely had a gabled roof of wooden beams and thatch, like most rectangular Inca buildings, but the form of the gable is unclear. The different heights of the two long walls might suggest an asymmetrical gable, with the peak closer to the higher south wall. However, the differing heights could have resulted from poor preservation. The symmetrical placement of the doorway exactly in the center of the end wall suggests, perhaps, a more symmetrical arrangement.

This building, clearly very different from local structures, represents a foreign architectural style and generally conforms to canons of Inca architecture. The building materials, the proportions, the niches in the walls, construction techniques—all brand this building as an Inca structure. There are some irregularities, however. For example, in most two-story buildings, usually built into steep slopes, the second story is entered directly from the outside (Gasparini and Margolies 1980: 172). Inka Chuklla, in contrast, is built on a flat location, and there is no obvious means of entrance to the second story. But despite this irregularity, a first glance might suggest that this building functioned as a residential structure, probably the house of an Inca official.

Several things suggest, however, that it is not a typical residence. In particular, the placement of the door in an end wall, rather than in the long front wall, is far from a common pattern. Although rare, a few examples of doors in end walls do exist at some Inca sites. For example, in the hillside house group of Pincuylluna at Ollantaytambo, doors are found in the end walls as well as in the front walls of the long narrow (storage) structures (Gasparini and Margolies 1980: 177–178). In this case the front doors may have been only for formality's sake; they may not have actually been functional, since the slope is so steep that ground level may be several meters below the door. So end-wall doors are used in concert with nonfunctional front doors where the houses are built on very steep slopes. This is not the case at Inka Chuklla. Another example is the temple of Huaytará, which probably had a door in the now-destroyed south end wall (Gasparini and Margolies 1980: 255–261). This structure is differentiated from Inka Chuklla by the high quality of its masonry, with unique double-jambed triangular niches. Like Inka Chuklla, though, it had a second story of adobe and a probably symmetrical gabled roof. The temple at Huaytará, clearly meant to impress, may have played some sort of ceremonial role in the Inca administration of this region. Likewise, we might suggest that Inka Chuklla may have had a ceremonial component to its function, although it is not nearly as impressive a construction as Huaytará.

At Callachaca, near Cuzco, is a structure with a doorway at one end. Located near the residential group at Callachaca A, it is built against a large stone outcrop (Niles 1987: 24). Both its form and its location argue that it was not a typical residence (Niles, personal communication).

Finally, located near Calca is a small complex of Inca buildings, illustrated by Squier (1877: 518; reproduced in Gasparini and Margolies 1980: 138) arranged around a large rock. Most of the buildings have doorways in their short end walls, rather than in the long walls. Perhaps the association with the large stone is significant here, as at Callachaca.

We must now take into consideration the location of Inka Chuklla with respect to Hatun Rumi, the large boulder next to which it is located. We know from numerous sources that the Incas venerated certain stones and called them huacas. In the area around Cuzco, Cobo listed the huacas located along the various *ceque* lines (a system of sacred radial lines originating in the center of Cuzco at the Qorikancha) and indicated what form they took (Rowe 1979). Quite a number of these were stones. Indeed, that the Incas left in place large stones, both worked and unworked, in otherwise carefully manicured and sculpted sites suggests that certain stones held great importance for them. At Apucara, we encounter a very large boulder, and next to it is located the only Inca building in the site. This positioning is rather reminiscent of Callachaca A and the site near Calca.

In sum, the combination of the location next to a large stone and the odd placement of the door in the end of the building—next to the stone—suggests some sort of special function beyond simple residence. Two suggestions, not necessarily mutually exclusive, come to mind. First, the structure might have served as a religious building, a shrine next to a sacred rock, functioning in a purely ceremonial capacity. (Interestingly, the Spanish chose to place their own Catholic church on the hillside just above this spot, perhaps to overshadow the old pagan religion?) Second, as conjectured above, this might have been the residence of an Inca official. Generally conforming to canons of Inca architecture, it would have been suitable for a royal resident. It stands out from the local architecture and is centrally located in the largest town—providing both the appropriate image and the locus of imperial power.

And it might have been a combination of the two, serving both as the royal residence and as a structure with ceremonial importance. Certainly Inca rule included a large component of ritual activity.

Huayhuay Puquio

This is the only site in the study area that is characterized by Inca-style cut-stone masonry. It is not the carefully fitted, fine Cuzco-style masonry, but rather what Niles has called fitted intermediate-style masonry (Niles 1987: 211–212). The walls we identified are retaining walls along the south edge of a large square raised platform, which today is simply an agricultural field with no evidence of other structures. For a length of some 35 meters, sections of the south retaining wall are visible (fig. 4.10). An additional short section is visible on the east side (near the southeast corner). Along the west side, at the southwest corner, the wall continues in a diagonal section, but has in it a doorway behind which is now dirt fill. The visible sections of Inca walls were uncovered in recent years by the local mayor. As part of this investigation, major portions of the long south retaining wall were pulled down in search of treasure behind the stones, revealing that the wall is a single stone thick and forms a slightly inclined retaining wall that rests directly against a deposit of dirt and stones that appears to be artificial fill (fig. 4.11). No retaining walls are now visible along the remainder of the east or west walls, or along the north wall. These areas are heavily overgrown and may be obscured by overburden, as was most of the south wall before the local investigation.

In sum, the retaining wall visible today probably formed one side of a square artificial platform. At the southwest corner there was a doorway in the diagonal wall that perhaps gave access to an interior room or, more likely, to a stairway to the top of the platform (fig. 4.12). Adjacent to this corner of the platform is a spring, which gives its name to the site. In deposits from the platform level eroding down over the retaining wall, and in areas below the site, is a quantity of occupational

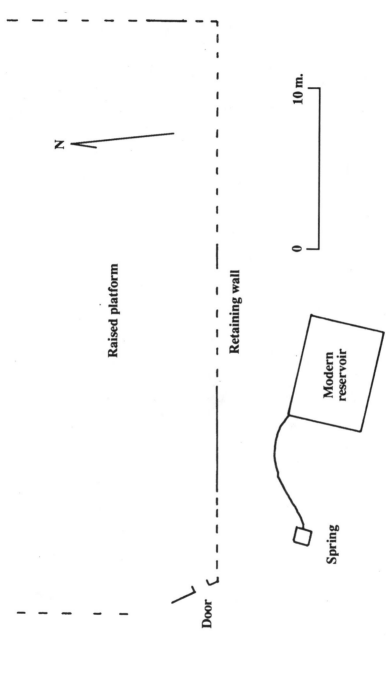

Figure 4.10. Plan of Huayhuay Puquio.

Figure 4.11. The retaining wall at Huayhuay Puquio, showing the pulled down section and fill behind it.

Figure 4.12. Possible doorway in Huayhuay Puquio.

debris. This debris includes a number of fragments of plates, a form that occurs on no other site in the survey area and that is distinct from local styles. But no clearly diagnostic Cuzco-style Inca sherds were found.

There are no remains visible on top of the platform. Today it is simply an agricultural field. But its very square shape, and its elevation above the surrounding areas, distinguish it from a typical field. It seems likely that the entire field was once a raised platform, held in place by Inca fitted intermediate-style masonry on all four sides. Further, given the amount of cultural material eroding off the platform surface, it seems likely that there may have been structures on top of the platform, which have since been destroyed.

What was the function of this site? I suggest three possibilities: a major shrine, the palace of the resident Inca, or a special-activity locus. The location of the structure next to a spring suggests very strongly that it may have been a shrine. Springs were often sacred to the Incas, and again, the list of huacas around Cuzco includes numerous springs that were shrines. In terms of architecture, it is somewhat reminiscent of the fortress at Ollantaytambo, where retaining walls of very fine cut stone surrounded the level on which was built the major temple— since destroyed by the Spanish. The destruction of whatever was on top of the platform at Huayhuay Puquio is consistent with its having served a religious function.

A second possibility is that this, not Inka Chuklla, was the residence of the Inca official. Certainly this structure, more than the building in Apucara, has the trappings of authority, built as it is in the Cuzco style. But the site lies about a kilometer from town. On the one hand, would not the Inca live in the town that was the designated capital of the province? Or would living apart, in especially impressive facilities, serve to reinforce his image as one who is apart from, and superior to, the local culture?

Interestingly, when the Spanish established the new town of Apucara during the *reducciones* (the relocation of indigenous people to Spanish-style towns) of the 1560s, they located the plaza of the town nearly adjacent to this site. Did they select that position so they could preempt the local shrine with their own Catholic church? Or were they pre-empting Inca rule by establishing their government headquarters adjacent to the old palace?

I would argue, however, that this site was not the residence of the Inca official. For several reasons it seems more likely that Inka Chuklla was his residence. Situated within the largest town and next to a major huaca, it was a distinguished structure in an important location. Moreover, its setting in the town, among the people, provided an appropriate forum from which to carry out administrative tasks.

But then, what of the function of Huayhuay Puquio? These retaining walls, along with the adjacent spring, are also reminiscent of the site of Tambo Machay near Cuzco, which was not a strictly religious structure; it was the hunting lodge of the Inca Pachacuti (Cobo libro 13, cap. XIV; 1964: 175). So the form might easily suggest a temporary residence as well, one with a reliable water source at hand. There is no evidence of a formal bath below the spring, but most of the area has been modified in modern times, and a reservoir now stands there.

We can draw a further analogy here, with the Inca town at Cajamarca. When Pizarro arrived in Cajamarca, he did not find Atahuallpa in the town. Rather, the Inca was at his royal retreat at the nearby baths. Perhaps such an arrangement of Inca towns with out-of-town facilities is a pattern that may be found elsewhere as well. Interestingly, there are two major entrances into Apucara from the Inca road. The town is not directly adjacent to the road but lies off to one side. A royal visitor might thereby go straight to the royal retreat and bath without entering the town, from whichever direction he came (from Cuzco or from Nasca). There he might be accommodated, fed, bathed, and refreshed, before making an entrance into the town.

In sum, then, I suggest that this site, located along the road about a kilometer from the designated provincial capital, may have functioned as a sort of royal retreat as well as a shrine. Not only could the resident Inca official retire to this suburban resort, with its (perhaps) fine bath, but royal or important visitors could also be accommodated there, rather than in the rather rustic small tambo up on the hillside. The presence of domestic refuse suggests some sort of habitation, and the architecture and artifacts indicate that the site was designed and used by the Incas.

Inca Building at Canichi

One other building of which I am aware is possibly Inca, but it is outside the survey area. Adjacent to the modern town of Andamarca is the old site of Andamarca, today called Canichi. Like other sites in the

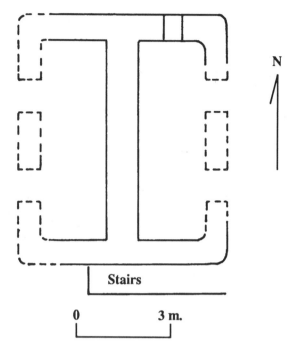

Figure 4.13. Plan of Inca building at Canichi.

region, Canichi is characterized by round stone buildings, sometimes arranged in small compounds. Small round *chullpas* (burial structures) are also found there, sometimes attached to houses. Centrally located within the site is a rectangular building divided into two rooms by a long wall down the center (fig. 4.13). The building, of fieldstone construction, is rather poorly preserved, but it is clearly distinct from local constructions. The center of the long wall is badly fallen down, so it is not possible to know if there was a door connecting the two rooms. At one end of the building is a stairway, built up the outside to a height of 2.7 meters, but no evidence remains of a doorway or even of a second floor. The two exterior long walls each had two doorways into the interior, and the corners of the building are slightly rounded. The building's exterior is 7.8 meters long and, if the two halves are the same size, 6.6 meters wide.

This building is clearly distinct from local architecture and is not a local construction. A building divided into halves by a long center wall is not an uncommon Inca form. The documents, however, say nothing

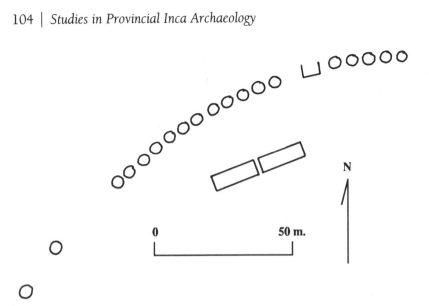

Figure 4.14. Plan of Inka Tampu.

of any Inca presence in this part of the region. The site lies away from the main centers of power and population and off the main Inca highway. The building might, however, have functioned as a temporary residence for the Inca when he came to visit and inspect this part of the region, or it may have housed a secondary functionary of some sort. Since Andamarca gave its name to this Inca province (Andamarca Lucanas), the area may have held some particular importance for the Incas. As I will discuss below, the terracing at Andamarca is truly remarkable and may be directly related to the Inca occupation.

Inca Tambo and Storage Sites

Three other Inca sites were located within the survey area. All include rows of Inca storehouses (colcas), and one has additional buildings as well, suggesting that it was an Inca tambo.

Inka Tampu

The site of Inka Tampu is located on a hillside above Apucara, along the Inca road entering the valley from the west. It comprises a row of probably twenty-five colcas, a small rectangular building within this row, and two larger rectangular buildings to the uphill side of the row (fig. 4.14).

There are today traces of only nineteen colcas remaining in the row. But they are very evenly spaced, and gaps in the row indicate that six more colcas originally stood there. The row of colcas follows a contour, as do most such Inca sites, curving around the side of the hill. The colcas at this site have an average interior diameter of 310 centimeters. A small, three-sided rectangular building, five colcas from the east end of the row, may have housed the caretaker of the site.

The two larger buildings, rather poorly preserved, measure 16.2 by 4.85 meters on the exterior and have traces of interior niches on the walls. The door (or doors) into each building was probably in the downhill-facing (north) long wall of the building. The small doors into the colcas also face downhill—away from these two buildings.

The site lies immediately alongside the probable route of the Inca road through the valley. The exact route is difficult to trace because of the proximity of modern villages; today it leads to the town of Cabana Sur. Originally the road probably led to Jincamocco, the Middle Horizon Huari capital of this region. The Huari site lies on the hilltop immediately above Inka Tampu.

There are no artifacts directly associated with Inka Tampu. In fact, most of the surface artifacts are identifiable as Middle Horizon remains that have eroded down from Jincamocco.

Culluma Baja

Across the valley in the area near Queca is Culluma Baja, an Inca storage site. It comprises forty-six Inca colcas, forty of which are in a single line, with the remaining six in a short parallel row (fig. 4.15). The line of colcas does not follow a contour as at other sites, but rather follows the edge of a ridge that extends out into the valley. The colcas at Culluma Baja are smaller than those at the other storage sites, with an average interior diameter of only 2.5 meters.

Again, no artifacts are directly associated with the colcas. It is interesting that adjacent to the line of colcas are the remains of an old rectangular enclosure site, dating to the Middle Horizon. As at Inka Tampu, the Incas chose to put their construction next to what had once been a symbol of imperial power. They also used the stones from the Huari enclosure to build the colcas at Culluma Baja, rendering the earlier enclosure nearly invisible on the surface of the ground. The artifacts in the area of the enclosure are diagnostic of the Middle Horizon.

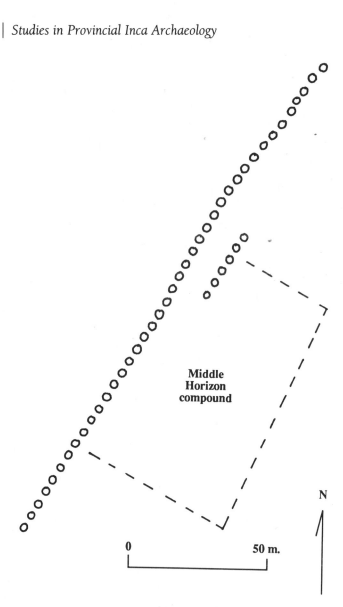

Middle
Horizon
compound

N

0   50 m.

Figure 4.15. Plan of Cullumba Baja.

Millpu

This site comprises a row of sixteen colcas (fig. 4.16)—the largest colcas of the three sites, with an average interior diameter of 3.3 meters. But most interesting is the fact that they are built into a terrace and the uphill portion of the colcas actually serves as a retaining wall. Short pieces of wall connect one colca to the next, thus completing the

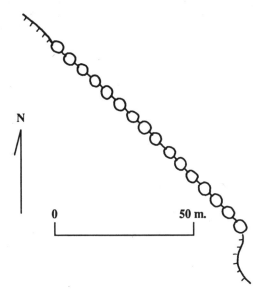

Figure 4.16. Plan of Millpu.

retaining wall. It is clear from details of construction that the terrace and the colcas are a single unit, built at the same time. This is particularly intriguing because most of the terraces in this valley were built in the Middle Horizon. In the region around Queca, however, there are several areas of terraces that suggest a later date of construction, as I discuss below.

There are no artifacts directly associated with the site. It lies below a medium-sized site, today called Santa Isabel. Adjacent to the site are some looted chullpas. Chullpas in the Queca region are rectangular with stone slab ceilings, sometimes with rounded interior corners, built singly or in small attached groups, located on small hillocks. In contrast, chullpas in the Apucara and Andamarca areas are circular in form, with corbeled ceilings. In Apucara they are sometimes attached to houses, and always occur within habitation sites. The same pattern is characteristic of Andamarca, but there they are sometimes found in isolated groups on hillsides as well. All chullpas in the valley date to post–Middle Horizon times.

Yanajocha

Outside the survey area, in the Andamarca portion of the region, are a series of spectacular terraces. Viewed from Canichi, several kilome-

Table 4.2. Comparisons of Colca Characteristics from Three Sites in Andamarca Lucanas

Site	Colca Area (m²)	Colca Volume (m³)	Colca Number	Colca Capacity (m³)
Culluma	4.91	17.19	46	790.51
Millpu	8.55	29.93	16	478.88
Tampu	7.55	26.42	25	660.50

ters away, some structures that may be colcas are visible near Yanajo-cha. If there was an Inca presence in Andamarca (e.g., as evidenced by the Inca building at Canichi), and if the terracing there was exploited by the Incas, then it would not be surprising to find storage facilities also in this portion of the region. However, this area, too, will have to await future research.

Summary of Storage Sites

The three storage sites in the survey area differ in several ways. One has additional structures, branding it as a tambo. There is a great variation in the number of colcas at each site, and the colcas at each site are of a different size, which might suggest that different work parties, and different supervisors, were responsible for their respective construction.

I have been able to estimate the storage capacity of each site by computing the total volume of the colcas (table 4.2). I estimate the height of the colcas to have been in the neighborhood of 3.5 meters. Some colcas have walls preserved to 3.1 meters; given some deposition inside the colcas and some deterioration of wall height, 3.5 meters seems a best approximation. (See D'Altroy and Hastorf 1984: 339 for a similar estimate in the case of colcas in the Jauja region.) As can be seen in table 4.2, the total storage capacity for all three sites combined is 1,928 cubic meters. Compared with such areas as Huánuco or Jauja, this volume seems fairly paltry. But this was a small province with a single resident Inca, not a valley with a major administrative center. It is also interesting that, although Culluma Baja has the greatest number of colcas, they are also the smallest. The total storage capacity is only about 20 percent greater than that of Inka Tampu, although Culluma Baja has nearly twice as many colcas. The location of the colcas in and adjacent to maize agricultural zones suggests that much of what was being stored was maize. This crop could be dried and transported to another location, or it could be made into *chicha* (beer) and used locally during state-sponsored feasting and celebrations. Other agricultural products, cloth, and craft items were likely stored here also (cf. D'Altroy and Hastorf 1984).

Terracing

The Carhuarazo Valley is very extensively terraced. Since the valley bottom is quite narrow and there is no flat bottom land that is suitable for agriculture, all agriculture takes place on the hillsides. There is hardly a hillside that is not intensively terraced—only extremely steep areas and rock outcroppings are devoid of terracing. Terraces extend up to an elevation of 3,400 meters in the main portion of the valley and up to 3,800 meters in the protected Andamarca river tributary. Terraces that are irrigated tend to be at lower elevations, where the microclimate is warmer and drier. In some areas the upper terrace levels, which are dry-farmed, have fallen into disuse, perhaps because of increased aridity in modern times as compared with prehistoric periods (cf. Thompson et al. 1985).

Dating Terrace Construction

In a recent article I defined several lines of evidence that can be used to date terrace construction (Schreiber 1987: 271–273). These include a variety of associations between terraces and sites, terrace location, construction style, similar technology used to level areas in habitation sites, the association with roads, and changing erosion patterns before and after terrace construction. I found that the presence of potsherds on a terrace is not a very direct or reliable estimator of date of construction, period of use, or date of abandonment.

Following these lines of evidence, I found that the vast majority of the terracing in the main portion of the Carhuarazo Valley was built during the Middle Horizon and was therefore probably related to the Huari occupation of the region (Schreiber 1987: 273–274). However, there are some portions of the valley that may have been terraced, or at least had the terraces rebuilt, during the Late Horizon.

Millpu

As discussed above, the colcas at Millpu were built into, and formed part of, a terrace retaining wall, indicating contemporaneity of terrace and colca construction. A nearby terrace has incorporated into it remains of a rectilinear structure. Since rectangular buildings were not introduced until the Middle Horizon, this terrace must postdate that period. I suggest that these two constructions are probably terrace repairs or revisions carried out during the Late Horizon.

Culluma

Below the colca site of Culluma Baja is a small area of terracing with a construction style uncommon in this valley. These terraces are formed by a retaining wall that extends about 50 centimeters above the level of the terrace surface, thus forming an enclosing wall on the downhill edge of the terrace.

The hillside behind Culluma Baja is also terraced in this same style. The only other place where the style has been observed is just below the site of Canichi—the Late Horizon town at Andamarca (Grosboll, field notes). The juxtaposition of these sites and these areas of terracing and the differing style of these terraces lead me to suggest that they may have been built during the Late Horizon.

Andamarca

Finally, for reasons that must for the moment remain largely subjective, I suspect that the spectacular terracing at Andamarca may date to the Late Horizon. First, although this area has not been systematically surveyed, the few sites with which I am familiar all date to post–Middle Horizon periods. I have seen no evidence of any Middle Horizon (or earlier) occupation in this small tributary. Second, the Andamarca terraces, although of the same basic construction style as terracing elsewhere in the valley, are in a better state of preservation than those elsewhere. Third, they are to my mind, and to other observers as well, simply more aesthetically pleasing than other terracing in the valley. And finally, to the people of the Carhuarazo Valley, regardless of which town they live in, the terraces of Andamarca are something special—somehow different from all the rest and considered the best terraces in all of Peru.

So, admitting that these criteria are very subjective, I remain with the distinct impression that the Andamarcan terraces are somehow different from those in the main part of the valley. A possible reason for this distinction may be that they were built at a much later date, perhaps during the Late Horizon, perhaps under Inca supervision.

Mitima Settlements

One site in the survey area, located just to the south of Queca (fig. 4.4), may represent a mitima settlement. As I discussed in an earlier paper (Schreiber 1987: 277), the presence at this site of ceramic styles distinct from local ones, as well as one Cuzco-Inca Polychrome A sherd, suggested to me that the site might have been such a settlement. The architecture is of entirely local style, which might be expected if a local community were moved to a new location outside the valley and another group moved into the site so abandoned. (As discussed above, there is documentary evidence that settlements of Andamarca Lucanas were found in other regions.) Thus a good case can be made that this was, in fact, a mitima settlement.

In the document dating to 1540, the list of villages in the valley includes one called Guanca Yuculla, located to the south of Queca. In this case, "Guanca" may refer to an ethnic group (Wanka) located to the north in what is today Junín, thus suggesting that the residents of the village were not of the local culture. This is the village closest to Culluma Baja and the atypical terraces. If the residents of Guanca Yuculla were responsible for the construction of these terraces, then perhaps they introduced the style from their region of origin.

Roads and Bridge

The final evidence of the Inca occupation and Inca constructions is the royal road that passed through this valley. Various sources, discussed above, agree that this was the connector road between the major coastal and highland routes. The route of this road was as follows: Nasca (intersection with coastal road)—Tambo Quemado—Lucanas—Apucara—Queca—Soras—Cochacajas (intersection with highland road). This road passed through the Carhuarazo Valley, adjacent to Apucara, and through Queca. Within the valley, the road is part of an intravalley network that mostly predates the Late Horizon. Between the valley and Nasca, the road was probably part of a Middle Horizon road system, controlled by the Huari empire. However, from the valley to the northeast toward Cuzco, the road dates more likely to the Inca occupation. The old Huari road north toward Ayacucho was probably also used by the Incas, as it connected this valley with the major Inca center at Vilcashuamán (Schreiber 1991).

The road entering from the west comes from Lucanas, crossing the puna called the Pampa Quilcata. The road is paved with flagstones, and during the rainy season it is still used to reach the modern provincial capital at Puquio. It is said that one cannot get lost because the road is paved all the way. The road drops into the valley down the Pichcapuquio *quebrada* and leads directly toward the modern town of Cabana Sur. The original route is unclear here; it may have passed through what is today the town or around the hills to the north of the town. In either case, it passed directly into or alongside the old Huari center at Jincamocco. The route can be picked up again next to Inka Tampu and followed across the quebrada, past Huayhuay Puquio, and alongside Apucara. From here it descends to the river.

At the river crossing was built a suspension bridge, with support pillars that can still be seen on the east side of the river. Approaching the bridge from the west, one descends a stairway cut deeply into a cliff face, allowing an easier descent to the bridge. The bridge was probably attached to a large rock outcrop at the base of the stairway, but no traces of the anchoring structures are visible today. The bridge extended from this outcrop, across to two stone pillars that secured the bridge at the same height above the east bank of the river. The distance spanned could not be measured, but I estimate it to be about 40 meters.

Above the pillars the remains of a retaining wall and buttress are still visible. At this point the road continued up the valley side and soon split into two branches: the old road to Vilcas and the royal road to Cuzco. Between this point and the town of Queca, it is difficult to follow the route of the royal road, as it is indistinguishable from other small trails that wind around and through the terraces. This, along with other data, indicates that the terracing already existed when the Incas established the road. From Queca the road extends up across the puna toward Soras and is reportedly paved with flagstones.

SUMMARY

Let me now summarize the Inca occupation of the province of Andamarca Lucanas, as it is known from the archaeological data, combined with information from the documentary sources. A good case can be made for a division of the province into four smaller units: Apucara, Queca, Andamarca, and Chipao. I suggest that before the Inca conquest there may have been four simple chiefdoms in the valley, centered on these four towns, and that there was no overarching political unification of the region.

Alternatively, there may have been only two chiefdoms, if Andamarca was subordinate to Apucara and Chipao to Queca. This position can be argued equally plausibly, given the historic and modern connections between these groups. For example, today Chipao and Queca are part of the same administrative district. At the time of the reducciones, Andamarca was moved into the main valley and combined with two other villages to become one called Cahuana—which in turn was subordinate to Apucara. And given the archaeological remains, neither Andamarca nor Chipao seems to have been a large town on the same order of magnitude as Apucara or Queca.

In any case, during the Inca occupation, Apucara was elevated to a higher administrative position and became the local capital of the province; Queca, Andamarca, and Chipao became subordinate to Apucara. And as the documents tell us, a single Inca was located in the province. I suggest that this resident Inca was placed at Apucara to supervise local elites who remained in power and were elevated to positions of control over the entire province. His presence and association with the Apucara elites added legitimacy to their new status as rulers of more than just their own chiefdom. In other words, the Inca was on hand to receive orders from Cuzco and to supervise local operations, but he was not directly ruling the province. If the Incas were directly ruling the province with their own people, certainly more than just a single individual would have been stationed there.

The Inca occupation for each of the four zones, respectively, may be summarized as follows. In the region of Apucara (fig. 4.3), before the Conquest, there existed a large town and several smaller villages. The Incas chose Apucara, lying along the major road through the region, to be the center of political power in the province and established a number of facilities in the vicinity. In the town itself was built an Inca-style building that probably was the residence of the Inca and also served a ceremonial function. Outside of town, but along the road, is a finer Inca construction that may have been some combination of shrine, bath, and royal retreat. And some distance farther from town, but still along the road, was a small rustic tambo with twenty-five colcas, a caretaker's hut, and two rest houses. So the Inca constructions in Apucara territory are largely designed for the maintenance of Inca political control.

In Queca, the situation is somewhat different (fig. 4.4). Queca, like Apucara, was a large town, and there were a number of smaller villages nearby that were probably subordinate to it. But the Inca occupation of this region seems largely devoted to agricultural production and storage. Repair of sections of terraces and construction of new terraces, along with two storage centers, indicate a more economic focus in Queca. Today this area is some of the most productive agricultural land in the valley, and likely it was so during Inca times as well. The location of a mitima settlement in this zone may have been to maintain high levels of agricultural production.

In Andamarca, the situation is less clear, given the lack of systematic survey. Andamarca was a small town, and there may have been another smaller village, or several, in the region. But this area, too, may have been important for agricultural production. The small Inca building at Canichi may have provided a temporary residence for an Inca official or some other supervisor, and the fine terracing may have been devoted to production of maize for the Incas. If this was the case, not only must it be shown that the terraces were built at this time, but there must be major storage centers located on or near the terraces.

The situation in Chipao is largely unknown, given the total absence of any archaeological data from this quadrant. However, the remains visible in air photos, and information available in documents, suggest that Chipao was a small town and that there were several smaller villages located in its vicinity. We have no evidence at this point for any Inca facilities in this region.

And what effect did incorporation into the Inca empire have on the local populace? As we have seen, no major changes were made in settlement location, and the system was largely left intact, except for elevating Apucara to the status of provincial capital. The documents tell us that the Andamarca Lucanas were the litter bearers of the Inca and supplied them with yanacona. Although they stressed to the Spaniards that they paid no other tribute, the archaeological data suggest otherwise. Certainly the people of this region had to provide extensive labor service to the Incas. They produced maize and other subsistence and craft goods to fill the storehouses. They provided labor for the construction of the various Inca houses and colcas. They built new sections of road, paved existing sections, and built and maintained a suspension bridge at Ñawpa Chaca. Villages were moved to new locations, as Andamarca Lucanas were sent out of the valley as mitimas. Mitimas from other regions were brought into the valley. In all, local life was very much disrupted by Inca control.

One important area is not mentioned in these documents and is not evident in the archaeological evidence either: the production of cloth. Making cloth involves several different activities, including (1) maintaining herds of camelids, (2) shearing the animals and producing raw wool, (3) spinning wool into yarn, (4) weaving yarn into cloth, and (5) storing the finished products for later use or transport. Certainly some of the colcas may have been devoted to the storage of locally produced cloth, but few of the other activities leave traces that can be discerned from surface remains.

There is, however, one mention of cloth with reference to the Lucanas (which may include the Andamarcas). Murra reports that chronicler Juan Polo de Ondegardo found that although "the Lucanas were preferred as litter bearers . . . he found in the quipus ample records of these 'provinces' contributing also the usual cloth and 'all the rest'" (Murra 1980: 71). As we have seen, the archaeological remains clearly support the contention that the Andamarcas were providing extensive labor service to the Incas, in addition to being litter bearers. And one activity that should have been included was the production of cloth.

The Carhuarazo Valley is located within a broad expanse of puna that today supports large herds of camelids. The Pampa Galeras vicuña preserve, established on the puna to the southwest of the survey area, has recently been extended to the edge of the Carhuarazo Valley. The puna in this region forms the boundary between the wet puna of the central highlands and the dry puna of the south highlands (Troll 1968). Today, because of the large numbers of vicuña grazing on the pampa, the ichu grass is badly depleted and *tola* shrubs are becoming increasingly prevalent.

Before modern overgrazing, the puna around the Carhuarazo Valley could have supported large herds of alpacas and llamas. Even today, alpacas far outnumber people in this province. And it was an excellent habitat for vicuñas as well. Thus Inca exploitation of this region very likely included maintenance of state herds of domestic camelids, as well as harvesting of wild vicuñas, and the production of wool, yarn, and cloth.

CONCLUSIONS

When the Incas arrived in the province that would become known as Andamarca Lucanas, they encountered probably four small chiefdoms, each centered on a town and including additional smaller villages. The Incas elevated the town of Apucara to the status of provincial capital and placed there a single Inca, a member of the royal family. In and around Apucara, they built the residence of the Inca, a royal retreat, and a tambo along the royal road. Elsewhere, Inca facilities seem designed to enhance agricultural production: new terraces, storehouses, and a mitima settlement in especially productive zones. Most of these aspects of the Inca occupation are visible in the archaeological evidence.

The fact that an Inca resided here is information that can come only from documentary sources. The documents also indicate one other aspect of Inca control not visible archaeologically: that the Andamarca Lucanas served as litter bearers for the Inca. Here we see an instance in which documentary information can be misleading without the corroboration of archaeological data: The natives of the region stressed to the Spanish visitor that their service as litter bearers was the *only* tribute (*mita*, or labor service) that they owed the Inca. The archaeological remains tell us that they served the Inca in many other ways as well.

5

THOMAS F. LYNCH

THE IDENTIFICATION OF INCA

POSTS AND ROADS FROM CATARPE

TO RIO FRIO, CHILE

EDITOR'S INTRODUCTION

Lynch concentrates on the distinctions that are present in this peripheral region of the Inca empire in contrast to the remains and documentary information relating to the core of the empire. A major difficulty
in studying the Inca occupation of this area is the relatively poor ethnohistorical information that is available. The research is oriented
heavily toward tambos and other sites on the Inca road that passed
through the region. That the Inca sites appear to be located on the road
rather than in the local population centers reflects the importance of
the road to the Incas. Lynch's work elaborates on the records for this
region in two ways. First, it suggests that Catarpe may have been an
administrative center for the region, rather than simply a tambo, and
second, his data suggest that there were more tambos present in the
area than are recorded on the ethnohistorical lists.

Some of the more significant information of Lynch's study comes
from the distribution of Inca ceramics and architecture. At sites like
Catarpe, which were clearly important Inca centers, Inca ceramics are

relatively scarce, although they were found in the associated cemetery. At the smaller sites that were probably tambos, Inca ceramics are much more prevalent. Nowhere is finely cut masonry found, although certain architectural features do signal an Inca occupation. These results contrast to those of other studies.

INTRODUCTION

Northern Chile's aptly named Gran Despoblado (Great Wilderness) is an immense, high, largely unwatered and unpopulated desert, rich in the well-preserved remains of both the earliest and the latest prehistoric periods. Unfortunately, modern use of the zone, especially exploration and development of its mineral wealth, threatens the delicate superficial features and requires that they be quickly recorded. Thus, for a number of years I have worked concurrently on the Inca occupation and the Early Holocene, Archaic use of the Atacama and Punta Negra basins (Lynch 1990). The Inca presence to the south, especially in the Norte Chico, is known from the pioneering studies by Iribarren and Bergholz (1971), Niemeyer (1962), Silva (1977), Rivera and Hyslop (1984), and more recently through the work of Stehberg and Carvajal (1988a, 1988b).

CATARPE

Although I began excavations at Catarpe, an Inca tambo and administrative center in 1976 (Lynch 1978), they were preceded by a reconnaissance by Grete Mostny (1948) and the casual cemetery excavations of Gustave LePaige (1972–73). In 1980 and 1981, John Hyslop, Hans Niemeyer, Patricio Núñez, Mario Rivera, Julio Sanhueza, and Klaus Schmidt (hereafter, the Inca Road Team) surveyed parts of a north-south segment of the Inca road between 23° 30′ and 25° 30′ south latitude (approximately to the modern towns of Socaire and Vaquillas) immediately to the south (Hyslop 1984; Hyslop and Rivera 1984; Niemeyer and Rivera 1983). In addition, in 1983 Rivera worked with me for a few days at Catarpe, as did Sanhueza in 1976 and 1983, identifying and exploring a segment of the Inca road leading into the tambo from the northeast (figs. 5.1–5.5).

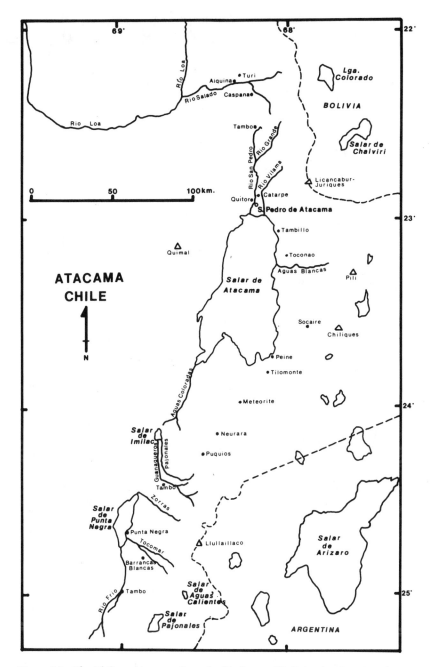

Figure 5.1. The Chilean Atacama, from the Río Loa to Río Frío, showing sites along the Inca road.

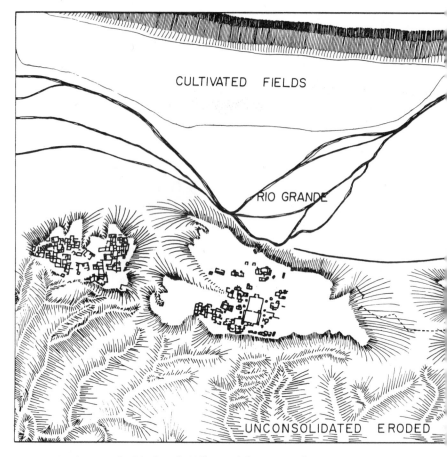

Figure 5.2. Catarpe, the Río Grande Valley, and the Inca road.

As the largest, most classically designed and strategically located tambo on the Atacama frontier, Catarpe is obviously important and will receive much more study. Some two hundred rooms and structures cover about 2 hectares, so the job has just begun, even though LePaige and others seem already to have exhausted the burials in the cemetery area. The site occupies three Pleistocene terrace remnants along the eastern margin of the Río San Pedro floodplain, about 7 kilometers north or upstream of the present-day plaza of San Pedro de Atacama. In Inca times the site probably controlled much of the water supply and an important route to the Bolivian and Peruvian altiplano.

The strategic location is parallel to that of the modern Chilean army

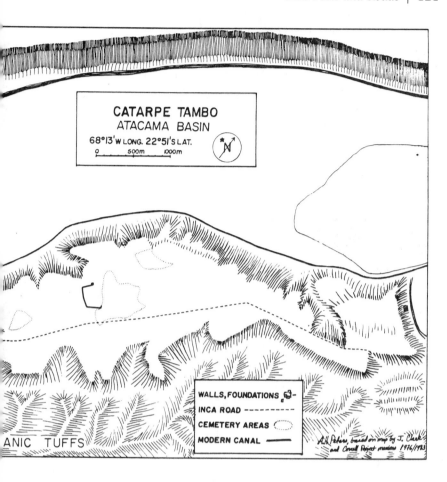

CATARPE TAMBO
ATACAMA BASIN
68°13' W LONG. 22°51' S LAT.
0   500m   1000m

WALLS, FOUNDATIONS
INCA ROAD
CEMETERY AREAS
MODERN CANAL

ANIC TUFFS

garrison, an equal distance up the Río Vilama and similarly at the edge of, but not in, this center of regional population, agriculture, and trade. Today the soldiers come mostly from Santiago rather than the Andean altiplano. The fields of Catarpe receive the first irrigation water and bear the best crops, while the old Inca roadway, with no active *chasquihuasi* (messenger houses) or customs stations, is still the preferred route for the exchange of Bolivian coca for Chilean chañar nuts. Llamas are again becoming an important, if illegal, commodity. (As Chile is certified free of hoof-and-mouth disease, Chilean llamas sell readily on the world market. The supply of "Chilean" llamas is augmented by llamas brought from Bolivia.) Transport of Chilean turquoise has

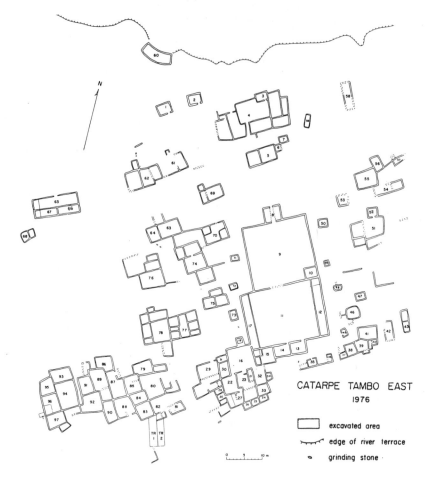

Figure 5.3. Catarpe East.

ceased, and copper goes by wheel on other roads. The archaeological presence of gold, copper artifacts, mold and crucible fragments, unformed copper, and even slag—at Catarpe but not at other tambos of the area—underscores my proposition that Catarpe is much more than a tambo.

Niemeyer and Schiappacasse (1988: 154–156) similarly have decided that Catarpe is "one of the most important administrative centers found on Chilean territory," from which the Incas planned and organized the conquest of the Copiapó Valley and regions to the south. They classify Catarpe as a small city or town and, following Ruppert

(1984), propose that turquoise from El Salvador and other southern mines was sent through Catarpe to destinations in Bolivia and Argentina. This view exceeds the evidence, in that little turquoise has been found so far at Catarpe itself, and there is not much reason to see the oasis of San Pedro de Atacama as "a center of manufacture for turquoise ornaments." On the other hand, I will say that one can follow the Inca road through the Gran Despoblado, by means of its turquoise litter, about as easily as Hansel and Gretel traced their route by bread crumbs. Perhaps turquoise was transshipped or forwarded through Catarpe but not fabricated there—or perhaps we have not yet found the turquoise workshop.

From even our limited excavations in 1976, 1983, and 1985, it is clear that copper was worked at Catarpe or somewhere nearby. Gold also occurs in the area, but the small bits of foil that we found may well have been carried in from elsewhere. On the other hand, the slag, unformed copper metal, and blackened bivalve mold and crucible fragments suggest copper metallurgy itself. The Catarpe crucible, although incomplete, resembles the one from the Copiapó Valley described by Niemeyer (1981).

Of the several finished copper artifacts, perhaps the most interesting are two copper plaques, or gorgets, about 10 centimeters square and 2 millimeters thick, with well-executed filigree designs of human faces and quadrupeds on either side (fig. 5.6). These were found stuck together in the shallow midden, accompanied by a depilatory tweezers. One cannot help but wonder how these important artifacts came to rest at Catarpe and why the human face in one case shows closed eyes, rather than the open eyes of the face on the obverse side. According to A. Rex Gonzalez (personal communication, May 19, 1984) the Catarpe plaques are very similar or nearly identical to others found at Rinconada, Jujuy, Argentina. They pertain to the Aguada style, which began well before Inca times. However, in northwest Argentina the religious cult in which they were apparently used persisted even into Spanish times.

In 1988, the archaeologist Torres Montesinos found a plaque closely resembling those from Catarpe, also 10 centimeters square, in a tomb near the "water temple" (or reservoir) at Sacsahuaman (Ascue 1988). This specimen also was accompanied by a "*depilador de barba.*" In that Cuzco Inca context, the open-eyed human face is considered a representation of the sun, while the quadrupedal animals are seen as felines.

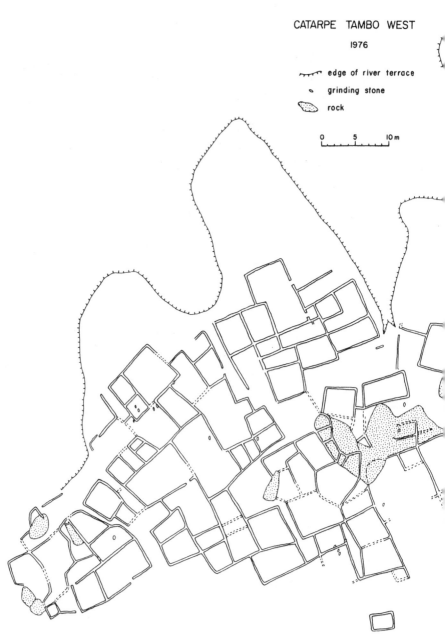

CATARPE TAMBO WEST

1976

⌒⌒⌒ edge of river terrace

◦ grinding stone

🪨 rock

0 ___ 5 ___ 10 m

Figure 5.4. Catarpe West.

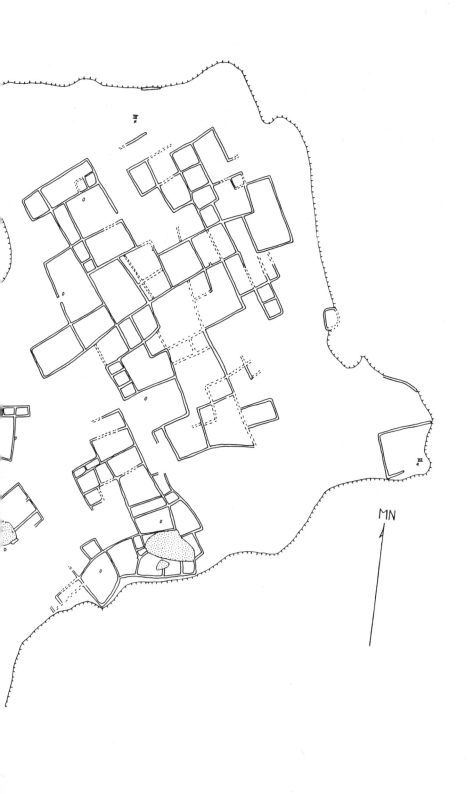

MN

Figure 5.5. Overview of Catarpe East.

A double-headed serpent is an additional Central Andean motif, but from the newspaper photograph it would appear that the Cuzco plaque also is in the Aguada style. One might ask whether artifacts of the Aguada style and cult were reused systematically in Inca contexts.

Niemeyer and Schiappacasse (1988: 156) propose that, like Tilcara in the Argentine Quebrada Humahuaca, Catarpe may have included a lapidary workshop where local artisans turned precious and semiprecious materials into objects of prestige and adornment, following the desired or required Inca models. As yet, we have no evidence of this. Neither can we substantiate their suggestion that Catarpe was the center from which Inca agents directed the construction of mountaintop shrines at Licancabur-Yariques, Chiliques, Pili, Pular (or Pullar), Llullaillaco, and Quimal—although investigations by climbers and archaeologists have established that such shrines are both Inca and important (LePaige 1978; Reinhard 1983, 1985; Reinhard and Sanhueza 1982).

Hyslop (1990: 240) notes that most four-sided plazas, whatever their other symbolic connotations, are found at administrative settlements outside of the Cuzco area. Seventy kilometers to the north of Catarpe, Turi is the first site of comparable scale to have an Inca plaza or kancha and kallanka, and it is similarly oriented (Castro and Cor-

Figure 5.6. Copper filigree plaques (obverse and reverse) and depilatory tweezers.

nejo 1990). In 1992 I located a small tambo or chasquiwasi midway between Turi and Catarpe, where the Inca road enters the Salado Valley tributary of the Río San Pedro. A probable kancha, as well as fine masonry construction and curbstones defining the road, suggests an important function for this station, although the orientation of the kancha is to the necessities of the terrain (fig. 5.7). To the south, the distance to the next administrative center is at least five times greater (more than

Figure 5.7. Salado Tambo, with road passing to the left (north) and probable kancha to the south, in front.

400 kilometers), with nothing larger than a tambo known between, probably because the road passes through one of the most barren and unpopulated areas of the Andes (Hyslop 1990: 253–254, 279). La Puerta, even further to the south in the Copiapó Valley, is about the same size (around two hundred houses) and has a slightly larger kancha with an almost identical layout—joined rooms on two opposing sides of the plaza and three "storage" rooms along a third side.

Turi, Catarpe, and La Puerta—all apparently administrative stations along the main north-south road—were placed within or near centers of indigenous population subsisting on relatively bountiful pastoral and agricultural resources: the Vega de Turi and upper Río Salado, the oasis of San Pedro de Atacama, and the ample resources of the Copiapó Valley. The indications of metallurgy at Catarpe are paralleled as well by the Inca mine at Caspana (just above Turi) and the proximity of La Puerta to (and presumed control of) the copper smelting at Viña del Cerro. Niemeyer concluded that La Puerta was the principal Inca administrative center for the Copiapó Valley (Hyslop 1990: 252). In general, according to Hyslop (1990: 270–279), Inca administrative centers were located with an eye to various environmental, cultural, and political concerns that included flat terrain, access to water and other natural resources, and strategic placement along principal routes. It seems to me that the Incas preferred to place their administrative centers near, but not actually within, concentrations of local ethnic groups. I am tempted to turn the usual interpretation around and visualize the Inca road as a connector of administrative centers, rather than of the nuclei of densest population, which often lay a bit off to the side on lateral access routes (Lynch 1989: 7). Following this line of reasoning, we might expect the administrative centers to be built more according to formula or master plan, than substantial towns or cities would be. Given the largely artificial origin and political purpose of such administrative centers (rather than economic origin and basis), it is no wonder that many centers were abandoned soon after the Spanish invasion and destruction of the Inca core.

We have found no European goods in our excavations at Catarpe: no bits of iron, glazed pottery, or broken glass. It may be that Catarpe already was abandoned, as speculated above, when the Inca road was traversed by conquistadores Diego de Almagro in 1536 and Pedro de Valdivia in 1540. The common presumption is that the fort or *pucará* stormed by Francisco de Aguirre, which they later named Las Cabezas (the heads) for the gory trophies that he displayed, is the same known today as Quitor Pucará. This identification, however, is based heavily on the opinion of Gustave LePaige, who presumed that the Spanish had burned the fortress during or after the assault (Hidalgo 1972: 32–35). While Quitor may show signs of having been burned, and Catarpe shows none, the description of the battle by our main source, Jerónimo de Vivar (1966 [1558], as interpreted by Hidalgo) could apply to either site. The fort taken by Aguirre was set upon a high hill and was approachable by a single pathway, according to Vivar. The ascent was too difficult for their horses, required an hour and a half, and was impeded by the arrows and slingstones flung by more than a thousand defenders. However, upon reaching the top, the Spaniards easily breached the walls and made their conquest.

Vivar's description of the battle fits Catarpe as well as Quitor. Quitor is higher, but Catarpe has equal or better defensive works and is flat and easily overrun once the top is reached. The ascent of Quitor can be made along a single but broad side; Catarpe could be approached by two narrow and difficult pathways, overlooked by emplacements in which we found piles of slingstones. Small arrow points were a relatively common find at Catarpe. Having led many groups of students, colleagues, and visitors up the ascents to both sites—they being as encumbered by their packs and cameras as were the Spaniards by their weapons—I would hesitate to say which site is more likely to have been the sixteenth-century Las Cabezas.

Catarpe in Comparative Context

Following Henderson (1987, 1992) we can see that there is a temptation, when working on the periphery of a strong and well-known culture area, to assume homogeneity in the cultural core and deal with the archaeology of the fringe in terms of oversimplified comparisons and contrasts with an implicitly monolithic Inca state or culture. There is "a natural tendency to focus on external similarities and to interpret them in terms of interaction" (Henderson 1987: 455). There are similarities and there are differences. I would like to overemphasize neither and to evaluate them comparatively in the contexts of this presumably important administrative center versus simple tambos, roads, wayside checkpoints, and boundary or "mileage" markers. Of course, the very assumption that I am dealing with tambos, chasquihuasis, *apachetas* (piles of stones serving as shrines), *hitos* (rock pile markers), and so forth violates Henderson's warning.

Be that as it may, Catarpe shares a number of features with other Inca installations, but only a few with Cuzco and the nuclear Inca area. The most remarkable of the latter is the orientation of the kancha 63° to 66° east of true north (fig. 5.8). This is essentially the same as the orientations of the Qorikancha (the Temple of the Sun) in Cuzco and the trapezoidal plaza and *Qori kancha analogue* (rectangular compound to the southeast) at Incawasi. To Hyslop (1985: 60–66, 1990: 232–237) these are significant astronomical alignments, although Dearborn (1986) has raised questions concerning their precision and utility.

I am satisfied with Hyslop's (1990: 234, 243) conclusion that, whether or not the Incas made extremely precise measurements and alignments for astronomical observations, they did likely orient buildings and plazas to azimuths in order to symbolize and define concepts in cosmology, social structure, and calendrical seasons. Attempted orientations may have been to the zenith sunset or to the June solstice sunrise and Pleiades (or May 25, solar) azimuths. In a number of cases

Figure 5.8. Excavations in the kancha at Catarpe.

(as at Turi, Catarpe, and Viña del Cerro), the east-west orientation may have been rather rough and ready at the moment of construction. Still, one might note that the similarities in size and conformation of the plazas at Catarpe, as well as orientation, are virtually identical to those of the double plaza at Anocariri (old Paria?), a tambo close by in Bolivia, near Oruro (Hyslop 1984: 144, fig. 9.4). At Tambo Colorado in the Pisco Valley, the kancha with joined rooms is virtually a mirror image of Catarpe's kancha or kallanka (structure 11) with associated rooms 12 through 17 (figs. 5.3 and 5.5).

Finally, we should note that the two large adjacent enclosures at Catarpe might well be considered a dual plaza, oriented at right angles to its component plazas, in that the two are joined by a well-built, formal doorway. Further, the main plaza at Cuzco had two parts, Haucaypata and Cusipata. Hyslop (personal communication, June 13, 1988) suggests I remember that "many other Inca plazas (particularly those outside of the Cuzco area) have physical evidence such as a road or an architectural axis which divides them, generally near the center. An idea worth playing with is that the plaza division separates *hanan* from *hurin* [the upper and lower moiety divisions among the Inca]."

The use of finely cut stone masonry is unknown in most of the

Figure 5.9. Cobble and mud mortar wall construction at Catarpe.

southern and western reaches of the Inca culture area. Instead, the Inca walls are built generally of double rows of fieldstone or partially worked stones, cemented with mud mortar. Raffino (1981: 77) lists this double-wall technique as a second-order attribute of Inca construction in Collasuyo. At Catarpe, the Inca builders used the river cobbles of the terrace surface (fig. 5.9). Many walls were demonstrably full height (that is, not topped with adobe or wattle) and at least the long subdivided structures (12 and 17) were covered with thatched roofs. These compose what may be the southernmost kallanka known. It is unlikely that large groups regularly traveled south into the Despoblado, but Catarpe may have had important storage and staging functions. The heavy walls of "storage" rooms 13 through 15 and the defensive works near the perimeter of the site suggest that Catarpe contained goods worthy of protection. Loopholes or embrasures (*troneras*) in some walls are both a possible sign of defensive function and, to Raffino (1981: 76, 124), a first-order attribute of Inca construction.

Catarpe was also a habitation area for local populations. This is especially clear in the western (perhaps hurin) sector of the site, which has more midden (fig. 5.4). There, the building plan was less regular

Figure 5.10. Earlier, underlying wall and blocked doorway in Room 15 at Catarpe.

and there are fewer massive walls. It seems to me that construction was to suit the terrain, with no effort made to follow a plan. I suspect that a local settlement may have preceded as well as coincided with the Inca occupation. Excavations in the eastern sector uncovered two instances of earlier walls lying unconformably under the planned Inca structures (fig. 5.10). It is also remarkable that, except in the cemetery, Inca potsherds, even Provincial Inca sherds, are extremely rare, although they do include the narrow-necked large jar (aryballos), which elsewhere appears to symbolize Inca rule and state-related activities (Carlevato 1988: 44). If we were to follow Hyslop's (1984: 292) advice to eschew a reliance on architecture in identifying tambos, we would identify Catarpe even more surely through its wooden spoons and spindle whorls than its pottery.

The situation is somewhat analogous to the interpretation of pollen frequencies in sites where windblown pollen from prolific producers may swamp the local pollen rain. In the sites I will discuss below, Inca pottery is, to the contrary of Catarpe, relatively common. It dominates the roadside situation where local population was previously unimportant or absent. The simple tambillos and chasquihuasi are less obviously Inca in conformation, orientation, and site layout—and, of

Figure 5.11. Peine Tambo.

course, local materials are expediently used in construction. An exception to this is the rather nice finishing of the walls at Peine, Meteorite, Puquios, and Guanaqueros. Otherwise, we must identify these Inca buildings chiefly by their associated artifacts, including the road itself, as suggested by Hyslop. Near the entrance to Catarpe, the road is a good determining artifact, in that it features well-defined steps, rare in Collasuyo, which are an excellent marker of Inca construction as well as Inca use (Raffino 1981: 77).

OTHER TAMBOS AND THE ROAD SOUTH

The next tambo south of Catarpe is at Peine, described first by Niemeyer and Rivera (1983). As the distance is close to 100 kilometers, there were probably two intermediate resting places, as yet unidentified. The first may have been at Toconao or the Quebrada de Aguas Blancas, both good sources of water, and the second perhaps below Socaire. Peine Tambo is well constructed out of fieldstones, sometimes in two rows, laid with straight faces outward (fig. 5.11). However, it is also rather small, consisting of seven rooms within a walled area of 60 by 15 meters. Like Salado Tambo and Catarpe, it overlooks a water-course and, from its slight elevation on a ridge, commands a view of the approaching road. Unlike Catarpe, it is unfortified and easy of access. Both the Inca Road Team and I collected Inca pottery and turquoise there.

At an altitude of 3,220 meters, Meteorite Tambo is 840 meters above Peine, as the road climbs south out of the Atacama Basin. Despite Hyslop's optimism, it would be a very difficult 44-kilometer hike for a single day. Thus, I calculate a midway stopover at Tilomonte, where there is an algarrobo grove and water of questionable potability, but no tambo (Hyslop 1984: 154). Meteorite Tambo also has seven or eight rooms on an area of about 60 by 10 meters, situated on an open plain with no source of water and no apparent effort made to prevent access. The construction methods are like those at Peine, but at Meteorite a trapezoidal doorway with monolithic lintel has survived. The lintel is similar to a fallen lintel at the entrance to the Catarpe kancha. The Inca Road Team collected both Inca and early Colonial sherds at Meteorite Tambo.

From Meteorite to a possible tambo at the Aguada de Puquios (3,730 meters in the Sierra de Almeyda) is another difficult journey of 42 kilometers, but there is an intermediate shelter at Neurara (3,350 meters), where Niemeyer collected Inca and Colonial pottery. No more than one room, this "tambillo" is unimpressive. The single room at Puquios is only 2.5 by 2.1 meters and would not seem to qualify this station as a tambo. Nevertheless, it is well built, in the customary Inca manner, and even has a monolithic threshold. The attached, walled courtyard has a formal rectangular hearth and an entry with four stairs. The only identifiable small artifacts were two preceramic tetragonal projectile points. Niemeyer (1962) supposes that flood deposits from the quebrada have covered the Inca midden. Hyslop (personal communication, June 30, 1987) further reports that the Puquios site has been partially dismantled and destroyed by heavy trucks carrying water from the springs.

From the Aguada de Puquios down into and across the Salar de Punta Negra is another 65 to 70 kilometers, but there are a number of protected quebradas with good waters, as well as a spring at the tip of the Punta Negra basalt flow. On mules it took two days for Niemeyer, Schmidt, and Núñez to reach the Quebrada de Zorras. The first night they made a dry camp in the upper Quebrada Pajonales, riding two

Figure 5.12. Chasquihuasi at Guanaqueros Tambo.

hours the following morning to the major pajonal with water, grass, and a building from the historic era. Apparently they missed the ascent of the Inca road out of the Quebrada Pajonales, where it departs south into the Vizcachas tributary of the Quebrada Guanaqueros. That section was identified and walked by the Cornell crew in 1985 and 1988.

The main Inca stop may have been not in Pajonales, as indicated by the Inca Road Team's guide, but in the Quebrada de Guanaqueros, where in 1985 I located another entry of the Inca road from the north. In the bottom of the quebrada is a strategically placed tambo of several rooms (at least seven—some were rebuilt), including a circular colca and one open-sided, classic chasquihuasi, built in the correct Inca manner (fig. 5.12). The massive 80-centimeter-thick walls are well faced, mud-mortared, squared and bonded at the corners, and they include stones that must weigh hundreds of pounds. The chasquihuasi, nearly 3 meters on a side, appears to guard the *chorro*—a narrow, hard-rock constriction of the quebrada walls, where an Inca path may have begun the climb up Mount Llullaillaco from 3,500 meters' elevation. At 6,739 meters (6,780 meters in some sources) this mountain is the third highest in the Western Hemisphere. Yet, having clearly been sacred to the Incas, it is capped by a shrine described by Reinhard (1983). Guanaqueros Tambo, which rests on the quebrada bottom, has been swept repeatedly by floods. There were no Inca sherds on the surface, but we found four black-on-red pieces on the difficult road descent from the northern quebrada rim. They appear to belong either to the Provincial Inca Saxamar or to the Copiapó Black-on-Red wares.

It is only 42 kilometers straight-line distance from Guanaqueros to the barely potable spring at the tip of the Punta Negra, at 2,950 meters, where Inca sherds have also been collected. This is Hyslop's maximum distance between tambos. From Punta Negra to an approximately fifteen-room tambo near the mouth of Quebrada Río Frío is another 42 kilometers up a gentle incline to 3,600 meters elevation. There are no intermediate water sources except, by way of a small detour, at Barrancas Blancas. There, Niemeyer's group found a few sherds (identified as Inca and Copiapó Black-on-Red) associated with a hardly Incaic, very small, walled-up rock shelter.

Niemeyer's Tambo de Río Frío is not likely a tambo, or even a tambillo. It is a single, roughly rectangular structure, about 3 meters on a side, which was probably not even roofed. The few associated sherds were of the non-Inca San Pedro series, with the exception of a modern glazed piece and one edge-sherd of an atypical Inca *escudilla* or plate (Niemeyer 1983: 125). This shelter has been much used in Colonial and modern times and, after Niemeyer's thorough surface collection, our crew may have camped in it as well. It is protected from the wind and was the only shelter we could find with a good view of Mount Llullaillaco at sunset.

The name Río Frío Tambo should probably be transferred to a much larger site, whose fourteen or fifteen structures cover an area about 40 by 12 meters. This tambo was missed by the Inca Road Team, whose mules had given out and who had transferred to jeeps. It is located on the wind-protected southeast side of a ridge separating the Quebrada Río Frío from the Quebrada de Laguna Seca. At this undisturbed site, we made a good collection of Inca pottery (figs. 5.13 and 5.14), an Inca obsidian point, turquoise, and even burned bone. With the exception of one large room or plaza, about 2.5 meters square, attached to two smaller rectangular rooms, the configuration of the Tambo Río Frío or Laguna Seca is hardly Inca in its architecture. The walls are poorly built of flat slabs of rock laid one upon the other and most structures are distinctly subrectangular in plan. However, the site merits further investigation.

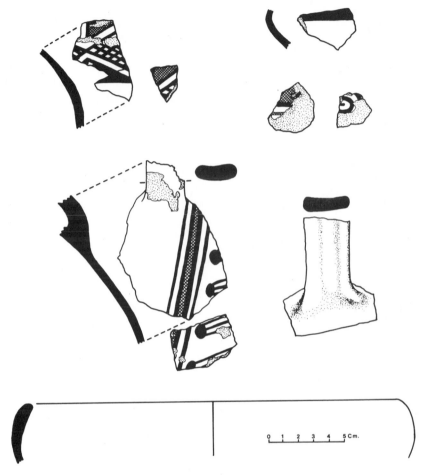

Figure 5.13. Inca pottery from Río Frío Tambo.

Apart from these tambos on the main Inca road, there are a number of apachetas and hitos, the latter set in pairs on either side of the road-way (figs. 5.15 and 5.16). Some are still piled in neatly columnar form. Hyslop's figure of 3 meters for the width of the Atacama road is not absolute and unvarying, but it represents a good average for the main road on the east side of the Salar de Punta Negra. However, there is also another, essentially unstudied, narrower road that runs along the west side of the Salar de Punta Negra, southward from the Salar de Imilac. Considerable quantities of turquoise and sherds of San Pedro Negro Pulido ware are associated with this single-track road and its

Figure 5.14. Inca escudilla *(plate) from PN 80, near Río Frío Tambo.*

Figure 5.15. Inca road structures and hitos (site PN 69) south of the Quebrada Tocomar.

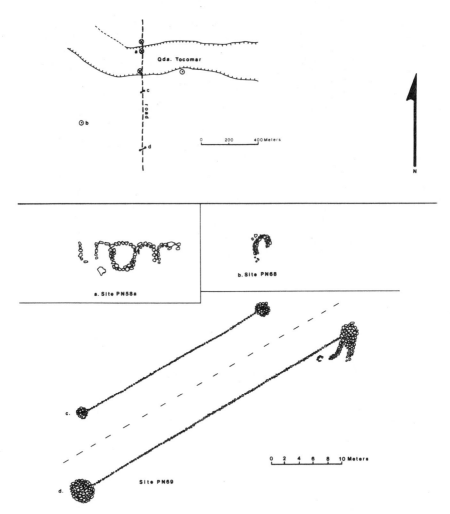

Figure 5.16. Inca road crossing the Quebrada Tocomar at site PN 58, with associated structures and hitos (sites PN 68 and PN 69) to the south.

structures, as well as occasional Inca sherds (figs. 5.17 and 5.18). It may be that the road from Imilac, along the eastern side of the Salar de Punta Negra, represents an earlier route than the "new" Inca road.

My interest in the Inca use of the Gran Despoblado began as an incidental aspect, or fringe benefit, of investigating the early Postglacial adaptation and settlement history of the Atacama Desert. Clearly, the continuing story, even into historical pastoralism and mining, is nec-

Figure 5.17. San Pedro Negro Pulido bowl from road on west side of Salar de Punta Negra.

Figure 5.18. Inca pottery, turquoise (sodalite) beads, and marine shell from various sites of the Salar de Punta Negra.

essary for a good understanding of the potential of this immense zone. Our next step should be a thorough analysis of the data available from Catarpe, supplemented by limited further excavation there and at other posts along the roadway. The exact route, too, must be traced in its entirety, as most of it has been unused and lost since the foot road was last followed by Diego de Almagro, Pedro de Valdivia, and perhaps a few mail carriers of the sixteenth and seventeenth centuries (Magallanes 1912). Much reading, museum study, and fieldwork remain to be done before we will have an adequate understanding of the Inca occupation of the Chilean Norte Grande.

ACKNOWLEDGMENTS

I thank the National Geographic Society (grant 4654–91), the National Science Foundation (grant BNS-8418815), and the Jacob and Hedwig Hirsch Fund for financial aid over the past ten years. Minera Escondida and the Universidad Católica del Norte (Instituto de Investigaciones Arqueológicas, San Pedro de Atacama) lent facilities, equipment, advice, personnel, and good fellowship, for which I am especially and personally grateful. Bev Phillips typed more than one draft, Mike Malpass gave valuable editorial assistance, while John Alden, Barbara Lynch, Ann Peters, and Camille Ward worked on the line drawings and maps.

Part II

TOWARD AN ARCHAEOLOGICAL

AND ETHNOHISTORICAL SYNTHESIS

Part II includes essays by Susan A. Niles and Catherine J. Julien and a concluding chapter by Michael A. Malpass. The Niles and Julien essays use an ethnohistorical perspective much more heavily than an archaeological one. Thus, they balance the archaeological emphasis of the earlier papers. In addition, both go beyond the analysis and comparison of archaeological and ethnohistorical sources to a discussion of fruitful directions for future research. Niles approaches possible means for discerning stylistic variability in the architecture of the provinces through a discussion of the data from the Cuzco area. Julien's analysis outlines a means of employing the ethnohistorical literature to generate hypotheses concerning Inca control in the provinces that are suitable for testing archaeologically. Malpass's final chapter summarizes the kinds of new information that have been obtained from the studies in the book.

6

SUSAN A. NILES

THE PROVINCES IN THE HEARTLAND:

STYLISTIC VARIATION AND ARCHITECTURAL

INNOVATION NEAR INCA CUZCO

EDITOR'S INTRODUCTION

Niles's essay focuses on the royal estates near Cuzco, continuing and elaborating on her earlier research (Niles 1982, 1984, 1987). The major contribution of this study is its review of the nature of these Inca estates, with a view to providing new interpretations of evidence from provincial areas. While some (e.g., Hyslop 1990) would argue that royal estates contain unique architectural features relatively unrelated to other Inca installations, Niles offers intriguing suggestions to the contrary. Her discussion of the variability in Inca architecture in the heartland, which ranged from the classic fitted stones and double jambs to more mundane fieldstone and adobe structures, is a warning to anyone attempting to identify the Incas in the provinces strictly on the basis of fine masonry. She also provides compelling evidence that distinct architectural styles identified from royal estates can be attributed to the individual Inca rulers who built them, whose handiwork might possibly be discerned in other regions. In addition, she discusses the idea that different architectural styles might reflect different perceptions of status or prestige. She likens the relationship between the royal estates and Cuzco to that between conquered provinces and Cuzco. Her suggestion that architecture might imply placement in the *collana-payan-collao* prestige system is one that merits further study.

INTRODUCTION

In examining the impact of the Incas on the provinces of Tahuantin-suyo, it is first important to consider one very special area: the region in the immediate environs of the Inca capital at Cuzco but outside the limits of the capital city. By looking at the way the Incas used this heartland area, we gain evidence that helps us to understand the Inca relationship to more distant provinces.

The land surrounding Cuzco in the Huatanay Valley and in the immediately adjacent Vilcanota-Urubamba Valley contains almost continuous tracts of terracing, roads, canalization works, and now-ruined buildings. This is the area that was closest to the capital and that was brought early into the Inca polity.[1] Early incorporations were by intermarriage and co-optation; later conquests were by force. The area under consideration had land that was put to immediate economic use, but for particular purposes: it was developed into Inca royal estates. The locations of the principal estates are shown in figure 6.1.

SOCIAL AND ECONOMIC ORGANIZATION OF INCA ROYAL ESTATES

The standard histories of the Incas comment on the development of such estates. Accounts by Sarmiento de Gamboa (1960), Cobo (1964), Murúa (1962–64), Cabello Balboa (1951), and Betanzos (1987), especially, describe the founding of privately owned lands. In addition to these histories, we have abundant land documents that supported the legal claims of local populations or displaced royal families, which can be used to examine the social and economic organization of estates (see, for example, Villanueva and Sherbondy 1979; Villanueva 1971a, 1971b; Rostworowski de Diez Canseco 1962, 1963, 1970; Rowe 1982, 1985b, 1990; Wachtel 1981). Most of these land disputes date to the first generation after the Conquest, and some continued into the seventeenth century. Such accounts contain good information on place

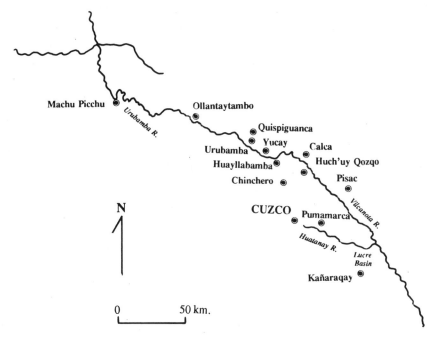

Figure 6.1. Selected royal estates near Cuzco showing their location relative to sites and places mentioned in this chapter.

names and productivity figures for lands of economic importance, and often mention the architecture to be found on the estates.

The country estates were developed privately by members of royal families, and the produce from the lands was likewise privately owned. All of the ruling Incas from Viracocha through Huascar had estates in the Vilcanota-Urubamba Valley, as shown in table 6.1. In addition to estates developed by rulers, there were parcels belonging to favored brothers and uncles and to significant women in the lives of rulers, for example, sisters, mothers, wives, and concubines.

The kinds of goods produced on estates near Cuzco were varied. Maize was the most abundant crop, but private lands were also devoted to the production of potatoes (lands of Mama Anahuarque) (Rostworowski de Diez Canseco 1962: 153) and *ají* (hot peppers) (Rostworowski de Diez Canseco 1962: 152). Additionally, stands of forested lands were owned privately (see Niles, in press) and used to collect *totora* reed and fish (Villanueva 1971a: 38), to hunt animals (Villanueva 1971a: 38, 52), to gather wood (Tierras de Sorama 1985), and to make

Table 6.1. Principal Royal Estates near Cuzco

Inca	Estate	Location	Source
Yahuar Huacac (r. ?–?)	Paullu	near Calca	Cobo (libro 12, cap. X; 1964: 75)
Viracocha Inca (r. ?–1438)	Paucartica	near Calca	Rostworowski de Diez Canseco (1970: 253)
	Caquia Xaquixaguana	site of Huch'uy Qozqo	Rostworowski de Diez Canseco (1970: 253); Cobo (libro 12, cap. XI; 1964: 77)
	Pumamarca	near San Sebastián, Cuzco	Pachacuti Yamqui (1968: 296–297)
Pachacuti (r. 1438–71)	Pisac	Pisac	Rostworowski de Diez Canseco (1970: 253)
	Ollantaytambo	Ollantaytambo	Rostworowski de Diez Canseco (1970: 253); Sarmiento de Gamboa (cap. 41; 1960: 247)
Topa Inca (r. 1471–93)	Machu Picchu	Machu Picchu	Rowe (1990)
	Chinchero	Chinchero	Rostworowski de Diez Canseco (1970: 253, 258); Sarmiento de Gamboa (cap. 54; 1960: 258)
	Huayllabamba Urquillos	Urquillos canyon	Rostworowski de Diez Canseco (1970: 253, 258); Villanueva (1971a: 38–39)
Huayna Capac (r. 1493–1528)	Amaybamba	Amaybamba	Rostworowski de Diez Canseco (1963)
	Yucay	Urubamba and Yucay	Rostworowski de Diez Canseco (1970: 253); Villanueva (1971a: 38–39)
Huascar (r. 1528–32?)	Calca	Calca	Rostworowski de Diez Canseco (1970: 253); Murúa (libro 1, cap. 46; 1962: 132–133)
	Muina	site of Kañaraqay	Rostworowski de Diez Canseco (1970: 253); Sarmiento de Gamboa (cap. 63; 1960: 265); Murúa (libro 1, cap. 39; 1962: 110)

salt (Villanueva 1971a: 36). Farther from Cuzco, lands for the production of tropical fruits and coca were held as private patrimony (see, e.g., Rostworowski de Diez Canseco 1963, 1988). The economic balance that prevailed in the economic organization of the Inca state is seen also in the range of parcels that were privately owned: Huayna Capac was said to have owned privately "minerals of gold and silver, quebradas of forests, country estates, terraces, herd animals, pastures, and cornfields" in a 1571 land claim launched by his descendant Doña Beatriz (*nona pregunta*; Rostworowski de Diez Canseco 1970: 257, my translation).

The goods produced on private lands did not go into state coffers; rather, such produce was sent to private storage facilities or carried to Cuzco. Some estates did have special parcels dedicated to the state religion, however. Topa Inca's holdings included small fields of the Sun (Villanueva 1971a: 34–35), and Huayna Capac's development at Yucay involved large tracts of terraced lands farmed for this divinity (Villanueva 1971a: 37–39, 53).

The economic importance of private estates to their owners was not a trivial matter. The produce supported the owners and their court in their lifetime and maintained the owners' descendants after death. In the case of ruling Incas, at least, the estates were also used to support the cult of the mummy after death. Inca Roca's mummy was maintained on his lands at Larapa (Sarmiento de Gamboa cap. 19; 1960: 224; Cobo libro 12, cap. XX; 1964: 73); Huayna Capac's mummy was kept at times on his estate at Yucay (Betanzos parte II, cap. I; 1987: 208). Indeed, some estates were developed for the owner after death (Betanzos parte I, cap. XLIII; 1987: 187).[2] We are told that Huayna Capac provided lands, *mamacuna* (chosen women) attendants, and yanacona for the mummies of both Pachacuti and Manco Inca (Betanzos parte I, cap. XLI; 1987: 182).

The demands attendant upon royal status were enormous and varied, and Inca royals used their estate lands to meet their needs. The production of foodstuffs to feed the court and to entertain guests was perhaps the most obvious of the needs met by the private lands, and the one that is most frequently articulated in the land claims of the late sixteenth and early seventeenth centuries. The magnitude of the entertainment obligations of royalty is hinted at in the argument seeking redress for the loss of land and yanacona which was presented by Doña María Manrique, mother of Doña Beatriz Coya, the heir of Sayri Tupac.

Doña María complained that she had insufficient means to eat and that she could not feed her servants or the other visitors that she was obligated, by her standing, to entertain.[3]

Most of the royal lands near Cuzco were devoted to the production of maize, a crop valued in its own right and particularly important as the source for the corn beer used in entertainment and in ritual. The ritual obligations of royalty must have consumed much of the produce of their lands. In addition to corn beer, coca and ají were required for the *purucaya* ritual, to complete the funeral obsequies on the anniversary of a death. Betanzos describes Huayna Capac's preparations for his mother's purucaya, noting that he spent the year between the death and the ceremony acquiring sufficient ají and coca to put on an impressive show (Betanzos parte I, cap. XLIV; 1987: 189).[4] Pachacuti and subsequent rulers owned estates in coca-growing lands where they could produce some of the stuff of ritual in quantity.

In addition to their economic importance, estates had political and symbolic value. They were built as part of the act of assuming office and were commissioned when a ruler's town palaces were built. The record of their construction forms an important part of the legacy of each ruler and is listed alongside his conquests of provinces in the histories recorded by Sarmiento de Gamboa, Cobo, Murúa, and Cabello Balboa. During the owner's lifetime, at least some court business was conducted on the estates. For example, Calca was Huascar's Camp David: he received the ambassador from Quito sent by Atahuallpa there (Cabello Balboa cap. 26; 1951: 413–416; unfortunately he also murdered the ambassador's party there). The chroniclers likened Huayna Capac's estate near Yucay to the Spanish summer palace of Aranjuez (Cobo libro 12, cap. XVI; 1964: 89).

When we think of an Inca king, we imagine someone with the ability to command any kind of resource desired, regardless of expense. We need to remember, however, that any goods acquired had to be gotten from someplace, using a claim that was legitimate in Inca terms. An Inca who demanded goods illegitimately ran the risk of annoying ambitious brothers or half-brothers, uncles, regents, and others with some claim to the throne. In Inca legal theory, a claim of private ownership was unassailable. Grants made by a king to his associates—living or dead—might be seen as a way to placate possible enemies and to reward loyal friends. Such grants would enrich the present and future members of a family and would exalt the position of an ancestral owner.[5]

THE CREATION OF ROYAL ESTATES

The designation of lands as royal patrimony and their development into economically useful estates reflects Inca diplomatic and administrative strategies. The early ruling Incas doubtless had relatively easy access to lands near Cuzco that could be taken through conquest or coercion of local lords. Pachacuti's principal holdings outside of Cuzco include Pisac, in the old Cuyo heartland (the Cuyos were the first group vanquished after he assumed the throne, and their capital was destroyed; see Sarmiento de Gamboa cap. 34; 1960: 239), Ollantaytambo (the Ollantaytambo campaign is the second listed by Sarmiento de Gamboa, and it also culminated in the destruction of their capital; see Sarmiento de Gamboa, cap. 35; 1964: 239), and properties at Machu Picchu and Amaybamba, along the route repeated in the story of his Vitcos campaign (Cobo libro 12, cap. XII: 1964: 79; and see Rowe 1990: 142–143). This latter venture culminated in the granting of gold mines to Pachacuti by local lords, "in order to further please the Inca and gain his favor" (Cobo libro II, cap. XII; 1964: 80, my translation). Topa Inca probably got some of his lands through his father, as fields owned together with his sister/wife, Mama Ocllo, are found adjacent to Pachacuti's holdings at Amaybamba (Rostworowski de Diez Canseco 1963) and Machu Picchu (Rowe 1990). Topa Inca's other properties near Cuzco (Chinchero, Urquillos, and lands of Cachi) must have been taken from local lords; at least some of the property was reportedly given to him by the chief of Cachi (Rostworowski de Diez Canesco 1962: 136), in the Urubamba Valley.

The later historical Incas may have faced greater challenges in developing lands for their estates. Huayna Capac focused his claims in the Yucay Valley on poorly drained land that had been overlooked by his predecessors. The meandering course of the Urubamba River was fixed through a large-scale canalization project that, according to Betanzos, required the work of 150,000 laborers, who were brought to Cuzco within six months of Huayna Capac's request (Betanzos parte I, cap. XLIII; 1987: 187). This previously unproductive stretch of valley had been in the hands of local populations, the Chichos (Villanueva 1971a: 38), Pacas, and Chaocas (Villanueva 1971a: 39), all of whom retained the use of lands that were left otherwise undeveloped on the estate. Huascar, who complained that all the good property had already been claimed by his ancestors (Pizarro cap. 10; 1986: 54), likewise resorted to reclaiming gravel bars and river-bottom lands by fixing the course of the Vilcanota-Urubamba River with the help of workers brought in from the four quarters of Tahuantinsuyo (Rostworowski de Diez Canseco 1962: 142, Manuscrito 1). For the construction and service of his palace at Calca he brought in "an infinite quantity of Indians" from Cajamarca and from París (Murúa cap. 46; 1962–64: 132, my translation).

THE SOCIAL ORGANIZATION OF ESTATES

Support populations on the estates were organized into small, permanent towns ("pueblos pequeños de a veinte y a treinta y cincuenta indios"; see Betanzos parte I, cap. XLIII; 1987: 187) which had some internal stratification. Such yanacona groups formed a tax-exempt class whose service was personal and who lived on goods that they produced on lands granted to them within the estates.

The organization of estates, although they were royal concerns rather than state business, was not unrelated to the endeavors of the Inca bureaucratic and military machine. Some of the strategies used by the Incas to further their imperial goals found their counterparts in the organization of estates. For example, the institution of selecting mitimas, colonists to be resettled from newly conquered regions to more established parts of the empire and to provide populations for under-used lands, was part of the Inca's strategy to pacify their domain and to maximize agricultural production at the state level (see Murúa libro 2, cap. 7; 1962–64, v. 2: 44–45; Cobo libro 12, cap. XXIII; 1964: 109–111; Sarmiento de Gamboa cap. 39; 1960: 244–245). But these goals also motivated the development of privately owned royal estates. It is perhaps not surprising that mitimas were also used to support these private endeavors (Rowe 1982). For example, Topa Inca's coca-growing lands in Amaybamba were settled by 1,500 mitimas "de todos nasciones [sic]" (Rostworowski de Diez Canseco 1963: 231), among them Chachapoyas, Yuncaybambas, and others from provinces in the yungas (low-altitude zones) (Rostworowski de Diez Canseco 1963: 237). According to a land claim launched by the descendants of one of these notables, the Chachapoya mitimas were brought in by Topa Inca at the time he conquered that province (Rostworowski de Diez Canseco 1963: 237). In this case, the relationship of the estates' populations to ongoing military concerns of the estate owners is clear: Topa Inca's early campaigns were to the Yungas of Antisuyu (Cobo libro 12, cap. XIV; 1964: 83–84), and a particularly hard-fought victory was won against the Chachapoyas (Cobo libro 12, cap. XIV; 1964: 84). Similarly, Huayna Capac's estate at Yucay included two thousand workers brought from the provinces and resettled there to form its permanent population (Villanueva 1971a: 139). One thousand of these workers had come from Chinchaysuyo; this was the region to which Huayna Capac's first major military campaign after ascending the throne was directed (Cobo libro 12, cap. XVI; 1964: 88–89). One thousand had come from Collasuyo, an area in which he had made conquests immediately after assuming the throne (Cobo libro 12, cap. XVI; 1964: 88–89), and in which he later traveled to settle local differences (Cobo libro 12, cap. XVI; 1964: 89). The estate at Yucay was built early in Huayna Capac's reign, just after he put down a rebellion of the Chachapoyas and toured the northern frontier (Cobo libro 12, cap. XVI; 1964: 89). At his death, a group of fifty *apuyanacuna* (royal retainers) from Tomebamba came to Yucay to care for his mummy (Villanueva 1971a: 129, 131, 135). This population probably reflected the king's military successes later in life in the northern reaches of the empire (Cobo libro 12, cap. XVII; 1964: 91–93).

The temperate lands of Amaybamba provided coca and tropical fruits for the estate owner; the transplanted support population was likewise from temperate lands, in keeping with the Inca policy of resettling mitimas in a climate similar to that of their home province. These colonists brought with them seeds of crops they were to grow: avocados, lucumas, maize, ají, coca, and the wherewithal to make a native beverage (Rostworowski de Diez Canseco 1963: 237). In addition to fostering greater genetic diversity in crops produced on estates, the requirement that farmers bring seeds with them was consistent with the protocol that governed the comportment of visitors to Cuzco: no one could enter that city without a burden, one appropriate to the station in life of the bearer (Rowe 1967: 62), nor could anyone, no matter how highly placed, appear empty-handed before the ruling Inca (Betanzos parte I, cap. XLVI; 1987: 193). The demand that mitimas enter estates with burdens from their homeland was a reminder that these lands were royal domains, just as Cuzco was, and that they were entering the personal service of an Inca. The requirement further restated the relationship of Cuzco and its lords to the goods—as well as the people—of the provinces.

ROYAL ESTATES AS SPECIAL PROVINCES

On the basis of the ethnohistorical sources, we can look at the relationship of the royal estates to Cuzco as being analogous to that of province
to capital. Like other provinces, estates provided economic support. In
contrast to the goods of other provinces, which were used to support
state enterprises, the goods of the royal estates sustained members of
the royal families and the cults they promoted. There were fields devoted to the production of goods required for ritual, such as coca, ají,
and salt, along with the ubiquitous maize for beer. Because many royal
cults surrounded the worship of ancestors, it should not surprise us
that grants of lands were made to dead as well as living lords (Betanzos
parte I, cap. XLIII; 1987: 187) or that fields specifically dedicated to
the cult of royal mummies should be designated (e.g., the lands of
Piscobamba at Amaybamba; Rowe 1990: 151). The economic needs of
royal families differed from the requirements of the army or administrators sent out from Cuzco; hence the nature of the goods provided on
estates differed somewhat from the goods provided in other provinces.

The social and physical design of estates modeled the relationship of
the Incas to conquered peoples and served the symbolic function of
laying visible claim to control of resources and of subject populations.
Like provincial administrative centers, the estates had facilities to provide for lodging and entertaining important visitors, to store goods,
and to house the populations in service to the Inca. A point of contrast
is that administrative centers such as Huánuco Pampa and Hatuncolla
served bureaucratic and military ends as well as economic ones, while
the estates appear to have been important chiefly to individual members of royal families, although their use as sites for entertaining dig-
nitaries or diplomats may have been significant. Because of their relationship to Cuzco and its resident royals, we might consider the areas
developed into private estates to be a special kind of province, "royal
provinces."

THE ARCHITECTURE OF INCA ROYAL ESTATES

If we can construct an ethnohistorical argument about the relationship
of the estates to Cuzco, what can we find out on the basis of the architectural evidence? Several aspects of the estates make them especially
fruitful for the study of Inca site planning. Because they are relatively

well documented, we sometimes know how particular parts of the estates were used. Further, we have good historical evidence to account for the attribution of construction to particular reigns, so we can begin to understand the changing expression of Inca style over time.

There is tremendous variation in the constructions built on royal estates. The variation is seen in engineering and agricultural works, as well as in the standing architecture. Structures differ in form and proportion, in technical details of construction and style of masonry, and in the disposition of buildings in groups. The variation is seen both within individual estates and between estates.

I shall focus my comments on two ways that we can contend with this variation. First, I shall consider chronology as a way to attribute some of the architectural variation among sites to stylistic change over time. Then, I shall examine variation within a site to suggest that we must consider how the relative prestige of the activities that took place in the buildings influenced their construction. Undoubtedly there are other sources of variation that could be considered—the availability of materials, the skill of workers, and the native tradition of construction brought to the endeavor by conscripted laborers come to mind—but they are beyond the scope of this essay.

CHRONOLOGY

The imperial part of Inca architecture covers roughly a century, from around A.D. 1440 to 1532, and the edges of Inca style can certainly be pushed a generation earlier, to Viracocha's reign, and perhaps a bit later, into the early Colonial Period. There is abundant evidence from the area around Cuzco that the style changed—and in no small fashion, an observation explored by Kendall (1978) and reviewed most recently by Hyslop (1990: 25–27).[6]

We could, in fact, arrange sites commissioned by individual rulers in a roughly chronological order. For Viracocha, we could consider Huch'uy Qosqo (Hemming and Ranney 1982: 45; Gasparini and Margolies 1980: 98, fig. 89) and probably Pumamarca near Cuzco (fig. 6.2). For Pachacuti, we could look at Pisac (Gasparini and Margolies 1980: 80–81, figs. 65–66; Hemming and Ranney 1982: 88–93), parts of Ollantaytambo (Hemming and Ranney 1982: 101–117; Gasparini and Margolies 1980: 69–75, especially figs. 52–60), and Machu Picchu (Gasparini and Margolies 1980: 86–93, figs. 72–80; Hemming and

Figure 6.2. Detail of the coursed masonry and double-jambed doorway of Puma-marca, near San Sebastian, Cuzco. The palace may have belonged to Viracocha Inca.

Ranney 1982: 118–163). For Topa Inca, we could look at Chinchero (Gasparini and Margolies 1980: 215–218, figs. 203–207). For Huayna Capac, we could examine his palace at Urubamba (Sawyer 1981; Niles 1987: 216, fig. 6.11; Niles 1988), and for Huascar, Calca (Niles 1988) and Kañaraqay. An examination of photographs of the standing architectural remains gives some impression of the complexity of the problem we face: how can we make sense of this enormous range of variation among sites? We might consider the sites developed by some of the rulers for whom we have good biographical information. As an interesting contrast, we can examine works attributed to Pachacuti and those built by his grandson, Huayna Capac.

Pachacuti was the first Inca to rule over an empire. He came to power by outmaneuvering his father, Viracocha Inca, around the year A.D. 1438. Sites developed by Pachacuti have some of the best-fitted masonry and the greatest regularity of style of all Inca sites. Most illustrations of Inca architecture focus on the handful of sites that were built during his reign in and around Cuzco: he developed estates at Machu Picchu, Pisac, and Ollantaytambo and undertook the rebuilding of Cuzco. Although it is difficult to characterize Pachacuti's architectural style briefly, we might note that it focused on the contrast between built and natural form (MacLean 1986). Pachacuti's works, more than those of other Inca builders, show the potential for mastery over stone in the skill with which blocks are cut and fit in such structures as the Qorikancha (Hemming and Ranney 1982: 81, 83, 86–87), the Torreón at Machu Picchu (fig. 6.3 and Hemming and Ranney 1982: 134–141), and the Intihuatana section of Pisac (Hemming and Ranney 1982: 90). Pachacuti's work often incorporates natural outcrops, embellishing them and elaborating them with walls, niches, and carving to make them cultural artifacts. One of the most spectacular examples of this kind of sculpture is seen in the "royal mausoleum" structure at Machu Picchu. Another example is the "Temple of Three Windows" at the same site (fig. 6.4), which both incorporates bedrock in the masonry wall and uses the architecture to frame important features of the landscape.

Various arguments have been offered to account for Pachacuti's interest in the architectural style he favored. Perhaps the cutting and fitting of monolithic blocks appealed to him because it reminded him of other holy places, such as Tiahuanaco (as suggested by Kendall 1978: 78). Perhaps the special setting which he chose for his sites and

Figure 6.3. Detail of the Torreón, Machu Picchu, showing the carefully fitted masonry of the structure and the bedrock carved into its foundation.

Figure 6.4. Detail of the Temple of Three Windows, Machu Picchu.

the provisions he made within them for the observation of ritual reflected his place in Inca history and his own spiritual orientation (MacLean 1986; Rowe 1987: 20). Perhaps his handiworks were tangible statements of his own place in the cosmos as reformer and reshaper of the world. What we can say is that the act of construction was particularly important to him and that his architectural taste is recognizable. The legends that tell of Pachacuti's works stress his role as reshaper of the physical and social world and rebuilder of the Huatanay Valley. Most of the accounts of Pachacuti's life make reference to his construction activities. Betanzos gives the most detail on his handiwork in and around Cuzco (Betanzos parte I, caps. XII–XIII, XVI; 1987: 55–63, 75–79). Whether such accounts are literally true is not important; it is significant that Pachacuti and his descendants chose to incorporate these details in their accounts of his reign.

Such structures are in sharp contrast with the palace built for Huayna Capac at Urubamba. Huayna Capac ruled about A.D. 1493–1525, and the initial construction at his estate dates to the earlier part of his reign. The architectural centerpiece of the estate was a palace called Quispiguanca (fig. 6.5). Built of adobe brick on crudely-fitted stone foundations, the palace appears to have been a walled com-

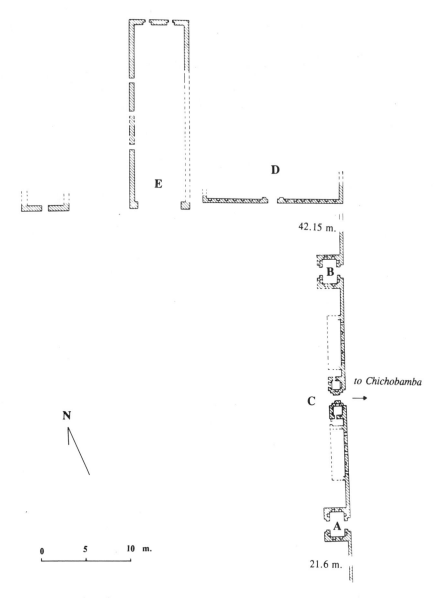

Figure 6.5. Plan of Huayna Capac's palace, Quispiguanca, near Urubamba. Visible remains include the gatehouse called Cuichipuncu (A); a matching gatehouse (B); a triple-jambed portal (C); remains known as Putucusi (D); and the remains of a great hall (E).

pound. Matching small gatehouses (3.55 by 5.90 meters) overlooked and guarded its eastern façade (the western façade is no longer standing), with formal entrance on that wall provided through a monumental portal. The double jambs of the gatehouse entryways (fig. 6.6) and the triple jamb of the portal use the elaboration of doorways that is part of the Inca architectural canon to suggest the importance of the compound. The buildings within its walls included a great hall (43.8 by 14.4 meters) with double-jambed entrances on its northern end and a wide entryway on its southern end. The presence of other buildings within the compound is suggested by wall stubs and niches, but it is not possible to complete a plan based on surface remains alone.

The gatehouses and portal are massive constructions with thick walls preserved to a height of the second (on one gatehouse) or third (on the portal tower) story. Undoubtedly, high thatched roofing would have made these structures appear even taller in antiquity. The whole compound is built on an artificially leveled terrace, overlooking similar surfaces which were devoted to agriculture. The compound was originally set in a park provided with a lake (Villanueva 1971a: 38), which, to judge from the surrounding water and land forms, must have been artificial. In contrast to sites built by Huayna Capac's grandfather, this palace is not oriented toward conspicuous aspects of the natural landscape; rather, the focus appears to be inward, toward the buildings contained within its surrounding walls.

Again, there is a very distinctive architectural style in Huayna Capac's estate, but one which is remarked upon in the ethnohistorical sources. Huayna Capac commissioned Quispiguanca, along with his Cuzco palace, the Casana, to be built by Apu Sinchi Roca, a half-brother. Sinchi Roca is described as a gifted and innovative architect (Sarmiento de Gamboa cap. 58; 1960: 260; Cabello Balboa tercera parte, cap. 21; 1951: 361–362; Cobo libro 11, cap. XVI; 1964: 89); Murúa cap. 30; 1962–64, v. 1: 76–77). There is no doubt that the structures he designed leave a very distinctive impression, based as they are on massiveness and height, rather than on view and form. Huayna Capac's estate included lakes and parks, a hunting lodge, and gardens that gave a uniquely cultural landscape to the area surrounding his buildings. These features certainly were partly the result of his place in the historical succession of the Incas: as a man who had inherited rule, he could indulge in pleasures (Rowe 1990: 144). But additionally, the overall design of his compound makes a much different statement

Figure 6.6. Cuichipuncu, the best-preserved gatehouse at Quispiguanca, viewed from the west.

about the place of humans in the natural landscape than does the work of his grandfather, Pachacuti.

The design and construction of palaces was important to ruling Incas and was one of their first concerns after they assumed the throne. In addition to the practical functions of housing the ruler and his retinue, palaces must have carried symbolic importance. This interpretation is suggested by the accounts that the construction of palaces was undertaken by both disputants to succession in the Inca civil war: Huascar built at Calca (Betanzos parte II, cap. III; 1987: 211; Niles 1988), and Atahuallpa built at Caranque (Betanzos parte II, cap. V; 1987: 215–216). Atahuallpa, in fact, ordered his architect to hurry with the construction in order to hasten his coronation ceremonies (Betanzos parte II, cap. V; 1987: 217). The fact that different kings commissioned structures of distinction suggests that stylistic innovation was not only tolerated but encouraged by ruling Incas. That we can recognize the handiwork characteristic of particular architects in the palaces built for their patrons suggests that we might look more closely at the structures they created in other parts of the empire, for example at administrative centers and important shrines.

In unraveling chronology and its effect on Inca architectural style, we have to do more than merely consider the kinds of ideas that may have been introduced from conquered provinces or from conscripted laborers. It is clear that we need to think about the taste of the person who commissioned the work and of the person who designed it. We must further take into account the ruler's vision of himself in relation to other people and to spiritual forces in the world. In short, it is a complex problem and one which is not yet solved.

PRESTIGE AND ARCHITECTURAL VARIATION

A consideration of chronology can help us to explain some of the stylistic variation among sites, but to understand the variation within sites we need to examine the activities that took place in particular building groups.

On estates, there is quite a range of building design and group layout. Most estates have a few structures or groups of some elegance. Component buildings may have relatively well-fitted masonry, multiple-jambed doorways, or a larger size or more complex layout than those

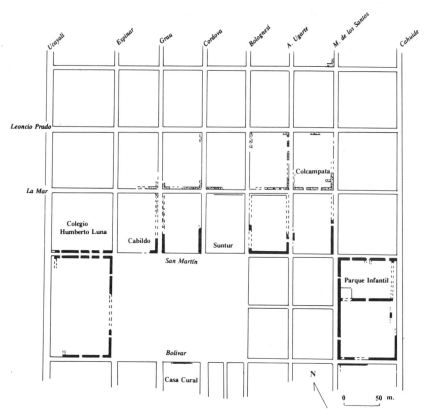

Figure 6.7. Plan showing the location of Inca walls in the modern town of Calca, site of Huascar's palace. The Inca plaza was within the area now defined by Bolívar, Espinar, San Martín, and Mariano de los Santos streets. The best-fitted masonry (indicated in black) is concentrated in the blocks that abutted the plaza. The less-well-fitted masonry (shown in stippling) begins in the block between San Martín and La Mar and continues one block above Leóncio Prado. Wall thickness is not drawn to scale.

of other groups. Huascar's estate at Calca is a good example of this kind of variation. In the grid-based plan of the estate, composed of blocks of courtyard houses, two of the blocks are larger and face each other across a huge open plaza (lower right and lower left in fig. 6.7). In construction detail, these two larger blocks are composed of better-fitting masonry than are others and also have double-jambed doorways that give access to the interior of the courtyard compound (fig. 6.8).

Figure 6.8. The fitted masonry of a double-jambed doorway giving access to a probable palace structure from the Inca plaza at Calca. (In 1986, this was the entrance to the Parque Infantil from Mariano de los Santos Street.)

These doorways have barhold devices on the interior. Other blocks at Calca are smaller, are composed of less carefully fitted masonry, and have single-jambed doorways.

A similar kind of stylistic contrast shows up at other estates. For example, at Pisac, the Intihuatana sector has several very fancy buildings constructed of coursed masonry and entered through a double-jambed doorway. Other groups at Pisac (for example Pisaca and Callacasa) are composed of buildings that lack these markers of high-style Inca architecture. At Callacasa, buildings have fieldstone masonry and adobe superstructures, and still-preserved clay plaster. Leaving aside the issue of whether the higher-quality buildings on estates all had the same function, I will note that most estates had some structures that were relatively nicer than others.

A reference to the design of Inca palaces offered by Guaman Poma suggests that the picture is even more complex than might be suggested by the architectural remains alone. He lists a large number of kinds of palaces, noting that different classes of nobles were permitted to have different kinds of palaces, in accord with their station (Guaman Poma f. 330; 1980, v. 1: 235). Such a statement suggests that we could anticipate a fair amount of architectural variation even within the relatively high-prestige building tradition. Some of the descriptive attributes of the palace types listed or depicted by Guaman Poma refer to form and layout (e.g., following his orthography, *suntor uasi*, "round house"; *carpa uasi*, "three-sided house"; and *quenco uasi*, depicted as a U-shaped house; see fig. 6.9). Such comments on building types as markers of rank are very much in accord with the evidence from royal estates: for example, at Calca, it seems reasonable to suggest that the more elegant structures were used by Huascar or his closest associates for high-prestige activities, while the less elegant buildings could have been used by more distant associates.

One of the dirty secrets of Cuzco archaeology is that there is a lot of crummy-looking Inca architecture. In a great deal of Inca construction, including carefully planned and built sites, the walls are of fieldstone masonry, and the structures are simple, with minimal ornamental detail.[7] An archaeologist counting the buildings on Inca estates would find many more of these simple fieldstone structures than buildings with fitted masonry. For example, at Callachaca, an estate of Amaro Topa Inca near Cuzco, there are remains of around seventy small fieldstone structures and no more than twelve extant buildings that might

Figure 6.9. Guaman Poma's illustration of selected types of Inca palaces.

be classified as having any of the attributes of high-prestige style (Niles 1987). At some sites which we have good reason to believe were parts of Inca estates, there are no buildings arrayed in kancha layouts or built of fitted stone. Such sites as Qotakalli, Wimpilla, Raqay-Raqayniyoq, and Cheqollo are typical of the support communities on Inca estates (see Niles 1987: 31–40 for illustrations of these and other sites). At these sites, the style of masonry and form of the buildings is simple, but the overall layout may be in a large, rigidly planned group. This style of architecture predominates in the houses of the support populations on royal estates and in storage facilities nearby, and it probably reflects the relative prestige of the occupants and activities to which these structures were devoted.

The distinction among various classes of buildings on estates also shows up in Spanish terms that inventory royal holdings. Topa Inca's and Huayna Capac's estates near Yucay, which were the subjects of visitas in 1551 and 1552 (Villanueva 1971a), included a number of construction groups, among them buildings belonging to Topa Inca and to his wife; Huayna Capac's palace and a hunting lodge; a house belonging to his consort, Rahua Ocllo; structures built later by Manco Inca; and the homes of the support populations of yanacuna workers. Part of this land also figured in a claim of 1558 (Rostworowski de Diez Canseco 1962: 143–151, Manuscrito 3). In these documents, the houses of yanacunas are usually referred to as *buhíos*, a term introduced by the Spanish and used in Peru to refer to small, one-room buildings, often of adobe.[8] Some buildings belonging to royalty or the Sun are likewise characterized as buhíos (for Guacha, Yucay, Curikancha, and Urcos-Pampa, see Villanueva 1971a: 35, 37, 53). Elsewhere in the visitas a distinction is made between building types, with Topa Inca's holdings at Guayllabamba including "una casa y bohío" (Villanueva 1971a: 36). Other structures belonging to rulers are characterized as *casas* (for Guayocollo, Chicón and Manco Inca's building near Patashuaylla, see Villanueva 1971a: 36, 38, 39–40), and Huayna Capac's palace compound at Quispiguanca is referred to as "unos tambos" (Villanueva 1971a: 38). The consistent linguistic distinction among the terms *buhío*, *casa*, and *tambo* might well be the Spanish interpretation of architectural distinctions that—at least in part—reflect the prestige of the activities carried out in the structures. Although we do not have any standing remains of houses of the support populations on Huayna

Capac's estate, the use of "buhío" to characterize such residences suggests that small and possibly impermanent huts were their lot.

Although humble structures from Inca provincial sites are rarely illustrated, they must exist. For example, in Huánuco Pampa, a provincial administrative center, there is variation in both masonry style and building layout among different groups at the site. Courtyard house arrangements are found only in restricted parts of Huánuco Pampa (Morris and Thompson 1985: 63–72). Storehouses at the site, although very different in form from the ones seen around Cuzco, are also simple structures of fieldstone masonry (Morris and Thompson 1985: 97–108).

Accounts of the social and physical organization of royal estates suggest that their designers followed very closely the dicta that new lands should include portions for the Inca and for the Sun; that each town should have provision for mamacunas of the Inca and mamacunas of the Sun; and that communities should be divided into hanan and hurin social divisions. For example, both Topa Inca's and Huayna Capac's estates in the Yucay Valley included generous provisions to the Sun on plots adjacent to lands of the Inca. (That the requisite portion due the state is missing from the estates is further evidence that these were royal, rather than administrative, concerns.) Both also mention the lands that were still to be under the control of the native populations (Pacas, Chaocas, Chichos, and Cachis). Huayna Capac's estate, at least, included grants made to the mamacunas of the Inca as well as lands managed by the mamacunas of the Sun. Finally, the inclusion of moiety divisions in the physical plan of support communities is suggested for Qotakalli and Raqay-Raqayniyoq, near Cuzco (Niles 1987).

DISCUSSION

Inca estates were not regular provinces in the Inca scheme of things. This point is made emphatically by yanacuna witnesses from Huayna Capac's estate who claimed that they lived in perpetual service to an Inca and were not therefore *suyuruna*, subject to Inca tribute (1574 *pleito* [lawsuit] of Doña Beatriz, testimony of Martín Cutipa; Villanueva 1971a: 131). But an examination of their organization and the principles of their design does permit us to reconsider how we might view the relationship of Inca heartland to province. More to the point, examination of the royal estates permits us to raise certain questions to keep in mind as we investigate the workings of the Inca state.

We might first consider architectural style. In light of the great variety of structures built by the Incas, what can we say about Inca architectural style and the relationship of the provinces to the Inca heartland? First, it is important to note that the whole range of stylistic variation has to be considered as part of Inca architectural style. It is important to look at fieldstone or adobe structures that might have been the homes of support populations, the loci of low-prestige activities. Even on estates, where we have relative good chronological control and reasonable attribution of function, many questions remain about organization. Particularly in using analogies to the design and architecture of provincial Inca sites, we must be careful to take account of the whole of their design and to consider their social context.

Other questions concern the relationship of provincial ethnic traditions to Inca ones. For example, might it be possible to look at the continuity of native traditions among the transplanted populations on royal estates or in mitima populations elsewhere? We know that Chachapoyas mitimas were brought with their native lord to Topa Inca's lands in Amaybamba, and that his heirs inherited both local rule and the lands given him by Topa Inca (Rostworowski de Diez Canseco 1963). Does this population retain any other traditions from their homeland? Would the sizeable populations of Collasuyo and Chinchaysuyo mitimas on Huayna Capac's estate keep alive the culture of their ancestors? Such inquiries might allow us to look at the relationship of provincial to imperial traditions, but in order to ask the questions we must have good control over both Late Intermediate Period and Late Horizon ceramic, textile, and architectural data.

Further, Inca sites must be considered in their historical context. Royal estates reflect the place of their owners in history, the tastes, ambitions, and changing imperial needs of those owners. Accounts of the construction of important buildings or the development of whole zones in provincial areas likewise mention their historical context: the builder, the circumstances of building, the circumstances of use—all are aspects relevant to understanding Inca provincial sites. For example, the Inca constructions on the Island of Titicaca were built by Topa Inca after a definitive conquest in Collasuyo, perhaps to placate local priests and to redirect the loyalties of the faithful to Inca devotions

(Cobo libro 13, cap. XVIII; 1964: 190–191). At this time, sizeable populations of colonists were brought to the island and the adjacent mainland to sustain the temple (Ramos Gavilán cap. XIII; 1976: 43–44). Topa Inca also set up mitimas in Quito at the conclusion of "a short, decisive war" (Cieza de León segunda parte, cap. LX; 1985; von Hagen 1959: 241), though we know that Huayna Capac spent much of his ruling life involved in consolidating and furthering the conquest of that region. Similarly, for the Cochabamba Valley of Bolivia, we are told that Topa Inca conquered the region and first established mitimas, but that it was his son, Huayna Capac, who actually developed the region (*Repartimiento de tierras por el Inca Huayna Capac* 1977: 25; Wachtel 1981: 298–299). We know that mitima policies were in effect at least as early as Topa Inca's early conquests, probably carried out during his father's reign, and as late as Huascar's. More than fifty years separate these regimes. Thus the historical context of the development—and even redevelopment—of sites or provincial areas must be taken into account. While I have focused here on the development of Inca style, one must consider the changes in local and provincial-Inca Late Horizon traditions as well. Theoretically, a mitima settled early in his reign by Topa Inca would bear different cultural traditions, or perhaps a different attitude toward the Inca state, than would one settled late in Huayna Capac's reign. That stylistic reflections of such larger cultural concerns can be seen in the material culture has been shown in Menzel's analysis of ceramics from the Ica Valley (Menzel 1976).

Returning to the architecture, it is also important to bear in mind appropriate comparisons in any discussion of remains from provincial Inca sites. When we think about "typical" Inca buildings, we must remember that we should not be thinking only of Cuzco itself or only of the structures commissioned by Pachacuti. (The latter are the ones most commonly shown to tourists and illustrated by experts.) We are only beginning to understand the changes in Inca architectural style over time. But we do have a body of data that we can use to consider aspects of prestige and building function as sources of variation in Inca architecture.

The construction of so many kinds of buildings in the estates near Cuzco, at places designed to meet the needs of particular rulers, must have been intentional. We are forced in the face of such variety to rethink the relationship of Cuzco to its surrounding area. The Incas were fully capable of commissioning Cuzco-style buildings wherever they wanted, but clearly they did not always want to do so. Cuzco was a special place, one not to be copied without good reason. Even the royal structures in the environs of the Inca capital did not copy it wholesale.

For the Incas, rank and prestige governed almost all interactions between members of different royal families, and between royalty and commoners. The prestige hierarchy of the Inca capital was based on categories of *collana*, *payan*, and *cayao*, from highest to lowest. In Cuzco the use of the terms was to rank royal families with respect to their genealogical distance from the reigning Inca (Rowe 1985a: 43–44). It might be possible to look at some of the architectural varia-tion encountered at Inca sites as premised on relative prestige. The relationship of Cuzco to its provinces is one which expresses physical distance as well as removal from the special activities of the capital. This relationship is analogous to the prestige terms: Cuzco is collana; royal activity away from the capital is payan. On the estates, the rela-tionship of the support population to the estate owner is also one premised on distance, in this case the distance between royal and com-moner and that between Inca and conquered tribe. If Cuzco and its royal activities are collana and the non-Cuzco royal activities are payan, then the nonroyal, non-Cuzco activities are cayao. Viewed in these terms, the range of architectural variation on estates makes sense as the visual manifestation of relative prestige differences.

If we consider the relationship of estates to capital in this way, we can change the way we look at provincial Inca architecture. Similar notions of distance and prestige must have prevailed for the state or-ganization as well as for the royal order (fig. 6.10). In an administrative sense, provincial administrative centers, the loci of Inca state activities away from the Inca capital, are less prestigious than is the capital itself; hence, they can be seen as payan, second in rank, to Cuzco's collana, first in rank. The activities of people other than ethnic Inca admin-istrators, such as local-level tributaries, might then be seen as cayao, lowest in rank, compared to the payan activities of the ethnic-Inca administrators.

We should expect that the design of estates will be different from that of administrative developments (see, e.g., Hyslop 1990: 298–300), yet there should be some similarities in the range of architecture to be found in these kinds of sites. In estates, there is a kind of archi-tectural variation that can be interpreted as indicating prestige differ-

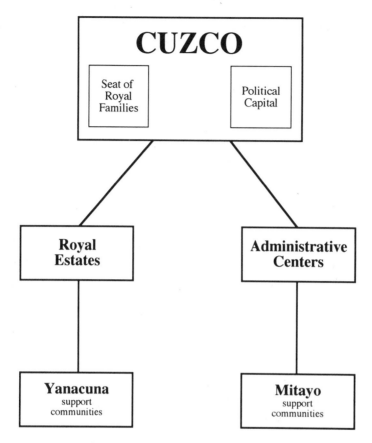

Figure 6.10. *Inca administrative and royal hierarchies.*

ences. In administrative centers and in provincial Inca sites, one might also look for such stylistic codes. Rather than measuring construction at provincial administrative centers relative to the high-prestige style of the capital, we might see them as intentional emulations of a particular style of planning, one which is payan (fig. 6.11). An appropriate comparison may be to royal estates, other payan sites, rather than to Cuzco itself.

I offer the suggestion that we should think a bit more broadly when we consider Inca architecture, to take into account the whole range of variation in planning form, building design, and ornamental detail. For instance, when we think of Inca masonry, we must expand the range of styles beyond carefully fitted stone blocks to include roughly con-

Prestige Categories	Royal Sites	State Sites
Collana	Cuzco	
Payan	Palaces	Administrative Buildings
Cayao	Yanacuna Communities	Resident Support Population

Figure 6.11. Inca prestige categories relative to the hierarchy of administrative and royal constructions.

structed fieldstone walls. Put in prestige terms, we must take into account cayao architecture and cayao activities that took place on sites.

Finally, we need to keep clearly in mind the function of the sites that we are studying. While some comparisons between royal sites and administrative sites can doubtless be made, the two are very separate entities. We need better descriptions of provincial Inca architecture, both from administrative sites and from royal holdings in areas far removed from Cuzco. Careful description and illustration of architectural detail might allow us to sort out the dating on some of these places a little bit better and to comment more fully on the social and economic organization of such sites. We might then really begin to understand what the Incas were doing in the provinces.

NOTES

1. The redesign of the Huatanay Valley is discussed by Zuidema (1990: 14–22). Some of the lands granted to royal women are mentioned in a

mid-sixteenth-century visita of the lands of Yucay transcribed by Villanueva (1971a). Discussion of these and other properties belonging to
royal women are offered by Rostworowski de Diez Canseco (1962), Silverblatt (1987), and Niles (ms.).

2. The passage that mentions the deeding of lands to the dead is given in the
   description of Huayna Capac's land reclamation projects in the Valley of
   Yucay: "y dio estancias a los señores del Cuzco ansi a los vivos como a los
   muertos que estaban en bultos para que allí pusiesen sus yanaconas mo-
   zos de su servicio para que les labrasen sus verduras y hortalizas y cosas
   de sus recreaciones" (Betanzos parte I, cap. LXIII; 1987: 187). This passage makes it clear that lands were given to living lords other than the
   ruling Inca.

3. See especially point five of Doña María's complaint: "Yten si saben que la
   dicha doña María Coya vive pobre y trabajosamente y apenas se puede
   sustentar para alimentos con los mil pesos que le dan sobre los indios de
   su hija porque tiene muchos indios que como a señora que es se la daban
   los cuales sustenta y tiene de ordinario un hombre casado con su mujer
   en su casa un mayordomo suyo asalariados a su costa, digan lo que saben"
   (Villanueva 1971b: 151). Witnesses who testified in her behalf offered
   their observations that she supported members of her "linaje" who visited
   (testimony of Diego de Segura [Villanueva 1971b: 157] and of Domingo
   de Artaza [Villanueva 1971b: 170]), or that her station required her to
   entertain many people: "estas señoras indias hijas de señores quieren mos-
   trar su calidad y hacer fiestas a los indios naturales que las van a visitar"
   (testimony de Juan de Pancorbo [Villanueva 1971b: 164]).

4. According to Betanzos, the coca and ají used for this ritual were acquired
   secretly from Chinchaysuyu province; he includes a somewhat puzzling
   account of how Huayna Capac obtained these products from the provinces in order to give his mother a good afterlife (Betanzos parte I, cap.
   XLIV; 1987: 189). It is not clear from the passage if he is describing trade
   or conquest.

5. The promotion of dead ancestors to a higher position was probably also a
   part of the Incas' early strategies of expansion in the Cuzco area, used
   along with co-optation and intermarriage. The list of the shrines of Cuzco
   includes several tombs that were said to be important to various groups
   that were Incas by privilege, rather than Incas by birth. Presumably in
   such a case more benefit would accrue to the living descendants of the
   dead person, rather than to the mummy, as would be the case of land
   granted to dead members of the royal families.

6. Some of the chronological changes are considered by Kendall (1978:
   78–86), who notes that changes in imperial Inca style may have come
   about as a result of contact with newly encountered provincial styles, a
   theme also addressed by Sawyer (1981) in his discussion of building at

Ollantaytambo. My conclusions will necessarily differ from those of Kendall because I am considering only one class of site—the estate—and have used land claim documents to supplement the chronicles as a way to establish the ownership of the estates.

7. I have also argued elsewhere that masonry style is related to prestige differences in the activities carried out in buildings (Niles 1987).

8. Hamilton notes the Taino origin of *buhío* but claims that it refers to a thatch-roofed house (Cobo 1979: 263).

7

CATHERINE J. JULIEN

FINDING A FIT: ARCHAEOLOGY AND

ETHNOHISTORY OF THE INCAS

EDITOR'S INTRODUCTION

Julien's essay reflects a level of synthesis between archaeological field data and ethnohistorical documentation that has rarely, if ever, been achieved in Andean studies. She uses an explicitly geographical approach to unite the two sources of information for each of the provinces discussed by the other authors in this volume. She goes beyond the simple evaluation of the sources, however, to indicate linkages *between* provinces that are useful for comparisons. Her ethnohistorical focus on an entire province, rather than a single site or valley, allows us a better view of the similarities and differences in the general features of Inca organization.

Julien's treatments of the provinces are roughly parallel. She first provides a method for reconstructing Inca territory from early Spanish administrative documentation, then looks at the evidence for the relationship between the Incas and the people they controlled. This approach demonstrates how the historical record is more than just facts in need of archaeological verification; it is also a corpus of data from which an image of the Inca whole is generated in a manner analogous to that by which archaeologists reconstruct cultures. Thus she clarifies why our views of the Incas drawn from each source are different. Her approach also identifies ways in which the ethnohistorical record can be used to generate research questions for archaeologists, not only in the regions already discussed but elsewhere as well. This essay should be of considerable value as a guide to future research on the Incas.

INTRODUCTION

Documentary sources have long served to guide archaeological investigation. To cite just one example, the search for Vilcabamba in the nineteenth century was fueled by documentary references to the last Inca capital (Hemming 1970: 474–500). Inca dynastic tradition, reflected in sixteenth- and seventeenth-century historical narratives written in Spanish, was the source of abundant references to places where the Incas had been active.

Using Inca dynastic tradition as a means of locating the physical remains of Inca activity had begun long before the nineteenth century, however. Pedro Cieza de León, who traveled through the Andean region in 1549, wrote a historical narrative based on Inca dynastic sources in addition to a travel account (Cieza de León 1984, 1985). Naturally he related what his dynastic sources told him to the sites he visited. He also collected information from native people as he traveled, though perhaps even in the provinces he chose Inca informants. His account of the Inca empire was the first attempt to test Cuzco dynastic tradition against the actual physical remains. When Cieza de León visited Cajamarca or Huamachuco, he did not doubt that they were the places mentioned by informants in Cuzco. Today his descriptions are critical in the identification of such sites as Inca centers. A carefully reasoned argument must be crafted to make the case that modern Huamachuco sits on the location of the Inca center Cieza de León visited (see the Topics' essay, chapter 2 above).

Not only the inhabitants of the Andean realm at the time of the Spanish arrival, but Spaniards like Cieza de León are foreign to us. Though we still assess documents for accuracy and truth, we now realize that there are far more serious distortions inherent in the written record. All narratives written about the Incas passed through the filter of Spanish experience. Even native accounts are not immune, as all of the native writers had had decades of contact with Europeans before writing and had learned appropriate forms of communication.

Administrative documentation, free of some of the covert messages inherent in narratives about the past, has its own defects. It addresses only a limited range of subjects. To a great extent, the information that was gathered deals with the period in which it was written and very seldom describes the past or ongoing processes of change. Moreover, administrative reports may just as easily strive to conceal as to reveal. As Franklin Pease noted some years ago, "historical information is often found in the margins of the paper, or perhaps between the lines, or above or below the level of discourse" (Pease 1976–77: 207).

The craft of the ethnohistorian is to collect the information that has survived and piece together a view of the past that is largely a hypothesis. The task is very similar to what the archaeologist does, and the differences are basically methodological (Deetz 1988: 13, 17–18). Since the ethnohistorian and the archaeologist have a common aim, the two approaches can and should be used together.

However, differences in the corpus of data familiar to each type of study make it difficult to find a fit between the two. Archaeology is bound to the material remains of human activity and necessarily focuses on sites and objects related to them. At times when ethnohistorical documents identify what went on at a site or describe physical remains in some detail, the two studies dovetail (Mellafe 1965; Thompson and Murra 1966). Road studies fall into this category as well, expanding the information found in documentary sources because of the nature of road networks (Hyslop 1984).

Another means of fitting the two classes of data together, beyond using documents to locate and identify sites, is to use the documentary record to reconstruct territory. Administrative records and travel accounts lend themselves to the reconstruction of cultural geography. At one point, I attempted to do this kind of study for the colonial district of Arequipa (Julien 1985). Anthropologists have called attention to a dispersed pattern of settlement related to resource control, and the Arequipa area had been used to define this pattern (Murra 1972). The Lupacas from the adjacent Lake Titicaca region had colonies subject to them in Arequipa, specifically in Moquegua, Sama, and Azapa. Whether the placement of these colonies was sponsored by Inca central authority or antedated the time of Inca control was a question that arose from the documentation, but which required archaeological verification.

To many ethnohistorians it is enough to note "Moquegua" as the locus of human activity. To an archaeologist, whose research is both more costly and more time-consuming than archival work, some idea of where to look for the people is necessary. Toward that end, I tried to relate population to resources, generating an overall picture of settlement (Julien 1985). This type of ethnohistorical study can be used to design and orient specific archaeological projects or, later on, to provide a regional framework for the interpretation of site- or valley-specific research (Stanish 1992).

An obvious territorial focus in the case of the Inca empire is the division into provinces. In most cases, whole provinces are larger than the territorial units of study most often chosen by archaeologists. Ordinarily, the archaeological focus ranges from a site to an entire valley. An ethnohistorical focus on provinces allows us to frame questions across much larger units of space. It is also a better base from which to generate comparison. Some features of Inca organization are common to all provinces, and we will be better able to see these features if we have a notion of where provinces begin and end. Not only similarities but differences should emerge as we compare territories defined by the Incas.

To prepare the review which follows, I examined written sources for information about territorial division in the six areas that were the focus of archaeological study. I have concentrated on several topics in my discussion, where source materials permit: territorial limits within the sphere of the nearest major Inca center, political organization of the area at the time of annexation by the Incas, and aspects of local economy that might shed light on boundaries. At times, I pose purely archaeological questions and marshal the physical remains into my review. The resulting discussion is somewhat awkward—largely, I hope, because archaeological and ethnohistorical methods and issues are juxtaposed. Moreover, my intent is to create a discussion. The discussion is contrived to address the myriad issues that arise from the archaeological research reported in this volume, not as an independently conceived piece of research.

The reconstruction of territorial division is based on methods I developed in my own work in the Lake Titicaca region, reviewed in the following section. It is the work of one ethnohistorian and is based on premises that are not shared by all. For one thing, it is based on the premise that the Incas had some notion of bounded space (but for other ideas about territoriality in the Andes, see Shimada 1985: xix–xx). I will return to this point in the conclusions.

I have also made use of Spanish narratives that were based on Inca dynastic tradition (but some would deny any historical value to these; see Zuidema 1964). When I use authors who drew on this body of tradition, I so note. I will assume that Cuzco sources give us one point of view on the political organization of the areas annexed by the Incas. Whether or not the rather short kinglist was a complete fabrication, the evidence of Inca expansion is conclusive, and we should listen to what Inca voices have to say about it, even muted as they are by translation into both a foreign language and a foreign historiographical tradition. Some of the people questioned by the Spanish were alive during the reign of the tenth and eleventh kings (Topa Inca and Huayna Capac). The information they gave had, therefore, not yet passed into oral tradition. Some were eyewitnesses; we should not ignore them.

Cuzco sources certainly contain bias and distortion. Still, they give us the only overview of the process of Inca expansion that we have. This view can be weighed against the information collected by the Spaniards from non-Inca informants, and perhaps archaeological means to validate or invalidate it can be found. For the latter reason especially, I am using these sources.

RECONSTRUCTING INCA PROVINCIAL STRUCTURE:
A LAKE TITICACA BASIN EXAMPLE

A special circumstance allows us to reconstruct Inca boundaries in the Lake Titicaca region and to identify several types of provinces. Spanish administrators first drew boundaries around native territories in the late 1560s and early 1570s, four decades after the European invasion. However, we can document boundaries between native territories in the 1540s, long before the Spanish system of rural provinces, called *corregimientos*, was implemented. The boundaries of the corregimientos are similar to the native boundaries we can detect from the early written sources (Julien 1983: 9–33). But there are differences that are important. We need to develop ethnohistorical methods that will generate a better image of Inca provincial territories than the image reflected in the corregimiento system.

For the Lake Titicaca region, I have developed such methods. Because the people of that region were subject to the labor draft for the Potosí mines, a second system of rural provinces was created, contemporary with and very similar to the corregimiento system (Julien 1983: 9–33, map 1). The territories were called *capitanías*, and each was headed by a local lord who was responsible for recruiting mine labor. The capitanías follow a local division of the Lake Titicaca region into Urcosuyo and Umasuyo and are more consistent with the boundaries noted in the 1540s than are the corregimientos. I have argued that they more closely approximate the territories of Inca provinces (fig. 7.1) (Julien 1983: 9–33). The capitanías were named, and their names suggest that some were composed of several native groups while others divided large groups into as many as four separate territories. This kind of "lumping and splitting" also suggests the intervention of a central authority.

Let us now look closely at what I am suggesting is the Inca provincial division of the Lake Titicaca region. First of all, it respects a division of the entire Collasuyo quarter into Urcosuyo and Umasuyo. Although the
· Collasuyo road, reconstructed from a 1543 list of tambos (Vaca de Castro 1908; Julien 1983: map 3), lies at the boundary between Urcosuyo and Umasuyo in the north, the road divides at Ayaviri into two branches, labeled Urcosuyo and Umasuyo, which rejoin near Caracollo. The boundary between Urcosuyo and Umasuyo appears to transect Lake Titicaca, though as I will mention below, the classification of several places at the boundary itself is ambiguous.

When named groups are split into territories, the split often follows the boundary between Urcosuyo and Umasuyo. For example, two named groups, Canas and Canches, were lumped together, then divided following the Urcosuyo/Umasuyo division. The Pacajes were divided into two territories along the same line. The Lupacas lay wholly within Urcosuyo (Julien 1983: 9–33, map 2).

The Lupaca territory was a formally organized province—that is, it was based on a native population that had entered into a tribute relation with Cuzco and had been structured by the Incas to generate the goods and services commonly found in Inca provinces (Julien 1988a). We know something about the structure of this province during the time of Inca control because of information preserved in an administrative survey of 1567 (Diez de San Miguel 1964; Julien 1982). Two *huno* (units of 10,000 subject households) were composed. A single site, Chucuito, functioned as the Inca center, and the Lupaca lords who supplied labor to meet Cuzco's demands resided there. Some of the households were permanently assigned to produce goods or provide

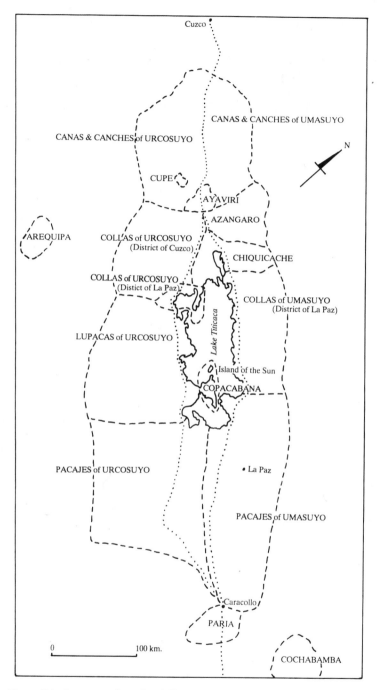

Cuzco

CANAS & CANCHES of UMASUYO

CANAS & CANCHES of URCOSUYO

N

CUPE

AYAVIRI

AZANGARO

AREQUIPA

COLLAS of URCOSUYO
(District of Cuzco)

CHIQUICACHE

COLLAS of URCOSUYO
(Distict of La Paz)

COLLAS of UMASUYO
(District of La Paz)

Lake Titicaca

LUPACAS of URCOSUYO

Island of the Sun

COPACABANA

PACAJES of URCOSUYO

• La Paz

PACAJES of UMASUYO

Caracollo

PARIA

0   100 km.

COCHABAMBA

Figure 7.1. Provinces along the Collasuyo Road from Canas/Canches to Paria.

services and were resettled in special communities near Chucuito (Julien 1982: 138–140; 1988a: 269).

Colla territory was also divided by the Urcosuyo-Umasuyo division, but at least a portion of it appears to have been reconstituted by the Incas along different lines than either the Lupaca or the Pacajes province. Within it were two smaller territories that were dedicated to the service of a particular Inca or the Sun.

A group of 4,500 households in Asillo, Azángaro, Quipa, and some of Carabaya was reported to have served Topa Inca, the tenth king of the official list. This estate appeared on a list of Topa Inca's holdings which included his palaces in Cuzco, his estate at Chinchero, and two other territories located at a distance from Cuzco (Rostworowski de Diez Canseco 1969–1970: 83; ADC 1558: ff. 886–886v; Julien 1991: 121). The estate may have passed to a son of this Inca who played a game known as *ayllar* with his father and won (Cobo libro 12, cap. XV, tomo III; 1890–95: 174–176; Albornoz 1989: 174–175). As described by Cobo, the state included Asillo, Azángaro, Pucará, Nuñoa, and Oruro (fig. 7.2) (Cobo libro 12, cap. XV, tomo III; 1890–95: 176). For ease of reference, I will refer to it as the Azángaro territory.

Arapa was dedicated to the service of the Sun (Polo de Ondegardo 1940: 182; 1872: 19). Arapa was part of a territory called Chiquicache, and perhaps all of Chiquicache was dedicated to the Sun (fig. 7.2).[1] Some of the people of Chiquicache were sent to the eastern lowlands as mitimas for the purpose of raising foodstuffs for their highland province of origin (Loredo 1942: 130).

The Urcosuyo-Umasuyo division split Colla territory into two parts. The colonial boundary between the districts of Cuzco and La Paz split each of these parts in two again (Julien 1983: map 2). This colonial boundary appears to have been based on a boundary that existed when the area was under Inca rule, since the recruitment of Collas to settle the Cochabamba area, a program effected by Huayna Capac, the eleventh king of the official list, respected it (Morales 1977; Wachtel 1982). The territories of Azángaro and Chiquicache fell entirely within the portion of the Colla province of Umasuyo that was part of the district of Cuzco. There may have been other territories within the three remaining Colla provinces which served particular Incas or supernaturals. For instance, there are indications that at least part of the Colla province of Urcosuyo that fell within the district of Cuzco was organized along the same lines as the Azángaro territory.[2]

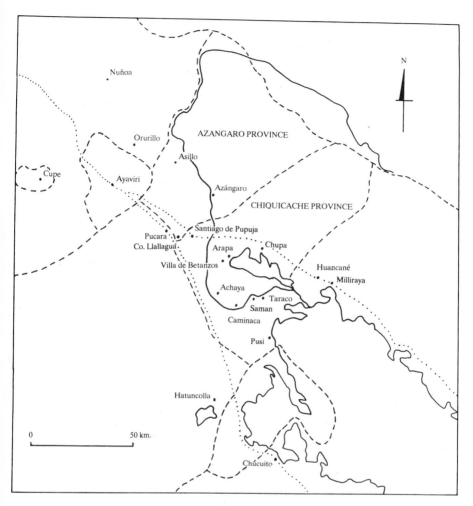

Figure 7.2. Chiquicache and Azángaro.

Within the Colla provinces, then, we can detect the development of estates dedicated to particular individuals or supernaturals, similar to those that have been studied in the Cuzco area. Because they served particular individuals or supernaturals, they may have been *yanaconas* (Rowe 1982: 97–102), as were the people who served on the estate of Huayna Capac at Yucay (Villanueva 1971a).

Huayna Capac's Yucay estate included two huarangas (2,000 households) who were mitimas as well, resettled from the Lake Titicaca region (Rowe 1982: 105–107; Villanueva 1971a: 139). While we can identify groups of *orejones*, who were initiated members of the Inca lineage, in the Azángaro territory (Glave 1989: 11–12) and mitimas from Canas territory in Chiquicache (Loredo 1942: 125, 130; AGI 1549–50: f. 32v; Hampe Martínez 1979: 91; Miranda 1925: 157), there is no evidence to suggest that these estates were not based on a largely local population.

Estates included substantial numbers of households, and so were granted as *encomiendas* (grants of the tribute owed by a particular native group) to particular Spaniards by Pizarro. Some or all of Chiquicache was granted to Diego de Almagro, Pizarro's partner, for example (Loredo 1942: 130). The people who had served on Inca estates were treated like any other group awarded in encomienda, whether they were located near or far from Cuzco. The Inca organization of these estates may have been similar in general outline to the type of organization usually imposed on subject peoples. This question will be taken up again below.

Copacabana was another kind of Inca territory: a sanctuary. The islands off the Copacabana Peninsula were important local shrines. The Incas took over the island cults and removed the inhabitants of the peninsula, resettling them at Yunguyo on the neck of the peninsula. Then they brought in mitimas from all over the territory unified by Cuzco, from Quito in the north to Copiapó in the south (Ramos Gavilán cap. IV; 1988: 39; cap. XII; 1988; Cobo libro 13, cap. XVIII, tomo IV; 1890–95: 56–64).

The source which allows us to classify the adjacent provinces into Urcosuyo and Umasuyo tells us that Copacabana was tacked on to the Lupaca capitanía so that its population could be included in the Potosí draft (Capoche 1959: 138). The Lupaca province was classified as Urcosuyo, but this classification may not have extended to Copacabana. Places at the boundary between Urcosuyo and Umasuyo appear to have had somewhat ambiguous status. The classification was ambiguous near Tiahuanaco.[3] Pucara is also located right at the boundary. The Incas authorized construction at all three places and may well have held them sacred. We do not know about the territorial limits of Pucara or Tiahuanaco, but the sanctuary of Copacabana did have a support territory. It was not an ordinary province.

Another type of province can be identified at the edges of what I have been calling the Lake Titicaca region, the territory Cieza de León called Colla (primera parte, cap. XCIX; 1984: 271; primera parte, cap. CVI; 1984: 286; Julien 1983: 42). Both Ayaviri and Paria were the centers of some kind of territory, but they were populated by mitimas and were not based on a subject local population. Information that was probably collected locally indicates that each was created following an Inca military campaign. Local people were vanquished, and the territories were reoccupied by mitima households (Cieza de León primera parte, cap. XCVIII; 1984: 270–271; primera parte, cap. CVI; 1984: 286; segunda parte, cap. LII; 1985: 150–151; segunda parte, cap. LXI; 1985: 177). Information about Paria indicates that it was an important staging area for the Inca army. Those recruited in Charcas were assembled first in Sacaca, then the forces were joined at Paria (Espinoza Soriano 1969: 25). Ayaviri was also on the Collasuyo road, the southern segment of the Inca road in the highlands, and may have served as a military depot, like Paria.[4]

Adjacent to the Lake Titicaca region, in the Cochabamba Valley, was another type of Inca province. Local residents were largely removed by the Incas, and people from the adjacent highlands and the northern Lake Titicaca region were resettled in the area in the time of Huayna Capac, as mentioned above. The agricultural production of this valley was organized to support an Ecuadorian military campaign (Morales 1977; Wachtel 1982).

Another, largely mitima population was established at Arequipa. Some of the population originated in the Canas/Canches province in the highlands near Cuzco; some were from Chilques, Chumbivilcas, and Yanahuaras territory in Condesuyo; and some were from Collaguas territory (Julien 1985: 194, table 9.4; Murúa libro 4, cap. XI; 1946: 397–398; Galdos Rodríguez 1986: 95–120). Some of the people—for example, the Collaguas—may have been settled there to harvest maize for their high-altitude place of origin, while others were settled in the immediate vicinity of what is now the city of Arequipa to serve the mountain of Putina (Albornoz 1989: 170).

What should be clear by now is that we have more than one type of province. Some were based on a local population, and some were not. Some had Inca centers, but others may not have. The archaeological characteristics of each may be quite different from those of the others. For example, Paria may have resembled Sacaca or Chucuito to a degree. All may have had a temple and the staff it required. But a center like Paria would have had special stores for provisioning armies, staff and facilities for serving a transient population for longer time periods, and perhaps, a larger plaza for assembly (Cieza de León primera parte, cap. LXIV; 1984: 186; segunda parte, cap. XVI; 1985: 44). A center like Paria could be expected to have a material tradition, in ceramics, architecture, and other media, that differed from the material tradition found at other types of Inca centers. A shrine like Copacabana may have had a material tradition that expressed its special nature as well.

Even provinces that were substantially alike may have had dissimilar structures. A study of the decimal structuring of the Lupaca province indicates that the preexisting structure of the Lupaca population was an important factor in its design (Julien 1982, 1988a). The Lupaca population was organized in two huno, but each had a differential distribution across the seven divisions of the population that appears to have been a preexisting feature of local organization. The huno may have been paired for administrative reasons. Each *huno curaca* (head of 10,000 households) kept a census for the whole province, which served to check the census held by the other. In the neighboring Colla provinces, the administrators of productive enclaves in one province resided in another. Elsewhere I have suggested that this type of dual division served as a check or promoted competition between productive forces and may have been institutionalized by the Incas for that purpose (Julien 1982). The dual division of the Colla provinces may have been drawn along the Umasuyo/Urcosuyo boundary and not internally as in the Lupaca province. The point to be noted is that the structure of neighboring provinces may be quite different owing to such features as previous organization or the relationship between the subject population and Cuzco.

The function of Inca centers associated with provinces of different types may also be far more complex than the ethnohistorical documents indicate. For instance, one Spanish administrator noted that Inca centers duplicated the shrine layout of Cuzco. Inca rulers often conducted military campaigns in person. They took some of the more important religious images with them and celebrated festivals of importance to the dynasty, such as *capac raymi*, while they were away from Cuzco. A native writer whose forebears had traveled with Huayna Capac on campaign in Ecuador mentioned that the Inca celebrated capac raymi in Vilcas and Quito (Pachacuti Yamqui Salcamaygua 1879: 301, 307).

Capac raymi was an elaborate round of ritual events that took place over a twenty-three-day period and required visits to three sacred mountains near Cuzco—Huanacauri, Anahuarque, and Yavira (Molina 1989: 98–110). Only young men related through the male line to Inca nobles were initiated, so perhaps the ceremonial landscape required for capac raymi, including the sites chosen to represent the three mountains visited during the ceremony, was re-created only at certain kinds of Inca centers. For example, this aspect of the ceremonial land-scape may have been re-created only where a permanent population of orejones resided, or where a large number of candidates for initiation might be expected occasionally, as at major Inca centers along the main roads that housed the Inca army during the time capac raymi was celebrated.

At the same time, a study of the structure of Inca administration (Julien 1988a) indicates that the Incas organized similar productive ac-tivities in each province. For example, productive enclaves of fine weav-ers and potters were established in all formally organized provinces.

Before turning to a consideration of the material remains, I want to review what ethnohistorical sources have to say about ceramic produc-tion in the area. A community of potters was settled at Cupe, located midway between Chucuito and Acora, in the Lupaca province. These people appear to have been organized to produce ceramics during the time of Inca rule. Another Cupe, near Ayaviri, may have also been organized for ceramic production, if the name Cupe is a clue to the occupational specialization of the people at that site. Such communities may have been located in the vicinity of Inca centers to alleviate the problem of transporting ceramics over any great distance. Hupi, near Huancané, was certainly the location of such a community (Murra 1978: 417).

Hupi is of particular concern in the context of the discussion which follows. A colonial lawsuit provides us with some information about the organization of ceramic production in the northern Lake Titicaca Basin (Murra 1978: 419–420). Hupi was settled close to Milliraya, a community of fine weavers, and these two communities appear to have been organized near the Inca center of Huancané. One issue in the colonial lawsuit was whether the people of these communities were originally from places in the Colla province of Umasuyo in the district of Cuzco or from the La Paz side of the boundary as well. As noted above, two Inca estates can be identified in the territory on the Cuzco side of the boundary. Although no archaeological survey designed to consider the material correlates of the ethnohistorical picture we have drawn was undertaken, we can learn something by reexamining the archaeological evidence that has already been gathered.

PROVINCIAL STRUCTURE AND ARCHAEOLOGICAL PERSPECTIVES

The Lake Titicaca Region: Chiquicache and Copacabana

Archaeological study will certainly amplify the image we have. A resonance between the ethnohistorical reconstruction we have just sketched above and archaeological material can already be found.

Survey in the Lake Titicaca region has identified several ceramic styles that are closely tied to the Cuzco-Inca style of the capital. Very finely made and stylistically innovative, these Titicaca Basin styles had an impact in Cuzco and elsewhere. When we consider their distribution in light of our ethnohistorical reconstruction of provinces in the Lake Titicaca region, a coincidence between their occurrence and estate or sanctuary territories becomes evident. Two styles, termed Taraco Polychrome and Urcosuyo Polychrome when they were first described (Tschopik 1946: 21, 31–32, fig. 18; Rowe 1944: 48, fig. 19 [5–7]; Julien 1983: 117), are relevant to our inquiry.

Taraco Polychrome consists almost entirely of Cuzco-Inca bowl and bottle shapes decorated with black, red, and orange pigments (Tschopik 1946: 21, 31–32, fig. 18, pl. 10g; Ruiz 1973: fig. 57). The vessels bearing Taraco decoration are often manufactured from a kaolin-type clay that fires to a very clear white color; if the kaolin clay is not used, a light cream-colored clay is chosen. Vessels are never slipped in any color, but the white or light color of the paste was probably an important aesthetic feature.

Taraco Polychrome was originally defined as a type with only a minimal description. The name Taraco was chosen because a fair quantity of fragments of it were found on the surface at Taraco in the northern Titicaca basin. A few fragments have been found at sites like Hatuncolla and Chucuito, but it is rare outside of the northern Lake Titicaca area. The fragments used to define it (Tschopik 1946: fig. 18) indicate heavy influence from the Cuzco-Inca style. Its distribution and other style features suggest that another type identified by Harvard Project 7, Sillustani Brown on Cream, is the probable local antecedent of Taraco Polychrome (Tschopik 1946: 27, fig. 11).

The type names Taraco Polychrome and Sillustani Brown on Cream belie the variability evident in white paste ceramic materials in the northern Lake Titicaca Basin. For example, the bowl material illustrated by Tschopik (fig. 7.2a–d; Tschopik 1946: fig. 18a–c, e) uses orange circumferential banding and cat-spot motifs (partly or entirely drawn in red). Another kind of bowl has an Inca-related pendant triangle band below the lip; these bowls are small and have very thin walls (Schmidt 1929: 300; Julien 1983: 193–194, fig. 122). A third kind of bowl has a bird handle, transverse band decoration and black and red line decoration only (Chapin 1961: 43, pl. 14e; Tschopik 1946: pl. 10e). All three of these bowl types show strong influence from the Cuzco-Inca style but, on the basis of stylistic and technological features, appear to represent the manufactures of more than one productive unit. Defining and tracing the evolution of these materials from local antecedents promises to be a complex task.

For the moment, let us consider only the Taraco variant that uses orange banding and the cat-spot motif. This variant formed the basis for the definition of the Taraco Polychrome type, and we can assume that it occurred with some frequency at Taraco. Both the use of the color orange and the cat-spot motif had a stylistic trajectory that reached considerably beyond the Lake Titicaca region.

Another Inca-related style from the Lake Titicaca Basin also had an effect beyond the local area. Orange banding is another style feature associated with Urcosuyo Polychrome (figs. 7.3–7.5 and color plates 1 and 2). Urcosuyo Polychrome was also defined as a type by members of Harvard Project 7 (Tschopik 1946: 32–33, fig. 19; Rowe 1944: 48, fig. 19[5–7]). Like Taraco Polychrome, it is a particular decorative mode that is used on Cuzco-Inca shapes, especially the bottle shape termed aryballos by Bingham and the two-handled dish. In both cases, the principal design areas are entirely covered with a composition of band and panel designs drawn both from the standard Cuzco-Inca design inventory and from a repertory of Urcosuyo bands and panels.

The style was named Urcosuyo because it was found most often on the surface of sites in the area traversed by the Urcosuyo road (Tschopik 1946: 32–33, fig. 19; Julien 1983: 234, n. 22 p. 241). A resemblance was noted between the materials used to define Urcosuyo Polychrome and ceramics recovered on the island of Titicaca in the last century by Adolph Bandelier (Tschopik 1946: 33; Bandelier 1910 pl. 21, facing p. 94; pl. 54, facing p. 222; pl. 67, facing p. 270; pl. 76,

Figure 7.3. Fragments from a Cuzco bottle from Llaq'aylli on the Island of the Sun. Red, black, white, and orange painted decoration. Bandelier Collection, 2104 (both), American Museum of Natural History.

facing p. 294). Sufficient Urcosuyo material was found in Cuzco itself that it was included as one of several modes characteristic of Cuzco-Inca ceramics (Rowe 1944: 48, fig. 19[5–7]).

While Urcosuyo decoration probably originated in the Lake Titicaca Basin, it is closely tied to Mode B decoration, one of the design compositions characteristic of the Cuzco-Inca style (Rowe 1944: 47, figs. 18, 21–22; pl. 5[4–6]). Pendant triangles and diamond bands that are the hallmarks of Mode B occur in the principal design space (fig. 7.3) or on the neck of a vessel (fig. 7.4), often in combination with Urcosuyo-style bands or panels. Sometimes the referent to Mode B is the use of a concentric diamond panel in a vertical position in the principal design space, the same position occupied by this panel in standard Mode B decoration. Urcosuyo may also use bands that are similar to standard Mode B bands in concept but are executed in a radically different man-

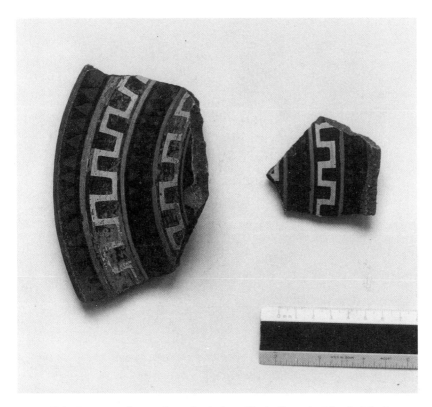

Figure 7.4. Fragments from a Cuzco bottle from Llaq'aylli on the Island of the Sun. Red, black, white, and orange painted decoration. Bandelier Collection, 2103 (both), American Museum of Natural History.

ner. For example, the diamond band that appears on the neck of a Cuzco bottle in figure 7.5 would be executed in black on a red background in Mode B. A band with red diamonds is a common decorative element in the Cuzco-Inca style, but it is not a standard element of neck decoration. While a minimal reference to Mode B (for example, the use of a concentric diamond panel to divide the principal design space) is frequent, Urcosuyo need not imitate Mode B in any obvious manner (see color plates 1 and 2; Bandelier 1910: pl. 76).

The type was tentatively defined by Harvard Project 7, since the number of fragments found on the surface of sites was not large, and they were "not very consistent in themselves" (Tschopik 1946: 32). As

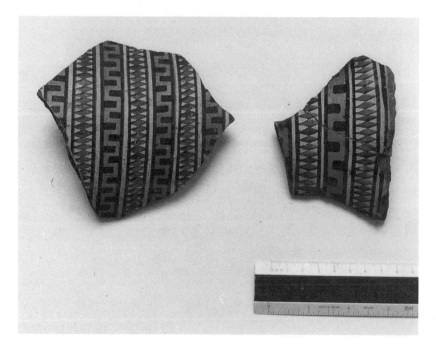

Figure 7.5. *Fragments from a Cuzco bottle from Llaq'aylli on the Island of the Sun. Red, black, white, and orange painted decoration. Bandelier Collection, 2103 (both), American Museum of Natural History.*

in the case of Taraco materials, the stylistic variation evident in Urcosuyo materials is sufficient to suggest that, again, more than one producing unit was involved in its manufacture.

For example, a variant of Urcosuyo was recovered from the chullpas of Sillustani (fig. 7.6 and color plate 3; Ruiz 1973: fig. 58). Although the variant is also based on Mode B decoration, it is clearly different from the Urcosuyo defined by Tschopik. The color orange is not used. Different band and panel designs are substituted for those characteristic of Urcosuyo. Also, the cat-spot motif and other small red-line motifs are used on white bands in a manner analogous to the red cross-hatch bands which appear on Mode B Cuzco-Inca vessels in the same contexts (compare bands in color plate 1 to Rowe 1944: fig. 18[21–22]), but entirely unlike anything which appears on the variant of Urcosuyo defined by Tschopik. This variant of Mode B appears to be a local development, although other variants of Mode B have been found in the Cuzco area (Bingham 1930: figs. 78, 81).

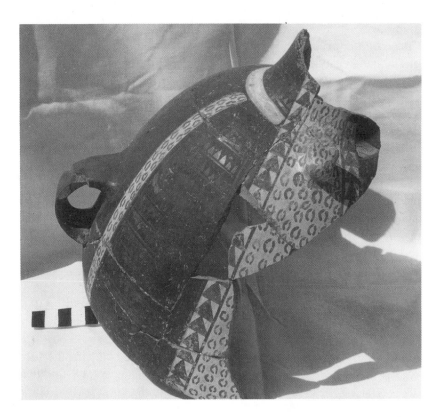

Figure 7.6. Cuzco bottle from Chullpa at Sillustani. Red, black, and white painted decoration. Sillustani Museum.

Let us discuss for the moment only the variants of Taraco and Ur-cosuyo materials that are characterized by the use of orange band decoration. Cuzco-Inca ceramics are typically decorated with black, red, and white. The introduction of the color orange into the color inventory of the Cuzco-Inca style appears to be related to Taraco and Urcosuyo influence. Orange is used for bands, bordered on either edge by black lines and also, in the case of the Urcosuyo vessels, in meanders and other linear designs of approximately the same width as the orange bands and for triangular motifs.[5]

If we ask what the stylistic antecedent of the orange band was, we discover a provoking possibility: the orange bands are similar to those used in the Tiahuanaco style, particularly as bands dividing the design space of tumblers and cups. The Incas were aware of the existence of

Tiahuanaco-style ceramics. A cup (color plate 4) and the neck of a Cuzco bottle (aryballos) in the Cuzco Museum imitate the decoration of Tiahuanaco-style ceramics but are executed in Cuzco-Inca paste and exhibit other technological features of the Cuzco-Inca style (Valcárcel 1935: 163–164, 166, 173; Buck 1935: apéndice 1, lám. i–1; Means 1935: 206–208). Both pieces use orange bands as design space dividers.

The cup is of particular interest because not just the decoration but also the shape is borrowed from the Tiahuanaco style. The mouth and neck diameters of local Killke-style antecedents are similar, and the profile varies from slightly concave to slightly convex (Bauer and Stanish 1990: 5, fig. 1). Cuzco-Inca cups have notably larger mouth diameters in comparison with their base diameters, producing concave sides and a marked flare toward the lip. In shape, they are more similar to Tiahuanaco cups than to their Killke-style antecedents. Because the cup shape appears to have been influenced by the shape of Tiahuanaco-style cups, it is of some interest to ask if the Inca copies imitated Tiahuanaco style cups from a particular area, since the Tiahuanaco style was widely distributed.

The answer is also thought-provoking: when we compare the Inca copy to Tiahuanaco-style cups that have site proveniences, we find that the design layout of the Inca copy is very similar to cups that come from the island of Titicaca. Cups from Copacabana and the island of Titicaca are divided on the exterior into two design panels by a pair of light-colored bands at the midsection (fig. 7.7; Eisleb and Strelow 1980: figs. 43, 63, 74). Sandwiched between them is a black band. The panel above the dividing bands is usually polychrome and more elaborate than the design in the panel below. Cups with Tiahuanaco site provenience usually have only a single light-colored band at the midsection and reverse the placement of the more elaborate polychrome panel.[6]

The light-colored bands from the Tiahuanaco-style cups of the Copacabana area are a fugitive white painted over a red-slipped surface, while the Inca copy uses the color orange instead. Perhaps the color orange is visually more similar to the fugitive white of Tiahuanaco cups than the dense white or cream pigments used on Cuzco-Inca vessels.

The question of Inca interest in the Tiahuanaco style deserves more attention, but it is enough for present purposes to note that we have evidence that Inca interest may be linked in some way to the island of

Figure 7.7. *Tiahuanaco-style cup from Ciriapata, Island of the Sun. Black and white painted decoration on a red-slipped surface. Bandelier Collection, B/2575, American Museum of Natural History.*

Titicaca. It is probably no coincidence that the variant of Urcosuyo which incorporates orange bands in its design composition is found in quantity in the same place.

It is time now to consider these stylistic relationships in light of our reconstruction of territory in the Lake Titicaca region. The archaeological evidence fits very well with our ethnohistorical image of the Inca organization of this region. Two very fancy decorative modes of the Cuzco-Inca style came into being in the Lake Titicaca region. One appears to be related to the sanctuary of Copacabana, and perhaps specifically to the island of Titicaca; the other may be connected to the development of Inca estates in the northern Lake Titicaca Basin.

If we interpret the appearance of orange band design in the decorative modes of the Cuzco-Inca style as being inspired by the Tiahuanaco style, we may also construct a hypothesis about the timing of this stylistic development. Sources which drew on Inca oral tradition tell us that the island of Titicaca was first visited by Topa Inca (Ramos Gavilán cap. IV; 1988: 39–41; cap. V; 1988: 45). Topa Inca also put down a Colla rebellion at the time of the death of his father, Pachacuti. The Collas had fortified the hilltops of Pucará, Asillo, Arapa, and Llallagua (Sarmiento de Gamboa cap. 49; 1906: 97; Rowe 1985b: 214). Two of these sites, Llallagua and Pucara, have been identified archaeologically (Rowe 1943). Since the Colla fortified sites are located exactly in the area where Topa Inca developed estates, we might also attribute the development of the Taraco style to the rule of this Inca or afterward.

This chronological placement accords well with what we know about changes in ceramic style during the period of Inca control. The evidence we have, though it is not conclusive, suggests that Mode B decoration was a late development in the Cuzco-Inca style (Julien 1983: 231, 253). The only stratigraphic placement for the color orange also agrees with a late placement (Julien 1983: 223–224, fig. 171).

Different lines of evidence meet fairly well in this case. The ethnohistorical reconstruction of territory, the mining of Cuzco sources for information about the Inca expansion, and the analysis of ceramic styles are more powerful tools when combined than when used alone.

Our reworking of the two bodies of data into a single framework raises rather than answers questions. For example, are the Taraco and Urcosuyo variants we have been discussing provincial Inca styles, or should we view them as additional decorative modes of the Cuzco-Inca style, even if we can substantiate that they were manufactured by Collas and drew on local stylistic and technological traditions? What do the other variants of Mode B decoration represent, at Cuzco or at centers like Hatuncolla? Where was the production center of the Taraco variant? Was it Hupi near Huancané or somewhere else? Assuming that these Taraco and Urcosuyo ceramics were produced by particular communities of potters, were other ceramics produced by these same people? Does the stylistic tie between the Taraco and Urcosuyo variants under discussion here indicate other kinds of ties between the Copacabana sanctuary and the estates in the northern Lake Titicaca Basin?

And, perhaps most important, what was the purpose of estates located at a distance from Cuzco? All of these questions can be addressed archaeologically.

The Vilcashuaman Region: Carhuarazo Valley

Schreiber surveyed the Carhuarazo Valley, part of the Inca province of Soras and Lucanas. Her specific goal was to obtain information about both the Huari and the Inca presence in the valley.

Soras and Lucanas was the name given to a corregimiento that included three encomiendas: two to people called Lucanas and one to Soras (Miranda 1925: 178–179). A good case can be made in this instance that the corregimiento territory was roughly the same as the Inca province. Some sixteenth-century authors give lists of Inca provinces, and Soras and Lucanas are listed together as a single province (Polo de Ondegardo 1916: 101; Pizarro cap. 29; 1978: 220).

We can sketch the structure of the Soras and Lucanas province in broad outline because a description of the territory prepared in 1586, one of a series known as the *Relaciónes Geográficas*, has survived (Monzón 1965a–c). The people of Soras and Lucanas were organized in three encomiendas. One was Soras, and it was composed of three parts: Hanansora, Hurinsora, and Chalcos. The town of Hatunsora was its principal center (Monzón 1965a: 220). The second encomienda, Hatunlucana and Laramati, was composed of two parts: Hananlucana and Hurinlucana. The principal site was Hatunlucana (Monzón 1965c: 226–227). The grant to Andamarca Lucanas was composed of four units: Andamarca, Apucara, Omapacha, and Huchucayllo. Apucara was the principal center in 1586; the people from Andamarca had been reduced (brought into Spanish-style settlements) at Cabana (Monzón 1965b: 237). Apucara in Andamarca Lucanas was the center of the Spanish corregimiento, but Hatunsora or Hatunlucana may have been more important centers under Inca rule, as their names suggest.

The composition of an Inca province probably depended on historical factors. The method of annexation, whether through military defeat or diplomatic bargaining, may have influenced the first structuring of the province under the Incas. Inca assessment of the value of local resources, previous political organization, the prestige of the enemy or the territory itself, and the requirements of persons or groups in Cuzco may also have affected the structure of a province. Here we are limited to what we can learn from Cuzco sources. Spanish narratives based on the Inca oral tradition describe military campaigns, but they also sometimes describe diplomatic co-optation—or we can detect it from them. Rather than compile information from several sources, I will briefly review what Juan de Betanzos, who appears to have gotten his information from members of Pachacuti's lineage, said about the annexation of Soras and Lucanas. Although his description is really just a backdrop for information about the victory rituals invented by Pachacuti, a war against Soras was clearly waged and won by the Incas.

The Soras campaign was important in an Inca version of their own expansion. It marked a turning point: after the Incas recouped their losses from earlier Chanca attacks, they organized their first military campaign aimed at expansion beyond the Cuzco area. The campaign was deliberate. It required the building of roads and bridges over both the Apurimac and the Pampachaca, and fortresses (Betanzos caps. XVIII, XIX; 1987: 87–97). The Lucanas and people identified as Vilcas who lived in what became the province of Vilcashuamán either joined in the fight or were peacefully annexed about the same time. The Soras were clearly the principal target.

No matter what the particulars were, the Incas also managed to clear a fairly large territory north of the Soras and Lucanas province where they founded the province of Vilcashuamán. The center of Vilcashuamán, like Hatuncolla, was a collection point for coastal tribute. But Vilcashuamán did not draw on a local population: the area surrounding it was repopulated with mitimas, as noted by Schreiber (cf. Cock 1981). Some of the Lucanas from the Andamarca group were resettled in the Vilcashuamán province along with people from Aymaraes, to the north (the northern Andamarca settlements shown in fig. 4.1; Monzón 1965b: 240, 247; Miranda 1925: 181).

Vilcashuamán was a major Inca center. It was situated on the main highland road. People from Andamarca Lucanas were also assigned to serve the tambo there, along with the Soras and some of the mitima groups in the province of Vilcashuamán. Although our information is about staffing the tambo in 1543, they were to serve as they had under Huayna Capac (Vaca de Castro 1908: 445, 455). Vilcashuamán appears to have been a military staging area and depot, like Paria and Ayaviri. A description of storage at the site noted that arms and clothing for the army were deposited there (Cabrera and Cháves 1965: 181). The plaza was said to have been large enough to contain 20,000 men (Carabajal

1965: 218). Vilcashuamán was the nearest such site to Soras and Lucanas.

The territory organized by the Incas as Soras and Lucanas had a different character. Its population had preponderantly local origins. We can study this local population in some detail because, in addition to the 1586 questionnaire, an encomienda award document dating to 1540 has been located (Cock 1981: 143–157). The early document lists the communities that existed before the resettlement program carried out under the administration of Viceroy Francisco de Toledo in the 1570s. Schreiber located many of the communities listed in the 1540 document, including places that were not mentioned in 1586. The Carhuarazo Valley was indeed the major focus of settlement in Andamarca Lucanas.

The documentation also notes the presence of people subject to Andamarca Lucanas in two other areas, in addition to the communities of Lucanas settled in the province of Vilcashuamán, noted above (fig 4.1). Other Andamarca Lucanas communities were located in quebradas along the upper reaches of the Yauca River. To reach these communities, one traveled from Apucara southward across the puna of Yauriviri, at the foot of the mountain Carhuarazo. This puna separated Andamarca Lucanas from Soras. Near the communities on the upper Yauca, just to the east, was the Inca province of Parinacochas.

A small number of Andamarca Lucanas were settled in Hatunlucanas at Uraguasi, known as Pueblo Quemado, above the Nasca Valley. This site was a way station on the road from Cochacajas to Nasca, but the Lucanas also raised cochineal in this area (Monzón 1965c: 234). To reach it from Andamarca Lucanas, one traveled first to the site of Hatunlucana, crossing the large expanse of puna which separated the two Lucanas divisions, and then traveled on the main road to Nasca (Monzón 1965b: 240, 1965c: 233). At Uraguasi, there was some territorial overlap with the Hatunlucana division, but otherwise Andamarca territory could be defined as a separate entity from all of its neighbors.

The separation between the population center in the Carhuarazo Valley and the communities in the upper Yauca makes the latter appear to be "islands" of settlement (Cock 1981: 145–146). But the punas which separated the Yauca communities from the Apucara Valley were part of Andamarca Lucanas. Lowland communities were located in a different production zone than the Carhuarazo Valley, but they were territorially contiguous with Andamarca Lucanas.

The large expanses of puna between the Carhuarazo Valley and other population nuclei appeared to the Spanish like large vacant territories, or "*despoblados*," but they were the economic core of Soras and Lucanas. The principal source of wealth was herding, and in 1586 camelid husbandry was important. With fiber and meat, the Lucanas obtained ají and coca from the lowlands (Monzón 1965c: 228, 235; 1965b: 238–239, 244, 247). Cieza de León, when he described the province of Soras and Lucanas based on his travels of 1549–50, noted its animal wealth (Cieza de León primera parte, cap. LXXXIX; 1984: 253). When Vázquez de Espinosa traveled across the puna separating Apucara and Hatunlucana in the early seventeenth century, he described only the *cabañas* (huts) of herders called *michis*. Vázquez, a cleric, described these people as irrational brutes who had no knowledge of the faith and who practiced idolatry. He also noted "an innumerable quantity" of wild stock, naming vicuñas and *guanacos* (wild members of the camelid family) in particular (Vázquez de Espinosa libro quarto, cap. 62; 1948: 489).

The population of Andamarca Lucanas was concentrated in the Carhuarazo Valley, where agriculture was practiced, though without much help from irrigation, since the river canyon was too deep to permit extensive canal systems (Monzón 1965b: 244). The same situation appears to have characterized the period of Inca control, based on Schreiber's location of places named in the 1540 encomienda award. However, the concentration of population in this area should not obscure the economic importance of areas that were sparsely settled.

Schreiber has a good grasp of the ethnohistorical picture, but I have expanded her presentation for several reasons: to establish the territorial integrity of Soras and Lucanas, to identify Vilcashuamán as the nearest major Inca center, and to review information about early economy. The image of Soras and Lucanas that emerges is itself a hypothesis, but it provides a starting point for comparing the Inca organization of Soras and Lucanas territory with Inca organization elsewhere.

First of all, Schreiber identifies features of Inca infrastructure in the Carhuarazo Valley. She identifies Apucara and Queca as stations on an Inca road that departed from the main highland road at Cochacajas, west of Abancay, and joined the coastal road at Nasca. Her work on Huari control of the area indicates that the major road from Huari to Nasca, via Vilcashuamán, also crossed the Carhuarazo Valley (Schreiber 1987: 274). The Incas reused this road (Schreiber 1984). The portion from Apucara to Vilcashuamán also served as an important link between Lucanas and Vilcashuamán, though it may not have had the facilities or staff to accommodate an army as the road from Cuzco to Nasca would have had.

Schreiber has also tentatively identified Apucara as the center of Andamarca Lucanas during the time of Inca control. A more certain identification awaits survey in the Andamarca area. The name Andamarca Lucanas suggests the prominence of Andamarca, even if it referred only to a huaranga and not to some type of pre-Inca polity. The structure at Canichi and the finely built terraces also suggest that this area had some prestige under the Incas.

Other archaeological features related to Inca control are minimal. Schreiber identifies several rectangular structures that provide a contrast with the local building tradition. In the Chupachos region (Thompson 1967), a similar construction has been identified as the residence of a local huaranga officer, and this pattern may well be found in other areas. The constructions at Inca Chuklla and Huayhuay Puquio are related to features of the landscape that may quite possibly have been sacred.

The structure at Canichi is a better candidate for the residence of a local officer. Cuzco-influenced ceramics were found at none of these places, however. Were there none to be found? Schreiber notes that the minute quantity of material related to the Cuzco-Inca style was probably imported from elsewhere. We are only beginning to understand the organization of ceramic production and consumption under the Incas, but a part of the labor obligation of each province involved gathering together a community of people "from all over the province" to produce ceramics, as at Hupi near Huancané (Julien 1988a: 267). We might hypothesize that one or more communities of this type were located in Soras and Lucanas territory, but perhaps near Hatunsoras and not in the Carhuarazo Valley. The Hupi community produced pottery that drew on local antecedents. The degree of Cuzco-Inca influence on the local product may have been considerably smaller in Lucanas than in Hupi.

The Huánuco Region: Chupachos

Grosboll surveyed part of the Inca province of Chupachos, or Guanca Chupachos. Her efforts were directed at assessing the impact of Inca control.

The province of Chupachos was located to the east of the main Chinchaysuyo road. The Spanish city León de Huánuco was founded in its midst in the early 1540s following an earlier attempt to found a Spanish city at the Inca center of Huánuco Pampa. The name Huánuco was transferred to the new site, and so Chupachos became Spanish Huánuco.

Whether it had been part of a province centered at Huánuco Pampa is in doubt. When corregimientos were established, Chupachos was incorporated into the corregimiento of Tarama (modern Tarma) and Chinchacocha. The corregimiento of Guamalíes, just to the north, included Huánuco Pampa, a band of lowland territory adjacent to it, and part of highland Guamalíes. The other part of Guamalíes was included in the corregimiento of Tarama and Chinchacocha (Miranda 1925: 201–204). Applying the perspective on Inca infrastructure that we gained in the Lake Titicaca region, we would hypothesize that all of Guamalíes was part of an Inca province that included Chupachos and Tarma. Huánuco Pampa, the territory around it, and the band of lowland territory adjacent to it were another province.

Huánuco Pampa was a major Inca center. Cieza de León described it as such and noted that it had a special function: Huánuco Pampa stood at the head of several provinces adjacent to the Andes, that is, to the eastern lowlands or *montaña*. He lists these provinces as Conchucos, Guaylas, and Tarma and Bombón (Cieza de León primera parte, cap. LXXX; 1984: 233).

Some major Inca centers were supported by a mitima population. What about Huánuco Pampa? An ethnohistorical reconstruction of the population around Huánuco Pampa during the time of Inca control depends in large measure upon its survival following the Spanish invasion. For example, in the case of Vilcashuamán, the documentation of the 1570s and later allows us to identify the origins of people resettled by the Incas. In the case of Huánuco Pampa, the situation is acute, because the Inca governor, Illa Topa, mounted his own campaign against the Spaniards, which lasted more than a decade, ending in the early 1540s. Cieza de León noted that the encomiendas awarded in 1539 when Spanish Huánuco was first founded at the site of Huánuco Pampa became worthless as a result of population loss in the area caused by Illa Topa's campaign. New grants had to be made. If a population was destroyed or abandoned its area of settlement in this early period, then administrative documentation generated in the next decades will not provide us with a means of studying settlement under the Incas.

Cieza de León also describes the annexation of the Huánuco area and indicates that the Incas organized Chupachos territory twice. He attributes the annexation of territory in the Huánuco and Chachapoyas areas to Topa Inca, and his story coincides with independent testimony gathered from local people in these areas (Espinoza Soriano 1967b: 291–292; Ortíz de Zúñiga 1972: 248, 258). During the reign of the subsequent ruler, Huayna Capac, people of the Chupachos region rebelled. This Inca, en route to an Ecuadorian campaign with an army of 200,000, left the army in Cajamarca, then backtracked to Chupachos via Chachapoyas. Chupachos had abandoned Inca organization, which Huayna Capac reimposed (Cieza de León segunda parte, cap. LXIV; 1985: 186–187).

We have excellent early information about the Chupachos province, collected in the course of two Spanish administrative surveys (Helmer [1549] 1955–56). There were four huarangas, and these were further divided into *pachacas*, or units of 100 households. An Inca labor assignment was also put on record (Helmer 1955–56: 40–41). It is of critical importance to the reconstruction of how Inca decimal administration operated (Julien 1988a). Because the labor assignment can be partially coordinated with information about settlement from the 1549 survey, we can also study the relation between labor assignment and settlement.

Despite the changes in settlement which surely occurred between the time of the labor assignment and the 1549 survey, the Inca productive organization of Chupachos can be traced on the ground. Not all of the communities can be located on a modern map, but the general location of each huaranga can be identified. Overlap in authority lines is found chiefly in the area labeled "mitima" (fig. 3.3), which appears to have been part of the territory of the huaranga of Marca Pari and the location of a number of communities that were not subject to his authority.

Overlap in authority also characterizes a number of occupationally specialized communities recorded in the 1549 survey. People who were occupationally specialized were known as *camayos* (Rowe 1982: 102–105), and they were resettled together in productive enclaves like the fine weavers and potters of Hupi near Huancané. There were camayo communities in the territories of all four huarangas (Helmer

1955–56: 24–39). In the 1549 survey, they were described as being composed of people "from all over the province," as we would expect, given what we know about Inca decimal administration (Julien 1988a: 267). Many of the occupations noted in the Inca labor assignment were represented by camayo communities in 1549.

Some communities produced goods for tribute in 1562 that were not listed in the Inca assignment. Productive activity may have been reoriented to some degree to meet new demands. Also, groups of occupational specialists were subject to particular curacas; this practice may not have characterized Inca organization. The ties between settlement in 1549 and the occupations listed in the Inca labor assignment are strong enough, however, to suggest continuity in a number of specific cases.

There were two such communities of potters, composed of people from "all over the province." One was Acochaca in Queros territory, and the other was at Payna, in the territory of Paucar Guaman. Another group of potters was settled in Yaros territory at Cachuchu. They had been there since Inca times, but in 1549 they were subject to Paucar Guaman. A group of *querocamayos*, who fashioned cups and other objects of wood, was located at Quero in the territory of Quirin. A group of "carpenters" at Guaychao in the territory of Paucar Guaman may have had the same assignment. Both groups were from "all over the province." A group of people who were herders "in Inca times" were settled on an *estancia* (ranch) in the territory of Paucar Guaman, and a second group on an estancia called Caracara in Yaros territory. People from "all over the province" assigned to tambo service at Ambo were settled at Tuculla in the territory of Quirin (Helmer 1955–56:24, 26–28, 30–31).

The camayos who washed gold from the river were located at Goucaquin in the territory of Marca Pari. A group of camayos *para hacer plumas* (featherworkers) was located at Latacocha in the territory of Marca Pari, and another group, who were camayos *de miel y pájaros* (collectors of honey and birds) was located at Malangalli. The latter settlement was outside the territory of Chupachos. The settlement of *cocacamayos* (coca cultivators) from "all over the province" was at Chinchao in the lowlands and outside the territory of Chupachos. Many of these people were surveyed within the territory of Chupachos, where they had their maize lands (Helmer 1955–56: 35–36, 38).

Other people from Chupachos were settled outside the province, in

Yaros territory, in addition to the potters and herders noted above. The town of Caxamalca, a settlement of camayos *de sal* (salt producers), was settled by people from the "suyo of Huánuco," probably in reference to the Huánuco province proper (Helmer 1955–56: 27–28).

Two places, Goallaura in the territory of Quirin and Maranbuco in the territory of Paucar Guaman, had people from "all over the province," but no occupational specialization was noted. Perhaps one of these places was the locus of *cumbi* (fine cloth) production. A large number of people were assigned to produce cumbi cloth, but this group is difficult to place. Pican, in the territory of Marca Pari, was a settlement of "*conbicos,*" a term that was probably shorthand for *cumbicamayos* (producers of fine cloth). Only seven households were counted there in 1549. Another five conbicos resided at Cochatama in the territory of Chinchao Poma. They were mitimas from Canto along with others who mined minerals for their home province and also served Chinchao Poma. The specialized weavers may have settled here near the source of minerals for mordants, since the dyeing and weaving of a textile is usually an integrated task. In the Inca labor assignment, a special group was assigned to obtain dyestuffs. These people were not mentioned in 1549 (Helmer 1955–56: 27, 30–31, 35).

The survey also puts into evidence groups of non-Chupachus in the area who were not covered by the labor assignment. These groups were concentrated in the area labeled "mitimas" on Grosboll's map (fig. 3.3) and just to the north of it, in territory that may have been under the jurisdiction of Huánuco Pampa, judging from the encomienda origins of some of the people residing there. Small groups of Incas from Cuzco were still there in 1549. The gold washing in the area might explain their presence. A group of mitimas from Chachapoyas, Cayambe, and Paltas resided at Malcunga, and another group from Cayambe was located at Llanguibamba nearby. Both places were in the territory of Paucar Guaman.

Grosboll notes that the huarangas were territorial units. The documentation permits us to draw rough boundaries around each huaranga and around the four together. We can define a Chupachos territory. A close reading of the 1549 survey allows us to identify people who are beyond the limits of this territory, resettled across the boundary in some other territory. Several communities were located just to the south, in Yaros territory (Helmer 1955–56: 27–28). Other communities were located to the north, "in the territory of the Andes." One of the communities located outside Chupachos territory was Malangalli, settled by the Incas to collect honey and birds.[7] At several sites within Chupachos territory (Pachancha, Uras, Pomayguaci), people subject to the huaranga officers of Chupachos, as well as Yaros from other encomiendas, had maize fields. These people also had coca fields in Chinchao, to the north and outside of Chupachos territory.[8] The territoriality of Chupachos is related to the huaranga structure of Chupachos and is an Inca, not a Spanish, creation. People were scattered across the landscape in this area of the Andes, and lines of authority crossed boundaries; however, a notion of bounded space is evident.

The Inca organization of Chupachos can be sketched from the documentation of 1549. A comparison with the survey of 1562 allows us to roughly estimate the pace of change after 1549. For example, only three households remained at Cochatama, the site in 1549 of sixteen households of mitimas from Canto who mined minerals and produced cumbi cloth. The three Cochatama households listed in 1562 contributed their share of the tribute assignment, including cotton clothing, chickens, potatoes, wheat, and maize (Ortíz de Zúñiga 1967: 108–109). Gone was any trace of specialized Inca production or foreign ethnic affiliation.

Other aspects of Inca organization are also difficult to identify. The 1549 survey, despite its detail on Chupachos communities, does not permit the identification of an Inca center. There may not have been one. The four huaranga officers resided in their separate territories. The residences of two of them have been identified (Thompson 1967: 359, 361; Morris and Thompson 1985: 138–148). One of these structures looks enough like a tambo to make us thankful that written information was available to suggest another interpretation. There were at least two local tambos, one at Ambo and the other at Chacaguacha, in the territory of Chinchao Poma (Ortíz de Zúñiga 1967: 92). One of the tambos may have served as the Inca center of Chupachos.

The site of Pillao also has Inca features that make it a possible candidate. It was divided into hanan and hurin, terms that characterize the division of Cuzco but which are uncommon in this area (Murra 1967: 398). Also at Pillao was a group of mitimas from Canta, Caxatambo, and elsewhere, there "to guard the doors of the Inca" (Helmer 1955–56: 34). They were to guard the doors of a house built by "the Inca when he came to conquer the lands of the Andes," here referring to the lowland areas below Huánuco (Ortíz de Zúñiga 1967: 239).

Settled at several sites near Pillao were Inca orejones and people from Quichuas province near Cuzco, who were to staff several fortresses to secure the Chupachos province. The Spanish administrator learned in 1562 that these people had been settled there by Topa Inca when the province was first organized (Ortíz de Zúñiga 1972: 248, 258).

We can outline the Inca organization of Chupachos because of the information we have about settlement and labor organization, but Chupachos may have been atypical. Two witnesses from Queros, interviewed in 1562, gave information about how the three pachacas of Queros came to be included with the Chupachus. These groups had been part of a huaranga of Yachas. Huascar, twelfth on the Inca kinglist, had separated them from Yachas and incorporated them with the Chupachus. They were his yanaconas, as were the Chupachus with whom they were joined (Ortíz de Zúñiga 1967: 91, 41). This group was part of the huaranga of Chinchao Poma, so his statement might have referred only to it. However, Diego Xagua, who had replaced Paucar Guaman both as head of a huaranga and as head of all Chupachus, testified that the Chupachus were selected by the Inca to be yanaconas (Ortíz de Zúñiga 1967: 25). The Chupachus, according to him, were yanaconas of Huascar.

Sources which drew on Inca oral tradition also note that the Chupachus served Huascar. At the same time that Huascar was building his palace at Calca, he reserved groups for himself in each of the four *suyos* (quarters of the empire): "At the time of an administrative survey, he removed a large number of Indians for his service called *aylloscas* who were Yanyos, Caxas and Huambos, which is near Cajamarca, the Chumbivilcas, Canas and Sorasoras, who are from Paria."[9] *Aylloscas* was the name used to describe these groups. *Aylloscas* were groups of people won in a game called "ayllar." Earlier we noted that the Azángaro territory may have been transferred in this way.[10]

What kind of a province was Chupachos? Was it an estate like the estate of Huayna Capac near Yucay and the estates of Topa Inca and the Sun in the northern Lake Titicaca Basin? The testimony gathered from local curacas, that the four huarangas of Chupachos were acquired by Huascar, indicates that it was.

If so, was Chupachos the organizational equivalent of other Inca provinces? When we examine the labor assignment, which should allow us to outline the organization of the province at the time of Huascar's rule, we find indications that it had been in effect since the time of Huayna Capac. For example, some of the people assigned to Cuzco were among the "Chinchaysuyos" who worked on Huayna Capac's estate in Yucay. The guards for Huayna Capac's body were chosen from this group, and they were already in Yucay at the time of his death (Villanueva 1971a: 108; Rowe 1982: 101). Their reassignment afterward is reflected in the labor assignment. This entry appears to be out of place, suggesting that an existing labor assignment was modified. Changes in the productive organization of Chupachos because of Huascar's activity appear to have been minor. The question of whether the Chupachus had yanacona status before Huascar's rule remains.

As a group, the documents allow us to hypothesize that three different Incas had their hands in the organization of Chupachos. Each round of organization would have had some effect on settlement. When the population movement implicit in the labor assignment is gauged, the number of people moved or absent is very large. First of all, 1,110 of the 4,108 Chupachos households were in Cuzco. Another 580 resided out of the province on a full-time basis. Another 918 were out of the province on at least a temporary basis, including the 500 assigned to army service. Those who remained, except perhaps the 500 assigned to do agricultural service, were permanently relocated to specialized communities within Chupachos territory.

Grosboll surveyed sites on both sides of the Río Pilcomayo but did not include the area of mitima settlement on the left bank of the Río Huallaga below modern Huánuco. Her main use of the ethnohistorical documentation was to provide a territorial focus for the several named groups—for example, Yachas, Chupachus, and Queros—and assess whether differences in cultural materials reflected ethnic differences. She found that differences across the boundaries between groups were often not as great as some of the differences within bounded territories.

She did not orient her survey to identify the Inca productive communities that were located within territory that she surveyed. That these were camayo communities established by the Incas is not directly mentioned in the 1549 survey; it is a hypothesis that arises from a consideration of the ethnohistorical data available from Chupachos and from other parts of the territory governed from Cuzco. The 1549 survey tells us only about communities that existed in 1549. Because local lines of authority were important, it also included the information that some communities were composed of people from all over the province (such communities were under the authority of all four huaranga offi-

Plate 1. Fragments from a Cuzco bottle from Llaq'aylli on the Island of the Sun. Red, black, white, and orange painted decoration. Bandelier Collection, 1938 (left) and 2008 (the remainder), American Museum of Natural History.

Plate 2. Fragments from a Cuzco bottle from Llaq'aylli on the Island of the Sun. Red, black, white, and orange painted decoration. Bandelier Collection, 2103, American Museum of Natural History.

Plate 3. Cuzco bottle from Chullpa at Sillustani. Red, black, and white painted decoration. Sillustani Museum.

Plate 4. Imitation Tiahuanaco-style cup from Sacsahuaman, Cuzco. Red, black, white, cream and orange painted decoration. University of Cuzco Museum, 1/577, Cuzco.

cers). The inclusion of information about occupational specialization and the Inca labor assignment appears to be entirely gratuitous. From it, we can infer the continuity of features of an earlier order and hypothesize Inca provincial organization.

Part of our hypothesis is that each decimal unit of local people was equally assessed and that one or more of its members was resettled in one of these productive units (Julien 1988a: 264–265). For example, one or more villages, composed of people from all over the province, produced ceramics. Both the production of the specialized ceramic communities and the distribution pattern of these materials can be studied archaeologically. Communities of resettled people may be archaeologically distinguishable from groups of local people who have not been moved, though the identification of differences may require very fine analysis.

Within the area that Grosboll surveyed and in the area of mitima settlement below Huánuco were communities of people brought from outside of the province. If this third type of community can be archaeologically identified, the pattern of consumption at these sites can be contrasted with the pattern or patterns identified at local sites. These people were settled in separate communities, so we can easily contrast patterns found at one site with patterns found at another. Also, it may be possible to locate communities of Chupachus located just outside Chupachos territory. Did these people participate in the same consumption pattern as the people within the territory did?

The Cajamarca Region: Huamachuco

The survey conducted by the Topics in Huamachuco was guided by sixteenth-century documentation that included information on Inca infrastructure and population movement.

Huamachuco initially formed part of the corregimiento of Cajamarca. It was granted as a single encomienda. The corregimiento included Cajamarca and Huambos, north of Cajamarca, as well as Huamachuco (Miranda 1925: 210). Our initial hypothesis, then, is that Huamachuco was a province within the orbit of a major Inca center at Cajamarca. The Topics find support for this hypothesis from the mitima settlement of Azancoto in the province of Chimbo, Ecuador, where people with origins in Huambos, Cajamarca, and Huamachuco were resettled, along with mitimas from other places.

The territory of Huamachuco comprised six huarangas, four composed of local population and two composed of people with origins elsewhere. Of the last two, one was made up of mitimas from highland provinces and the other of mitimas from the lowlands (Espinoza Soriano 1974: 291). All of the huarangas were subject to a single curaca and were assessed alike in 1567: they paid their tribute in silver, chickens, and maize, although they were allowed to substitute gold, which they could mine in their territory. In a brief description of Huamachuco in 1549, the author noted that the value of the encomienda had been based on this mining activity (Loredo 1958: 250). Huamachuco was the most valuable encomienda in the entire district of Trujillo, which included not only a large section of coast but also three corregimientos of Chachapoyas. Animal wealth and "tapicería," probably cumbi production, were also noted (Loredo 1958: 250, 255–256).

A second group of mitimas, referred to as "yungas mitimaes y chaupeyungas," was mentioned in the 1567 documentation. They paid the bulk of their tribute in cotton cloth, and the amount they owed in silver was less than a third of what the other group paid (Espinoza Soriano 1974: 293). Their number can be estimated because they were required to provide the Spanish with one cotton garment per tributary household. No one else was assessed in clothing, and a total of 330 cotton garments was supplied, suggesting a population of 330 tributary households. Their assessment in cotton cloth and the connotation "chaupi yungas" indicates that these people were settled at a lower elevation in the coastal valleys and not in highland Huamachuco.

Clearly there were different categories of mitimas in Huamachuco. Those who were settled in the highlands were reduced (brought into new settlements) in 1565. The lowland mitimas appear not to have been reduced at that time. A list of places where these mitimas were settled was given. Usually the names of early reductions were a composite of a saint's name and of a native name. In 1567, the names of the towns where people from the six huarangas were reduced are composites; the saints' names were not given for the "yungas mitimaes y chaupeyungas."[11]

The structure we have outlined for Huamachuco can be compared with the organization of Cajamarca. There the population was organized in seven huarangas, including one composed of mitimas with highland origins. Some groups of people from the lowlands were separately accounted and were not part of the huaranga structure of the province (Espinoza Soriano 1967a: 33–39). One of the separately accounted groups in Cajamarca was a pachaca from Collique that produced ceramics for deposit at Cajamarca but was still subject to the curacas on the coast. Cajamarca was a center for the collection of coastal tribute, as noted above, and the activities of unattached coastal mitimas at or near this center were probably related to that function.

The question of the relationship between Cajamarca and Huamachuco is important to our consideration of Inca control in the region. The descendants of Topa Inca noted that their forebear used military force against both Cajamarca and Huamachuco, annexing these territories in the same campaign (Rowe 1985b: 209). They did not provide us with a measure of the relative difference in status between Cajamarca and Huamachuco. Sarmiento de Gamboa, who had access to Inca dynastic tradition, identifies the lord of Cajamarca as Cuysmanco Capac. The word "capac" following a proper name meant "hereditary king" (Sarmiento de Gamboa cap. 38; 1906: 79; Betanzos cap. XXVII; 1987: 132). These lords occupy an important place in Inca accounts of their expansion. The conquest of this lord and the annexation of his territory was accomplished with military force and resulted in substantial population loss, followed by large-scale resettlement with mitimas and the construction of a monumental Inca center (Cieza de León primera parte, cap. LXXVII; 1984: 225–228).

Cajamarca and Huamachuco were not equals in Inca eyes, even after annexation. Cajamarca was one of the most important Inca centers north of Cuzco. Like Huánuco Pampa, it served as the center for neighboring provinces (Cieza de León primera parte, cap. LXXVII; 1984: 225). Like Hatuncolla, Vilcas, and Cuzco, it was designated to receive coastal tribute. A local population of six huarangas was subject to it, and so an important element of its pre-Inca polity may have remained.

Cieza de León's description of Huayna Capac's trip to Ecuador, mentioned above, conveys an idea of the relative importance of Cajamarca among Inca centers. Huayna Capac left Cuzco with an army of 200,000, but beforehand his delegates and governors in the Inca centers in the provinces were instructed to have on hand all of the things that were usually collected and kept to supply military campaigns. Road stations, located every four leagues (20 kilometers) along the route, were supplied with what his army would need as well as a surplus. Huayna Capac traveled with the army, stopping a few days at Vilcas, a bit longer at Jauja (where he had a dispute to settle), again for only a few days at Bombón, but for a longer period at Cajamarca, where he left the army while he waged a military campaign against the Chupachos, mentioned above (Cieza de León, segunda parte, cap. LXIV; 1985: 186–188).

As in Soras and Lucanas, camelid husbandry was a major focus of the local economy of Huamachuco. To a similar or perhaps greater degree, some of the puna was devoted to range for wild game. Cieza de León describes an Inca hunting precinct in this province and large hunts which took great numbers of wild animals, particularly guanacos and vicuñas (Cieza de León primera parte, cap. LXXXI; 1984: 236). These preserves were economically important as these animals were sources of fiber, particularly fine vicuña fiber, and meat, which was conserved and stored for the army (Cieza de León primera parte, cap. LXXXI; 1984: 236; cap. CXI; 1984: 295; segunda parte, cap. XVI; 1985: 43–44).

The Inca center of Huamachuco had a large plaza and a number of Inca buildings (Cieza de León primera parte, cap. LXXXI; 1984: 236–237). When Cieza de León singled out structures for mention, he described two kallankas, as noted by the Topics in their review of documentary material. He supplied measurements that compare well with the measurements of similar structures at both Huánuco Pampa and the tambo of Tunsucancha. Huánuco Pampa had a much larger number of kallankas, and even at Tunsucancha there were three (Morris and Thompson 1985: 54–55, fig. 5; p. 111, fig. 19). Huamachuco was not a major Inca site.

The Topics, on the basis of archaeological evidence, arrive at the same conclusions. They identify modern Huamachuco as the site of the Inca center. Although the continued occupation of this site appears to have all but obliterated the architectural evidence, the argument they make, based on the location of an Augustinian convent and finds of ceramics, is entirely convincing.

The Topics use the number of colcas to measure the relative importance of the Inca site of Huamachuco. Quantitative comparisons are difficult, however, since perishable materials were sometimes used to construct storehouses (González Holguín 1952: 54). Also, certain types of storehouses may be associated with particular products, and therefore be a measure of expected output of that product alone. To the degree that we are measuring the capacity of storehouses that kept basic Andean foodstuffs, we may have some ability to compare Inca centers along the major roads that were designed to accommodate large groups. Given what we know from the ethnohistorical documents, the Topics' comparison of Huamachuco with Jauja and Huánuco Pampa is apt. Stone storage structures may give a relative measure of the importance of these sites.

As in other areas, Inca domination is not particularly evident in the cultural materials away from the centers, tambos, and roads that are the infrastructure of Inca control. Besides these basic categories, the Topics' survey suggests that we may expect to find materials that are more closely related to Inca styles in the communities of mitimas.

The Topics have begun the painstaking search for differences among the communities of Huamachuco related to Inca organization. In addition to communities of mitimas incorporated into the huaranga structure, we should someday be able to identify groups of people with local origins who were moved by the Incas within the province of Huamachuco to form communities of camayos. We should also be able to find the groups of mitimas located in the middle coastal valleys.

This latter feature of organization may be an Inca accommodation allowing joint use of this area. Before Inca annexation, the situation may have been quite different (Netherly 1988b: 115–117, 122). Archaeological survey and excavation undertaken in this area with the aid of a finely divided ceramic sequence would be of great interest to both archaeologists and ethnohistorians. Locating the communities of "yungas mitimaes y chaupeyungas" mentioned in the 1567 assessment would offer an excellent point of departure.

The Atacama Region: Catarpe

Lynch examines the site of Catarpe in the Inca province of Atacama.

Two corregimientos formed in the 1570s include territory that is now part of Chile. The corregimiento of Arica included the coast and a portion of the adjacent highlands from Tacna in the north to Loa and Tarapacá in the south (Miranda 1925: 172–173). The corregimiento of Atacama and Lipes lay to the south of it (Miranda 1925: 141–142). Although a corregimiento had been formed, the people had not been reduced and no tribute could be collected because the majority of the people were in revolt. Very likely only the coast was under Spanish control.

Other methods, then, must be used to reconstruct the southern border of Atacama and Lipes and the Inca organization of territory to the south. The account of Jerónimo de Vivar, who traveled to Chile with Pedro de Valdivia in the early 1540s, contains useful information for our purposes. He does not describe local construction except for several fortresses and an occasional reference to the local house type. However, his descriptions of the populated valleys are fairly systematic; he either notes that the inhabitants practiced rituals learned from the Incas or that they practiced the rituals but had no temple. He therefore indicates indirectly that there was Inca construction in the former case. Using Vivar's account to reconstruct territory, we would place the southern limit of Atacama and Lipes at Chañar, where the Incas had a small settlement of people from Cuzco. There were Inca centers at Copiapó, which he notes was conquered by Huayna Capac, and at Coquimbo (Vivar cap. XI; 1988: 71–72; cap. XV; 1988: 80; cap. XVI; 1988: 83–84; cap. XIX; 1988: 87–88; cap. XXII; 1988: 91–92).

The most important Inca center appears to have been at Aconcagua, however. Diego de Almagro spent seven months in the Aconcagua Valley in 1536 where, according to Vivar, he made friends with the Inca governor and so earned the enmity of Michimalongo, a local curaca. In 1541, when Valdivia arrived in the area, he met Quilicanta, the Inca governor, in the Mapoche Valley just beyond Aconcagua. Quilicanta had had to leave Aconcagua, taking the people loyal to him to Mapoche (Vivar cap. XXV; 1988: 99; XXVII; 1988: 102). The Inca center, then, had been at Aconcagua. Vivar puts the southern boundary of Inca territory at a place called the Angostura, 7 leagues (35 kilometers) south of modern Santiago. He notes that this place was the northern boundary of a people known as the Pormocaes or Picones, whose territory extended south to the Maule River (Vivar cap. XCIII; 1988: 240–241).

Sources that draw on Inca dynastic tradition also describe the Inca annexation of this area. Topa Inca, after subduing the Colla revolt that occurred after his father's death, went further south with his army and annexed Charcas. From Charcas he went to Chile, where he defeated the lords Michimalongo and Tangalongo and annexed their territory (Sarmiento de Gamboa cap. 50; 1906: 97). At the Maule River, Topa Inca was said to have erected some type of monument to mark the southern limits of Inca territory (Sarmiento de Gamboa cap. 50; 1906: 97). Then he returned to Cuzco. His son, Huayna Capac, returned to

Chile, also traveling into the region from Charcas. He removed the Inca governor that his father had installed and left the province in the hands of the two lords his father had defeated. He then returned to the highlands by way of Coquimbo, Copiapó, Atacama, and Arequipa (Sarmiento de Gamboa cap. 59; 1906: 105).

Topa Inca's descendants also focused on the province centered at Aconcagua. After the Colla revolt was put down, Topa Inca went to Charcas, Chichas, Yamparaes, Chiriguanos, and Tucuman. Then he traveled down to the coast to the province of Chile, the name the Spanish used to describe the Aconcagua and Mapoche area (Vivar cap. XXV; 1988: 100; cap. XXVII; 1988: 101). He headed north and returned to the highlands by way of Tarapacá. The people he saw in this area were poor, and so he did not campaign in the area (Rowe 1985b: 215). The testimony of his descendants, like the account collected by Sarmiento, indicates that the Aconcagua area was organized, and perhaps reorganized, before the annexation of Atacama.

Sarmiento's account describes Michimalongo and Tangalongo as the local lords of Aconcagua in the time of Topa Inca and Huayna Capac. When Vivar was in Aconcagua in 1540, Michimalongo was curaca of the upper part of the valley and Tangalongo was curaca of the lower part. This arrangement may reflect Inca organization of the valley. The use of the same names by Sarmiento's informants for people living three generations earlier may be an example of the telescoping of time that can happen in oral tradition (Vansina 1985: 130–133). If the names reflect the Inca structure of the province, they may tell us little about the political organization of the valley before Inca annexation.

Sarmiento's account also lists the places Huayna Capac passed through on the way north: Coquimbo, Copiapó, Atacama, and Arequipa. The first three names on this list are places where we would hypothesize from the account of Vivar that Inca centers were located. Arequipa was certainly an Inca center. Sarmiento's informants were Incas, and they would have described the territory from the point of view of Cuzco. We could hypothesize, then, that the Inca centers on the coast south of Arequipa were Arica, Atacama, Coquimbo, Copiapó, and Aconcagua. Vivar's account would support a similar list.

Missing is any description of the Inca annexation of the province of Arica or, for that matter, any of the coastal area south of Oçoña in what is now Peru. These arid coastal valleys were not densely populated in the late sixteenth century. Population was concentrated in the upper coastal valleys, between 1,500 and about 3,400 meters. The valleys adjacent to the Lake Titicaca region may have been controlled from the lake region before Inca annexation, perhaps by a single lord. Under the Incas, the Lake Titicaca provinces maintained special productive enclaves in the upper valleys of this part of the coast (Julien 1985: 202–207, 216–220).

Because of the lack of Spanish control, we do not have early census data for the population in the provinces south of Arica. The coastal valleys south of Tarapacá to Copiapó, that is, the desert coastal portion of the Atacama province, were even drier than those to the north. The pattern of concentration of population at higher elevations may well characterize the Atacama province. The first corregimiento defined in the area, although it had a short duration, included Lipes. By the early seventeenth century, Lipes and Atacama were separated into two corregimientos. Some kind of census had been taken while the two were joined, as 902 tributaries were reported, but tribute had still not been assessed. Our best hypothesis, then, is that the Inca province of Atacama included the highland territory of Lipes. The people of Atacama clearly had ties to the adjacent highlands during the Spanish colonial era that suggest a long-term pattern (Hidalgo 1985: 163, 166–167).

Lynch's study focuses on a portion of the Inca road from Catarpe south to Río Frío, within the Atacama province. He identifies Catarpe as more than a tambo, noting its resemblance to Inca centers at Paria and Tambo Colorado. The comparison is apt and suggests that the main Inca installations were located in this area and not in the adjacent highlands. Lynch's study is part of a body of recent studies that expand our information about road systems through the Atacama Desert and further south, including the transverse route across the Andes east of Aconcagua (Stehberg and Carvajal 1988a) that would have been used by the two Incas who campaigned in the area according to Inca dynastic tradition.

The network of roads, particularly in the desert of northern Chile, is an obvious focus for archaeological activity and a necessary first step. The resettlement of people to comply with the provincial labor assignment, Inca restructuring of ceramic production, and the introduction of mitima communities await future study. This task will be a challenge, since the Spanish central authority lost control of most of Atacama and Lipes and the province or provinces to the south during a period in the 1560s and 1570s that was critical for the generation of documentation that facilitates the reconstruction of pre-Spanish territorial organization.

The Cuzco Region: Inca Estates

Niles examined architectural styles on Inca estates in the Cuzco area, located in the Cuzco and Urubamba valleys (fig. 6.1).

Defining provinces in Cuzco itself is not a simple matter. The corregimiento of Cuzco was an urban province, established more than a decade before corregimientos in rural areas. Native residents and Spaniards were organized in parishes. It focused on the urban area and did not extend much beyond the Cuzco Valley. Was Inca Cuzco just the city and the immediate vicinity, or did it have a larger territory subject to it in the same way as, for example, Vilcas?

The latter option is indicated. Juan de Betanzos, who drew on sources from Pachacuti's *panaca* (a group formed by individuals related through the male line) describes how this Inca organized the area around the capital. Oral tradition can collapse events which took place over a long period into a single flurry of activity or perhaps reorder sequences entirely (Vansina 1985: 130–133, 176–178), but the description of how Cuzco was organized may approximate reality. In the following summary of Betanzos's account of the activities of the Inca ruler, our concern is with the image of Cuzco that he generates, not with the focus on a particular individual.

Betanzos describes a major building campaign undertaken by Pachacuti in the Cuzco Valley. He rebuilt the city itself, including a major remodeling of the Qorikancha, and developed several canal projects in the valley (Betanzos cap. XI; 1987: 49–53; cap. XII; 1987: 55–56).

During this time Pachacuti ordered the lords from the provinces around Cuzco who had sworn obedience to him to come to Cuzco. He had devised a system to provision the capital and to permit the people in the territory around it to be gone on long campaigns without losing their means of supporting themselves at home. The plan involved distribution of land, marking permanent boundaries, and construction of storage deposits. It also involved the provisioning of foodstuffs to Cuzco. Initially these provisions were to support the people working on building projects in the valley. Soon after, Pachacuti organized the production of tribute clothing, including cloths for carrying loads of earth and stone so that the people working on the building projects would not have to use their own (Betanzos cap. XII; 1987: 55–58; cap. XIII; 1987: 59–63).

Part of Pachacuti's plan was to marry the lords to women of his own descent group. Their descendants, who were to inherit the lord's authority, would thus be tied by affinal bonds to the Inca dynasty (Betanzos cap. XII; 1987: 57). He also sent his representatives to the territories of the lords and married the young men of one group to the young women of another, cementing bonds between groups. The people who were married received gifts of clothing and the household items they would need (Betanzos cap. XIII; 1987: 63).

The result of this activity was a hinterland of discrete groups, tied to Cuzco and to each other, who would supply the basic needs of the urban population. Every four months, the people dependent on Cuzco received what they needed from the tribute that was supplied from this hinterland (Betanzos cap. XIII; 1987: 63).

What Betanzos does not tell us is who these lords were, except that they had sworn obedience to Pachacuti. We know that Inca status was extended to a number of groups who resided in the territory around Cuzco. They were referred to as orejones, since they were initiated into Inca status and wore ear spools, but they were not members of the Inca dynasty—that is, they were not necessarily related through the male line to the Inca lineage that traced descent from Manco Capac (Guaman Poma 1936: 84, 117–118, 337, 740). They have been called "Incas by privilege."

These groups were widely distributed in the territory included in the colonial corregimientos of Abancay, Yucay, Andes, Quispicanche, and Chilques (Miranda 1925: 158–159, 160–162, 166–168). As a hypothesis, then, I will suggest that the support territory we have identified from the narrative of Betanzos coincided spatially with the distribution of these groups of orejones and that the unit comprising these five corregimientos gives us a rough approximation of the territory of the province of Cuzco.

The royal estates surveyed by Niles occupy only a certain area within this larger territory. They are found in and above the Cuzco Valley, the Urubamba Valley, and the highlands between Cuzco and modern Urubamba. The creation of Inca estates in Urubamba may relate to the circumstances under which this area was annexed. Sarmiento, who created a joint account of Inca history by interviewing members of the eleven panacas, descended from Inca kings, described the conquest of the Urubamba Valley from near Pisac to below Ollantaytambo. It was undertaken by Pachacuti in retribution for an attempt on his life. This campaign resulted in substantial population loss in the valley, particularly in the area near Pisac (Sarmiento de Gamboa cap. 34; 1906: 71–72; cap. 35; 1906: 72–73). The Urubamba Valley had a number of Inca estates, and it may have been the most coveted location for these properties. The step that established particular Inca claims to this territory appears to have been Pachacuti's campaign, which largely cleared the valley of local population. We do not know how the Incas established similar claims in the Chincheros and Lucre areas, for example, or how later Incas obtained estates near Cuzco. The dynastic sources consulted by Sarmiento describe no further armed conflict in the province of Cuzco after the local campaigning in the first years of Pachacuti's rule.

Except for the concentration of Inca estates in certain areas, Cuzco appears to have been surrounded by elements of local population that had resided in the area before the Inca expansion. There was no wholesale depopulation and resettlement as there was in the case of territories where other major Inca centers, like Vilcas, were established. Even so, I would argue that the analogy between Cuzco and the major Inca centers was a strong one. Guaman Poma includes a series of ordinances that he attributes to Topa Inca: "Let there be other Cuzcos in Quito and another in Tumi[pampa] and another in Huánuco [Pampa] and another in Hatuncolla and another in Charcas, and the head of all of them would be Cuzco" (Guaman Poma 1936: 185).

While there was no immediate depopulation, Inca resettlement policies may have tended to create a negative balance in the population of rural Cuzco, since orejones were often used in the resettlement program (Cobo libro 12, cap. XXIII; 1894–95: 222). Groups of orejones also figured prominently in military campaigns, probably out of proportion to their number relative to the population of the empire as a whole.

Inca estates functioned within the larger territory that provided support for Cuzco. The nature of these holdings differed fundamentally from other types of holdings. Estates were attached to a particular individual. They included women, retainers, land, animals, and personal goods. They are basically similar to the holdings of important supernaturals, both in Cuzco and in the provinces. Spanish administrators repeatedly asked about the property of the huacas, and although they often got nowhere with their questions, we know that such estates existed (Albornoz 1989: 169–171).

Was the relationship between individuals, whether members of the Inca dynasty or supernaturals, and the resources that supported them similar to the relationship between province and capital, that is, between the support territory around Cuzco or other major Inca center to the center itself? Were the claims to the land and its resources the same, or did they have a fundamentally different basis? Niles poses an analogy which begs this question. An answer, however, is tangled in our reconstruction of the nature of property under the Incas, an issue which has occupied ethnohistorians for the better part of this century (Trimborn 1923–25; Rostworowski de Diez Canseco 1962; Pease 1986). The nature of property is tied to other domains since, as I have already indicated, supernaturals had claims similar to those of living beings.

These individuals had claims of some sort, but can they be equated to private ownership of the land and its resources? Titles were established under a Spanish juridical structure through reference to claims that existed under an Inca tenure system. It is worth noting, however, that these estate holdings did not pass neatly from one system of tenure to the other. Inca wealth was generated by retainers, and the retainer populations on estates were uniformly granted as encomiendas by Francisco Pizarro. Encomiendas appear to have been given exclusively to Spaniards under Pizarro, and only later, under the viceroys, to members of the Inca dynasty and other native lords. If anything, Inca estates were initially lost by their holders. Claims in the Cuzco area were partially reconsolidated through the joint accumulation of encomienda and land titles. Claims to holdings outside the Cuzco area, with one possible exception, were never reestablished.[12]

Inca estates were not confined to the Cuzco area. In the case of estates attached to particular Incas, we have already cited a reference to palaces held by Topa Inca in Huánuco Pampa. This ethnohistorical reference can be tested against the stylistic sequence for Inca architecture that is emerging from the work of scholars like Niles (1987). The architectural sequence may also be amenable to correlation with studies of ceramic style during the time of Inca rule, since we are beginning to identify stylistic attributes with the holdings of particular Incas and to order stylistic events in time.

Niles makes stylistic sense of the most impressive architectural works authorized by particular Incas. She also notes the heterogeneity of Inca construction and the mixture of fine styles of construction with rustic ones. Some classes of Inca architecture appear to be analyzable in terms of ideal or standardized forms, like the kancha or kallanka. Even the ideal forms are not immutable, and the structures which suggest them coexist with a heterogeneous corpus of architectural forms spanning a considerable range of status differences.

WORKING WITHIN A GLOBAL FRAMEWORK

Although we have every reason to seek a global view of the Andean territory articulated by the Incas, reconstructing this picture is an immense undertaking. Here I have suggested that one means of linking the disparate bodies of data generated by archaeologists and ethnohistorians is through an explicit geographical approach. The regions included in this review were chosen because archaeological research had been related in some way to the body of ethnohistorical sources. The sample is admittedly arbitrary. However, we could not, even if pressed to do so, define what is representative. An obvious omission is the Peruvian coast. A recent study of this region that approximates a global view can be consulted, though its purpose was not to reconstruct territorial limits (Netherly 1988a). Also, I am concerned only with the definition of territories formally organized by the Incas, and not with the external limits of the space controlled by Cuzco (but see Dillehay and Netherly 1988).

All six of the archaeological investigators framed their studies within "provinces" or referred to Inca "boundaries." These are the terms that appear in historical narratives in the sixteenth and seventeenth centuries, but the narratives are written in the Spanish language, and ethnohistorians no longer assume that the spatial terms used in Spanish documents in any way reflect native ideas about the organization of space. There is a basic question, however, that we should not ignore: did the Incas have some notion of bounded territory?

Even without understanding the foreign system of thought which underlay Inca territoriality, we can detect that the Incas did have a notion of bounded space and defined provinces with reference to specific limits. Both Guaman Poma de Ayala and Polo de Ondegardo describe the physical marking of territory with boundary markers (Polo de Ondegardo 1872: 22–23, 42–43, 54–55; Guaman Poma 1936: 852; Julien 1991: 112–113). But what kind of boundaries were they marking? This question is difficult to answer; we must look to sources that are less likely to reflect the point of view of Europeans.

The two administrative surveys (1549 and 1562) of Chupachos territory allow us to examine this question in terms of the physical location of Chupachos communities. Not only Chupachos, but each of the four huarangas that composed it, appears to have made up a territorial unit of some kind. The physical location of people subject to the Chupachos curacas is not at issue. Fully three-quarters of the population had been moved, some beyond the limits of Chupachos territory. In 1549, decades before Spanish involvement with delimiting rural provinces, people could be described as residing "outside of Chupachos" in nearby Yaros or in the adjacent lowlands at coca plantations.

Limits between provinces can be reconstructed, as I have shown in the case of the Lake Titicaca region. By casting the descriptions of Inca centers in the Lake Titicaca region against the reconstruction of Inca territory in the same area, differences between provinces begin to emerge. The provinces served a variety of purposes, but they can be divided into two general classes: either they were based largely on an original population or they were composed of settlers following the destruction or removal of all or most of the original population. These composite provinces were often merged with a neighboring province when rural corregimientos were formed or, less often, became the core of a corregimiento themselves. The special purpose of the composite provinces was no longer important. For example, the inhabitants of the Copacabana peninsula, resettled there by the Incas from all over the Andes to maintain an important shrine, were assigned by the Spanish administration to the Potosí mita in the same numbers as their neighbors and had a similar assessment in dried fish.

Because the differences were no longer important, the written record only occasionally supplies us with the kind of information we need about the nature of these provinces. For example, in recent years documentation has been located that allows us to identify Cochabamba as a composite province, created by the Incas to cultivate maize on an industrial scale. The settlement of mitimas in Arequipa may have fulfilled the same purpose, at least in part, but we have not located nor can we necessarily expect to find parallel information about Arequipa.

To deal with the uneven generation and preservation of the written record, we need innovative ethnohistorical methods that derive images of the past from superficially unpromising sources. A case in point is an onomastic analysis which found that Inca Quito lacked the articulation with a local population that characterized neighboring highland provinces (Salomon 1988: 68–69).

While I have created a contrast between centers which drew on a local population and centers which did not, I do not wish to subscribe to a rigid classification along these lines. A center could have a number of purposes. For example, Hatuncolla was a repository for coastal tribute along with Cajamarca, Vilcashuamán, and Cuzco (Cieza de León primera parte, cap. LXXV; 1984: 223: Julien 1983: 79). Both Cajamarca and Hatuncolla appear to have been the centers of Inca provinces based on substantial local populations, while Vilcashuamán was not. Cuzco was an exception, but may have been organizationally more analogous to Vilcashuaman than to the other two centers listed.

I have also used the term "major" to refer to an Inca center that was the focus of more than one province. Centers like Huánuco Pampa, Cajamarca, Vilcashuamán, Hatuncolla, Ayaviri, and Paria qualify for reasons having to do with tribute collection or military assembly. We can begin to detect a hierarchy among Inca centers. Until we learn more about the nature of the provinces around these centers and other features of Inca infrastructure, however, charting the organizational hierarchy of Inca centers or provinces is premature. There may well have been measurable status differences among the places that I have qualified as "major" Inca centers in this review.

We can already detect that provinces were multifunctional. Some may have had special or unique functions. As noted above, Cieza de León wrote that Huánuco Pampa was head of neighboring provinces that bordered the montaña. The archaeology done at Huánuco Pampa has helped us to shed assumptions about the general character and spatial requirements of major Inca centers, but we have not yet developed archaeological methods for testing and expanding the very sketchy picture of regional and macro-regional articulation evident from the ethnohistorical documentation (Morris 1982, 1988b).

When we think of Huánuco Pampa, located at more than 3,900 meters of elevation, we do not readily imagine the economic integration of this puna site with the warm, humid lowlands to the east. But Huánuco Pampa was ideally situated for storage purposes. Coca, for example, was transported away from the lowlands as soon as possible after harvesting. If it was not dried immediately or if it became damp, it turned brown and lost value. In the cold, dry highland environment, it kept for a considerable period, though it was no longer considered fresh after a year (Matienzo cap. XLV; 1967: 167–168).

When we read the report of the 1549 Chupachos survey, we can see the involvement of Chupachos people in collecting or growing a number of lowland products that were destined for movement away from their sources and not for local redistribution. Coca was sent to Huánuco Pampa and Cuzco. Maize and ají grown within Chupachos territory and shoe soles and wood were transported to Cuzco. Ceramics traveled to Huánuco Pampa (Helmer 1955–56: 40–41). While we would like to know what became of the goods that were generated in the provinces, the Chupachos example may prove to be unrepresentative, since the movement of products away from Chupachos territory may be related to its estate status.

In other cases, the product may have been redistributed locally on a much larger scale. But to the degree that groups who were settled in the montaña served important individuals or supernaturals, we could hypothesize that centers like Huánuco Pampa, Tunsucancha, and Bombón warehoused or processed, if only on a temporary basis, the portion of the lowland harvest destined for distribution elsewhere. Were these products held in stone storehouses away from the central precinct of the Inca center or were there other types of storage facilities for coca, feathers, honey, wood, etc.?

The parts which composed the Inca empire were not uniformly alike, despite Inca organization of the population into units of standard size (Julien 1988a). Most of the studies included in the present volume deal with territories, like Huamachuco or Andamarca Lucanas, that were beyond the immediate orbit of a major Inca center. Evidence of Inca control was found, but on the whole the studies dealt with the material remains of local people, not that of Incas or substantial groups of foreigners. No monumental construction that was clearly authorized by the Incas was identified. Away from major Inca centers and roads, and away from territories that were developed as estates or sanctuaries, the visible symbols of Inca control were scarce.

The physical remains in these areas do not live up to our expectations, which for a long time have included the introduction of a governing class of officials and garrisons (Menzel and Rowe 1966: 66).

These expectations generate archaeological correlates: the officials should live in some type of center; a special class of materials of an intrinsically foreign nature should be associated with them; and a type of architecture that suggests their administrative role should be present. The studies in this volume reflect a certain tacit change in long-held assumptions about the structure of Inca central authority (Morris 1982: 162). We have been looking for the remains of an interposed bureaucracy, but the relationship between a subject population and Cuzco appears to have been mediated largely through a chain of local political authority.

In many provinces, we can expect that the physical remains of construction authorized by Cuzco would be engineering projects such as roads, bridges, and terraces. The remains of tambos and temples associated with Inca-sponsored cults may be the only architecture even tacitly authorized by Cuzco in such provinces. The stylistic influence of Cuzco is apparent in structures that have been interpreted as the residences of particular individuals with strong ties to Cuzco or shrines, but in these cases the construction may have resulted from local initiative and not from a Cuzco mandate.

A related assumption, that Inca control can be measured by the degree of influence of Inca styles on local material traditions, is also untenable. The evidence from Chupachos is a case in point. Despite the absence of strong Cuzco influence on local materials, the ethnohistorical evidence for organization by the Incas is ample. A wholesale movement of the population occurred. Many people were relocated within the limits of Chupachos territory to facilitate production orchestrated by the Incas, and the movement may well have altered many aspects of local economy unrelated to the operational needs of the Inca state.

However, the restructuring of this population was not mirrored by an increase in the penetration of imperial symbols. As a counterbalance to studies of provinces like Huamachuco and Andamarca Lucanas, I presented a case from the Lake Titicaca region to show that, at least in some areas away from Cuzco and away from major Inca centers, the influence of Cuzco symbols was strong. However, these territories were not ordinary provinces; they were rather estates or sanctuaries. Grosboll may be dealing with an estate in Chupachos, but she did not find similar evidence of the penetration of Inca influence. If the Chupachos province only became an estate on the eve of the European invasion, then perhaps there was little time for this special status to receive material expression. Some other factor, however, may be responsible for the difference.

The appearance of Cuzco symbols in the provinces may be associated with wholly different phenomena than our crude methods have been able to detect. Our preoccupation with identifying Cuzco influence on the basis of the presence of imperial symbols could be misleading. Though we have only begun to unravel the complex interrelation between Inca styles and local material traditions, we can already see that we must go beyond the assessment of the penetration of Inca styles if we want to understand Inca control.

Of course, studies of ceramic style provide the type of finely divided chronology that will permit us to describe changes in settlement patterns through the period of Inca rule. Thus far, the presence of Cuzco-Inca features has been the most important, if not the only, method of identifying an occupation contemporary with Cuzco control. Several of the present studies went beyond this elementary mode of analysis to use ceramic sequences developed locally which document changes in the local ceramic tradition that may or may not have been stimulated by contact with the Cuzco-Inca style. The local sequences that have been developed are very rudimentary, however, and nowhere has a definition of any of these style units been given.

The definition of style—that is, a sensitive study of the inventory of shapes contemporary with each other and the decoration appropriate to them—is essential to the study of changes in settlement as well as to archaeological identification of the communities created by the Incas. Not just the communities of people brought from a long distance who, by our currently rough measures, appear to have left their own ceramic tradition at home but also the communities of local people resettled by the Incas may be identified through differences in the mix of ceramics. Since, according to our ethnohistorical sources, people were resettled in communities and not mixed with local residents, we should take the time necessary to explore the intricacies of style for information about social identity.

Just what we will learn depends on what there is to be found. For example, before the ceramic styles of Chincha and Ica were defined on the basis of shapes and appropriate decoration, the two styles were confused because of what happen to be superficial resemblances (Menzel 1966: 63). Careful attention to ceramic style revealed differences in the responses of Ica and Chincha to Inca annexation. Moreover, the definition of style permitted the identification of more than one provincial style in each valley. Inca control resulted in the creation of divisions within the local population that were manifest in the ceramics.

Menzel's studies were based on grave lots which provided contextual information that was important in both the analysis of style and the identification of social units (Menzel 1976: 221). A chronology was developed through defining stylistic units with reference to a single "master grave lot" (Menzel 1976: 6). A finely divided chronology for the period of Inca expansion was achieved for several south coastal valleys. By refining local chronologies, we gain the tools we need for studying Inca expansion as a process.

This same type of study can be done with excavated refuse or with surface remains of a short-term occupation. The refuse associated with a living group reflects a selection of material from a larger range, though the selection of material for daily use may be quite different from what the living group might have selected for the burial of any of its individual members. Still, materials from the same layer of a refuse deposit that is associated with a living group can be used in a manner analogous to the use of burials to define stylistic subunits. The association pattern is also symbolic in a general way of the identity of the living group. The communities of people moved from a long distance, camayo communities brought together "from all over the province," and those who remained in a community of long standing should be differentiable through careful comparison of the consumption patterns found at different sites.

If we consider our reconstruction of Inca provincial organization, the situation is even more complex. We may document patterns of consumption at sites, but to the degree that specialists produced ceramics, the range of materials available was limited. Even the people who continued to live in communities of long standing may have consumed a different selection of ceramics after the Inca organization of ceramic production, and their consumption pattern may have been very similar to the pattern of recently created communities. Differences between communities of local people and mitima settlers may be more in evidence, based on the Topics' survey in Huamachuco and my own in one of the Colla provinces (Julien 1988b: 52).

A pivotal concern is the archaeological identification of ceramic producers. Only when these communities are identified will we be able to interpret the consumption patterns that we find. The documentation

and archaeological survey reports already available to us raise important questions for future research. For instance, were the potters of
Hupi near Huancané producing the kaolin paste Taraco material or was
there a production center elsewhere—for example, in Chiquicache?
We know that Huancané was an Inca center of some importance, but
we have no idea yet of what role it played. If we develop a strategy to
identify production and distribution of ceramics in this area, we will
be doing work that is fundamental to a study of Inca Huancané.

The variation in Taraco materials indicates a degree of complexity
that will require a sophisticated approach. If the kaolin paste Taraco
material with orange band decoration occurs in refuse, at which sites
is it found? Is there a different distribution for the Taraco variant executed in a paste that fires to a cream color? Perhaps the variation is
household-specific rather than site-specific. How do the distributions
of Taraco variants compare to the boundaries we have reconstructed in
this area?

A study of production centers could also be profitably pursued in
Chupachos, since we know the names of three places where ceramics
were being produced, two of them composed of people "from all over
the province." The Chupachos communities may be structurally equivalent to Hupi, if the Incas everywhere created camayo communities to
produce pottery (Julien 1988a). However, even if the production of
ceramics was similarly organized, we may find that patterns of distribution and consumption were altogether different. Such differences
will have a marked effect on the archaeological record.

Through careful comparison of sites like Hupi and the Chupachos
communities, as well as through establishing the linkage between
sources of ceramics and the places where they were consumed, we can
begin to explore more general questions, such as, for example, Inca
involvement in local economy. It is too soon to conclude that Inca-
organized production benefited only the state (D'Altroy and Earle
1985: 189).

Perhaps the most important reason to reconstruct a native territorial
framework is that it allows us to identify, and hence to compare, equivalents. If we were working only with the archaeological record, the
equivalents would be far more difficult to identify. We might think to
compare Pikillacta and Huari, for example, as sites of Huari activity,
but we would not have a ready means for equating less monumental
sites across a broad expanse of territory.

In the Inca case, the equivalents can be entire provinces. For example, we might compare the Inca administration of Lucanas and Soras with that of Huamachuco. In both provinces, substantial areas were devoted to camelid pasture and range for wild game. We might contrast these provinces to Chupachos, where agricultural production played a more important role than camelid husbandry did and resources from the tropical forest were nearby. The lowland portion of Chupachos territory was occupied by a substantial number of people resettled from outside the province. Fully three-quarters of the people of Chupachos had been moved. Did the Incas alter the economy of the puna to the same degree as they did that of the lowlands adjacent to the tropical forest? Would they have had reason to create regions of mitima settlement, like the one we can identify within the boundaries of Chupachos territory, in the puna?

. The Incas orchestrated the articulation of disparate parts (Morris 1988b: 132). Cuzco itself was the center of a province. By working with the territorial framework they authored, we may yet reconstruct this articulation.

ACKNOWLEDGMENTS

This essay was drafted in 1990 while I was a Humboldt Fellow at the University of Bonn. I gratefully acknowledge the time I was able to devote to complex undertakings like the present one. Editorial comments from Patricia J. Lyon aided in the revision of the manuscript. I especially thank Michael Malpass for his constant effort to see this project through to completion. While at times he seemed to have been cast as Sisyphus, he turned in a Herculean performance and deserves his laurels.

NOTES

1. Chiquicache (also referred to as Chuquicache) was originally granted in encomienda to Diego Almagro, Francisco Pizarro's partner in the overthrow of the Inca empire (Loredo 1942: 122, 130). Chiquicache was first mentioned in 1543 in the *ordenanzas de tambos* (list of tambos) of Vaca de Castro because two tambos (named Pupuja and Chiquicache) were

located along the Umasuyo road which passed through this territory (Vaca de Castro 1908: 432–433). In order to come up with an approximate map of this province, encomienda tenure has been traced backwards from the 1570s, the time when native peoples were reduced into Spanish-style towns. Early references do not always give the names of encomiendas, and often tenure has to be traced through the holder. The following are the encomiendas that could be traced:

Taraco (Loredo 1942: 122, 130; Maúrtua 1906: 76; AGI 1549: f. 26, 1550: f. 30)

Achaya (Maúrtua 1906: 76; Miranda 1925: 154; AGI 1549: f. 29v)

Saman y Pusi (Maúrtua 1906: 76; Miranda 1925: 154)

Camanica (Maúrtua 1906: 76; Miranda 1925: 154)

Caquizana (Maúrtua 1906: 76; Miranda 1925: 154; AGI 1549: f. 27v, 1550: f. 15)

Arapa (Maúrtua 1906: 76; Miranda 1925: 154; AGI 1549: f. 27v, 1550: f. 15)

Checa [mitimas from Canas province]

2. This tentative statement is based on the manner in which encomiendas were granted in this area. Many of the grants awarded were mixed—that is, they included people from the immediate Cuzco area with the grant to a group from the Colla province of Urcosuyo (district of Cuzco). Examples are Lampa/Quispicanches (Hampe Martínez 1979: 88), Urcos/Juliaca (Vaca de Castro 1908: 430 [substitute Bachicao for Machicao], 436), Arapa/Tambochilques and Mascas (Hampe Martínez 1979: 89), Caracoto/Yanahuaras (Hampe Martínez 1979: 90), and Accha/Cabanilla (Hampe Martínez 1979: 89). This type of award is similar to the Papres/Achambi/Carabaya award (Hampe Martínez 1979: 89), which included part of the former estate of Topa Inca (Julien 1991: 91, 121).

3. Tiahuanaco is part of the Pacajes province of Umasuyo in the capitanía listing but is listed as an encomienda in Umasuyo in another source (Julien 1978: n. 23 pp. 229–230).

4. Fine Cuzco masonry can still be observed in the modern town of Ayaviri, which very likely occupies the location of the Inca site. Hyslop has identified the site of Anocariri as Inca Paria (Hyslop 1984: 143–145). This site is considerably less monumental than one would expect, given the descriptions of Inca construction found in Cieza de León.

5. An early colonial style, termed Kuychipuncu by John Rowe (personal communication), recombines the color orange and the cat-spot motif in new design compositions.

6. Eisleb and Strelow (1980: figs. 24, 24b, 25a, 26, 28a, 29, 30, 52). There are some cups with Tiahuanaco provenience that have the elaborate polychrome panel in the upper position, but only one light-colored band at

the midsection (Eisleb and Strelow 1980: figs. 56, 57). There are also three cups from Tiahuanaco that are like the Copacabana cups (Eisleb and Strelow 1980: figs. 70, 72, 73). If Tiahuanaco was a capital of some kind, like Cuzco, we may have the same problem trying to isolate the style of the capital from variants of it.

7. Helmer (1955–56: 33). This community also included people from the encomienda of Hernando Alonso Malpartida, who had a grant to people who were probably part of the province surrounding Huánuco Pampa. The reconstruction of territory is a complex problem in this area. These people may have been the group identified as Guanca, who were awarded with the Chupachos when the first awards were made, but who may have been some kind of separate entity (Loredo 1958: 229–230.) A community called Guanca was nearby, and they were subject to curacas named Condor and Marca Chare, who may or may not have been under Chupachu authority (Helmer 1955–56: 32–33).

8. Helmer (1955–56:35–56). Chinchao was in the territory of the encomienda of "yanayungas" of Hernando Alonso Malpartida (see n. 7).

9. Murúa (libro 1, cap. 46, tomo I; 1962–64: 132): "y saco juntamente con vna vissita ynfinita cantidad de yndios para su seruicio llamados. aylloscas que fueron los yanyos caxas. y huambos que es junto a caxamarca-los chumpiuilcas-canas-y çoraçoras que son los de Paria."

10. "Aylloscas" appears to denote how an estate was obtained. In this case, it was obtained through a game of chance. Another province transferred in this way was Parinacocha, which was won from the Sun by Topa Inca (Albornoz 1989: 175, 182). People who became part of an Inca estate because their province had fought an Inca and lost may have been called yanayacos (Sarmiento de Gamboa cap. 51; 1906: 98–99). The Azángaro territory may have been annexed initially by this mechanism.

11. Espinoza Soriano (1974: 293). These people may have been tacked on after the original grant was defined. Later awards may sometimes be a better reflection of earlier territories because the Spanish administration had learned more about who was included in earlier political units.

12. The exception is the encomienda of Pucara y Quipa, which formed part of the encomienda award used by the Marqués de Cañete to lure Sayri Topa out of Vilcabamba (ADC: f. 23). This encomienda was only part of the estate of Topa Inca's lineage in the northern Lake Titicaca Basin (fig. 7.2) (Rostworowski de Diez Canseco 1969–70: 83; Julien 1991: 91, 121).

8

MICHAEL A. MALPASS

VARIABILITY IN THE INCA STATE:

EMBRACING A WIDER PERSPECTIVE

In this book we have identified methods for studying the relationship
between the Incas and the people that they subjugated through the two
principal means at our disposal, ethnohistorical documents and archaeological investigations. These two sources generate distinctive images of the Inca empire, yet the information from one can often be used
to clarify the image from the other. In addition, each source provides
information not available in the other; thus an elaboration of our
knowledge can often be achieved by using the two sources together.
As Julien notes, the ultimate goal of future research is to merge the two
images into one.

Regarding the analytical focus of the volume, the essays demonstrate
the utility of a combined ethnohistorical and archaeological approach
to understanding the Inca empire. Where the emphasis is placed depends on the availability and quality of both documents and archaeological research. In areas like northern Chile, where documentation is
not as abundant as in the central Andes, archaeological data provide
the bulk of our information. Here we find that even lists of tambos are
in need of elaboration. This situation is probably a result of the fact
that native informants were more familiar with the central Andes and
consequently had less information about peripheral areas. In addition,
as Julien points out, the unsettled early colonial history of this region
has left a dearth of administrative documentation, hindering our un-

derstanding of the pre-colonial cultural configuration. Given the relative scarcity of both human and natural resources in this province, it is not surprising that the historical documentation is scanty. Therefore, archaeology will have to fill out the details of the Inca impact in such areas.

Standing in contrast to northern Chile is the province of Chupachos, where a wealth of historical documents can be exploited for their information on the Inca occupation. Some of these documents were specifically addressed to how things were done "at the time of the Inca," and the information was actually provided from Inca quipus still in the possession of local leaders (Murra 1982). Yet there can still be sources of confusion in these documents. As Pease (1982: 180) notes, some of the patterns presented may be pre-Inca, while others were imposed by the Incas. Here, archaeology can help clarify the situation by identifying the pre-Inca patterns, as indicated by Grosboll's results.

The articles by Schreiber and the Topics both exemplify how the ethnohistorical and archaeological records are complementary sources of information. Schreiber's identification of agricultural terracing and storehouses indicates that this region provided much more to the Inca empire than the litter bearers that the documents mention. Her review of the structural evidence of Inca control sheds light on the governance of provinces like Andamarca Lucanas. However, the importance of this region, suggested by the fact that these people were chosen to be the Inca king's litter bearers, could not have been revealed by archaeology.

Similarly, the Topics indicate that the basic historical picture of the Huamachuco region could be identified archaeologically, but important details about Inca control of this region are found only in the written documents. Here, the specific manipulation of territories for political purposes, as suggested by Netherly (1988a), is also indicated: the addition of chaupi yunga lands formerly controlled by the coastal Chimu to the highland province of Huamachuco decreased the power of the Chimu lords.

Thus, the essays presented indicate the importance of utilizing both written documents and archaeological investigations to provide a more complete account of the Inca presence in provincial areas. Niles's and Julien's articles suggest that the potential of this dual approach is far from exhausted. The former provides some intriguing ideas concerning how the Inca organization of the areas around Cuzco might mirror Cuzco's relationship to provincial regions. Given the fairly good documentation relating to these "provinces in the heartland," these ideas might be useful for interpreting similar variability in material remains thoughout the empire. In addition, Niles's tentative identification of a stylistic chronology of architecture could be important in explaining variability in the provincial regions.

Finally, Julien calls for a more comprehensive analysis of the Inca empire, using a geographical approach. She suggests that reconstructing specific Inca territories with the help of colonial Spanish documents could provide a better idea of the variability in Inca rule between provinces. Her application of the model to the areas discussed by the other authors demonstrates the potential of such an approach. By testing the reconstructed territories using archaeological data, we could then be able to know more about exactly how the Incas organized the disparate polities under their hegemony.

The second focus of this book was an empirical one: to provide the means of identifying Inca activities in provinces. Related to this focus was an interest in differentiating material remains related to the time of Inca control from material remains generated in the same areas before Inca expansion. An important contribution of the essays in this volume is the documentation of the many different ways of making such distinctions. As indicated, there is an enormous range in the visibility of Inca material remains in different areas. This variation includes not only the amounts of different artifact types, such as pottery, but also the kinds of material remains themselves: the Inca occupation is recognized by architecture (Grosboll, Lynch, Schreiber, Topics), site layout (Lynch, Schreiber, Topics), the presence of the Inca road (Lynch, Schreiber, Topics), mitima settlements (Grosboll, Schreiber, Topics), colcas (Grosboll, Schreiber, Topics), and even agricultural terraces (Schreiber, Topics).

As mentioned in the introductory chapter, the most important means of identifying Inca influence traditionally has been the presence of Inca ceramics, including both forms (such as aryballos, plates, openmouth jars, and pedestal-based ollas) and decorations (such as rows of triangles, the Maltese cross, and zoomorphic motifs like llamas and birds). However, these kinds of pottery are relatively rare in the provinces studied in this volume. The same is true for other areas not covered in this volume, for example, the South Coast (Morris 1988b; Sandweiss 1989).

In fact, most of the authors in this volume point out the relative scarcity of ceramics that closely resemble the Cuzco-Inca-style ceramics of the capital or imitations of it like the provincial Inca ceramics found at such major centers as Huánuco Pampa. Much more common are continuations of local ceramic traditions as seen in the Andamarca Lucanas, Chupachos, and Huamachuco regions. Studies of provincial Inca ceramics and heavily influenced local styles remain an important avenue of investigation, to be discussed below.

What we do see from the regions discussed in this volume is clear evidence that pottery derived from local traditions continued to be made after the Inca incorporation of local groups. In some areas, such as the Lake Titicaca region, Inca forms and decoration were incorporated into local traditions, while elsewhere—such as Andamarca Lucanas, Chupachos, and Huamachuco—they were not. In Huamachuco, provincial Inca pottery is identified from the forms (aryballoid), animal head lugs mostly associated with aryballos forms, and distinctive pastes. In Chupachos, the presence of aryballos forms is also seen, and it is suggested that such forms are associated with tribute payments. Thus, new forms that appear with the Inca conquest would appear to be associated, at least sometimes, with direct control of the regions. This may be related to the Inca practice of forming camayo communities that produced materials such as pottery for the provinces.

Architecturally, an Inca occupation is often identified by the presence of kanchas, trapezoidal doors and niches, and, especially, finely cut masonry. The last item, considered a hallmark of Inca architecture, is certainly much less evident in the provincial regions discussed here than in other areas. Its scarcity underlines Niles's caution that the majority of structures even in the Cuzco area were typically constructed only of fieldstone. Thus, while all finely cut masonry may be related to Inca activity in the provinces, not all Inca masonry is finely cut. This caution applies to both domestic and nondomestic structures, as Niles points out.

Lynch observes that there is *no* finely cut stone in his study area and makes the further comment that such architecture is relatively rare anywhere in the southern or western parts of the empire. Could this situation have resulted from the relatively late annexation of these regions, while much of the finely cut masonry was the work of Pachacuti, as Niles indicates? Lynch's comment that the massive walls at Catarpe suggest important functions might be true, but it also might reflect Nile's suggestion that such architecture was more reflective of Huayna

Capac's architectural style. While the question of who organized the northern Chilean provinces, Topa Inca or Huayna Capac, is still uncertain, it is possible that the latter did. The massive walls of Catarpe might thus reflect the architectural style of the last Inca ruler.

In other regions studied we also see a lack of "classic" Inca masonry. Schreiber found only a single structure of cut stone, Grosboll found none, and even at Inca Huamachuco very little cut stone was found. In these regions, Inca architecture is identified by the structural forms and, in the case of Ichu in the Chupachos region, the presence of trapezoidal niches. Schreiber found only three structures which were probably related to Inca activity and all were identifed by their nonlocal forms, although one did have cut stone. Here, however, most niches were rectangular. Grosboll identified possible Inca influence in structures by their rectangular configuration, which contrasted with the round houses of the local inhabitants. Lynch identified kanchalike structures at Catarpe by their similarity to others in the empire and by their orientations of 63 to 66 degrees, which is similar to the orientation of the Qorikancha in Cuzco. Thus, formal differences in structures may be used as indicators of Inca-authorized construction in the absence of finely cut masonry.

One important result of the empirical studies presented here, as Julien notes, is a change in the tacit assumption regarding the structure of Inca authority: investigators have been looking for an interposed bureaucracy governed by Inca rulers from Cuzco, when in fact, Inca rule was most often mediated through local authorities. Hence, the lack of the imperial symbols should not be so surprising; perhaps it should be expected.

Lynch and the Topics also used site layout to identify Inca-authorized construction. The presence of a four-sided plaza at Catarpe with kancha and storage structures around it is suggestive of Inca administrative centers outside of Cuzco (Hyslop 1990). The Topics argued effectively that the modern town of Huamachuco is located on the site of the Inca center by a careful analysis of the size and shape of the main plaza, together with other nonarchitectural evidence.

Finally, several other methods were used by the authors to document the Inca impact in different provinces. The presence of the road with its associated support installations is of course a well-known means of documentation. The appearance of colcas and support structures is also documented by Grosboll, Schreiber, and the Topics. The identification of these structures as features of Inca administration must be supported by other evidence, such as, for example, the style of masonry used, or artifacts. In like fashion, the presence of mitima settlements, which are indirect indicators of Inca control, must also be corroborated by additional data. The identification of these settlements is especially problematic: without close attention to chronology, it will be difficult to distinguish the remains of earlier settlements (hypothesized as economic enclaves in an archipelago-type pattern) from the remains of Inca-authorized settlements (Sandweiss, personal communication).

One of the most interesting means of discerning the Incas' presence, discussed by some of the authors (Schreiber and the Topics), involves the archaeological identification of agricultural systems, especially terracing and irrigation works. We know from ethnohistorical sources that the Incas constructed new agricultural fields in many areas to increase productivity, yet few investigators have discussed using this information as a means of identifying Inca-sponsored activity in the provinces. Both the Topics and Schreiber indicate that Inca-built terraces are different from earlier ones, a conclusion also reached in my study of the Colca Valley (Malpass 1987). This finding also emphasizes the importance of looking at architectural features other than villages and structures when attempting to identify Inca activities in the provinces.

It is difficult to generalize about the nature of Inca control from the evidence presented in this book. This conclusion is in harmony with the analytical focus presented above: that the nature of Inca control was quite varied in different provinces. In some places, like northern Chile, the evidence for Inca control is quite clear and abundant, in terms of both architecture and artifacts. Then there are intermediate regions, like Huamachuco, where there is some evidence but not a lot. In other areas, like Chupachos and Andamarca Lucanas, the evidence is relatively rare.

We have assembled a considerable body of information pointing to the variability present in the Inca provinces. But how can we account for this variability? What factors were operating? What does this information tell us concerning the nature of the Inca empire?

One distinct kind of variation that is evident involves the locations of Inca settlements. As Julien points out, and as has been amply documented by Hyslop (1984), the Inca road system, with its associated administrative centers and tambos, formed the infrastructure of Inca control in the provinces. Yet the relationship of the road system to conquered populations varies considerably throughout the empire. In northern Chile, the road seems to skirt the main indigenous population centers, linking the Inca-built settlements instead. The same appears to be true of the Chupachos region. In contrast, in the Andamarca Lucanas region, the road goes through major population centers, with Inca structures occupying prominent locations amid the local populations. Finally, in the Huamachuco region, a new Inca center was constructed near the pre-Inca center of Marcahuamachuco, which was then abandoned. Why the differences?

Unfortunately, our information is not detailed enough to allow us to answer this question unequivocally. Several factors were probably important. The difference could be due to the nature of the earlier political development, as Julien points out. The evidence presented in this volume suggests that where groups incorporated into the Inca empire were politically undifferentiated, such as in northern Chile or Chupachos, the Incas created an infrastructure for controlling them. A similar kind of political development is described for the South Coast region by Menzel (1959) and for the Mantaro region by D'Altroy (1987). The information from Chupachos also appears similar to that described by Pease (1982) for the Chachapoyas region.

However, where there was some sociopolitical complexity, such as in the Andamarca Lucanas or Huamachuco regions, the situation appears to be more complicated. For Andamarca Lucanas, the Incas chose to elevate one of the two largest preexisting settlements to be the regional center, while in the Huamachuco region they chose to build their center near, but not in, the earlier political center. Such variability is also indicated in Pease's (1982) discussions of the differences between Inca rule in the Chimor and Lupaca regions, both of which were areas of highly complex pre-Inca polities.

Economic factors were clearly important considerations in the locations of Inca centers as well. The Topics suggest that Inca Huamachuco was located to be closer to the food-producing areas of the valley. Schreiber also suggests that the construction of an Inca building at Canichi and the agricultural terraces in Andamarca were due to the importance of those regions for maize production. Such was the reason for the Inca-induced changes in the Upper Mantaro region as well (Earle et al. 1980).

It is also possible that other factors influenced the locations of Inca centers. Moving the Huamachuco elites down from the hilltop site of Marcahuamachuco to a lower location may have been a psychological ploy to symbolize the power of the empire over the local political leaders or to punish them for their resistance. Such punishment is suggested for the abandonment of Tunanmarca, a comparable Late Intermediate Period site located in the Upper Mantaro region (Earle et al. 1980).

It is also possible that the location of Inca centers and the road itself followed portions of earlier highways constructed by the Huari state of the Middle Horizon (A.D. 600–1000) (Schreiber 1987). In this case, the Incas chose to build on earlier constructions rather than begin anew.

These possibilities indicate that the factors important to decisions concerning site locations in different areas varied with local circumstances. The diverse methods used by the Incas to tailor their political control to fit the social, political, and environmental conditions of different regions are again highlighted.

Another important feature of Inca control was their resettlement of local and nonlocal peoples in an area after its conquest. Such mitima settlements served various purposes for the empire, some specialized and some generalized (Rowe 1982). The reasons for moving people around the empire were both economic (to expand productivity in zones that were underutilized) and political (to decrease the resistance of politically restive groups). However, the degree to which groups were resettled is often unclear in the ethnohistorical record.

All the authors in this volume except Lynch discuss the nature of such settlements. In some areas, mitimas were brought from considerable distances. While none of the studies here provide evidence of dramatic relocations like those for the mitima settlement at Cochabamba, Bolivia (Wachtel 1982), Schreiber suggests that one mitima settlement in the Andamarca Lucanas region was composed of people from the Upper Mantaro area who were ethnically Huanca, and the Topics discuss evidence for an influx of coastal groups to the Huamachuco region. Grosboll only briefly mentions the substantial mitima settlements in Chupachos, as they were located outside of her study area. However, in contrast to the foreign mitimas relocated to other provinces, she suggests that there were relocations of local people strictly within this territory. Julien also notes that there were a number of mitima settlements within the territory studied by Grosboll, composed of artisans brought from inside Chupachos territory. Thus, both interprovincial and intraprovincial movements of people were a part of Inca policy. The information provided by the authors indicates that both economic and political factors motivated the mitima occupations. The settlements in Chupachos were probably founded for economic purposes, although the ethnohistorical documentation does not contain direct statements to this effect. Julien notes that it is conceivable that the Incas created craft production centers to rationalize local production, not just to produce goods for the state. Sandweiss (personal communication) makes the further suggestion that through the creation of specialized craft centers the Incas controlled the production of prestige items and hence controlled local leaders. Thus, political motivations may also have been operating.

In like fashion, the one mitima settlement identified by Schreiber is located near a series of colcas, suggesting an economic focus, although the group who lived there may have been Huanca, a group who fiercely resisted the Incas. Thus, both political and economic reasons for this settlement may be inferred. The Topics mention that highland mitimas were probably concentrated in the center of the Huamachuco province for political purposes, to control the heart of the province. Thus, the variation in both function and purpose of the mitima occupations is confirmed by the studies here.

The lack of covariance in the data sets from different provinces also suggests that Inca control was variable. One of the reasons for this might well have to do with what Julien points out: that the provinces were different with regard to the functions they served for the Incas. Some might have been central places for gathering armies and foodstuffs, while others were not. Such disparate functions would result in very different kinds of archaeological manifestations in different provinces.

Other possibilities are suggested by Niles's essay. Is the architectural variability due to the distinctive styles of different rulers? She mentions Pachacuti as being the source of most of the finely cut masonry usually associated with Inca rule. Using Rowe's (1945) chronology of the conquests of each ruler, one can see that the area conquered by Pachacuti between the southern shores of Late Titicaca and Lake Junin do contain many of the finest examples of cut stone. Schreiber found a single example of a cut stone structure in the Andamarca Lucanas region, an area annexed during the rule of Pachacuti according to sources drawn from Inca historical tradition. Given that the focus of Inca governance in that area was Vilcashuamán, perhaps it is understandable that more fine stone masonry is not present.

Grosboll found no high-quality cut stone architecture in the Chupachos region, although it is abundant at Huánuco Pampa. According to Cobo (1979: 138) and others (see Rowe 1946: 206ff.), this was an area conquered by either Pachacuti or one of his generals, but apparently only consolidated during the time of Topa Inca. Others (e.g., Guaman Poma 1980a) indicate that the palaces at Huánuco Pampa were Topa Inca's. Does this mean that the latter shared some of Pachacuti's vision of architectural style, or was this region in fact organized by Pachacuti? The same questions can be asked of the Huamachuco region studied by the Topics.

While the question of personal architectural styles cannot be adequately addressed here, some association does appear possible. Perhaps more intriguing is Niles's suggestion that the provincial and local centers might have functioned in the Inca tripartite social hierarchy. She indicates that administrative centers could have been payan to Cuzco's collana status, with local settlements being cayao. How, then, to describe sites like Huayhuay Puquio, in Andamarca Lucanas, where some intermediate-style masonry is found, or Ichu, where Cuzco-style architecture appears? These could be considered extensions of the payan status to the individuals residing here, which accords with the interpretations presented. Perhaps the prestige factor, coupled with the personal style of the ruler at the time of the conquests, can account for much of the variability in Inca construction.

A final point of relevance to any discussion of the nature of the Inca presence in provincial areas is that the expansion of the empire took place in less than one hundred years. One reason for the lack of an Inca presence in many areas might simply be that they did not have sufficient time to make a greater impact. Given more time, perhaps they would have made their presence in all areas more evident. Still, the great variability seen in the archaeological visibility of the Inca cannot be explained simply as a result of the brevity of their rule. The essays presented here attest to the complexity of the factors involved in their presence or absence.

All of this evidence emphasizes the importance of using multiple sources of data in order to confirm the presence of the Incas in provincial areas. Also, it is important to note that the archaeological manifestations of Inca activity are as diverse as the historical evidence for Inca control. Inca studies have made great strides in recent years but much more can be learned through combined archaeological and ethnohistorical collaboration. It is hoped that future researchers will go beyond the investigations discussed in this book to expand our understanding of the Incas and their interactions with other Andean ethnicities. Julien provides several lines of potentially productive inquiry. And as Pease (1982: 190) notes,

> It would be possible to have the impression, which has grown stronger in recent years, that the Tawantinsuyu is more a complicated and extensive network of relationships than it is the apparently monolithic and showy apparatus of power that the chroniclers described in the sixteenth century. The description of these relationships, which can reveal macrosystems of interchange greater than we are accustomed to handling, may well provide better understanding of the relationships of the Tawantinsuyu with the Andean ethnic groups.

BIBLIOGRAPHY

ADC (Archivo Departamental del Cuzco)
 1558   Provisiones del Marqués de Cañete a favor del Inca Sayri Tupa. Archivo Departamental del Cuzco, Colección de Papeles de Vicente José Garcia, vol. 7, pp. 20–24.

AGI (Archivo General de Indies)
 1549–50   Cumplimiento e diligencias que la justicia de la villa de plata hizo cerca de la libertad que los yndios que estan en las minas de Potosí tienen de yrse a sus tierras sin que nadie se lo impida. Archivo General de Indies, Justicia 667. Seville.

Albornoz, Cristóbal de
 1989   *Instrucción para descubrir todas las guacas del Piru y sus camajos y haziendas* [c. 1584]. In *Fábulos y mitos de los incas*, edited by Henrique Urbano and Pierre Duviols. Historia 16, Crónicas de América 48: 163–198. Madrid.

Anonymous Conqueror
 1929   *The conquest of Perú as related by a member of the Pizarro expedition.* Edited and translated by Joseph H. Sinclair. New York Public Library. Reproduced in facsimile from 1534 edition.

Ascue Sarmiento, Javier
 1988   Hallan restos de uno de los últimos Incas. *El Comercio*, March 16, pp. 1 and 6. Lima.

Auger, Reginald, Margaret F. Glass, Scott MacEachern, and Peter H. McCartney, eds.
 1987   *Ethnicity in complex societies.* Calgary: Archaeological Association of the University of Calgary.

Bandelier, Adolph
 1910   The islands of Titicaca and Koati. New York: Hispanic Society.

Barnes, Monica, and David Fleming
 1989   Charles-Marie de la Condamine's report on Ingapirca and the development of scientific field work in the Andes, 1735–1744. *Andean Past* 2: 175–235. Ithaca.

Bauer, Brian
 1990   State development in the Cuzco region: Archaeological research on the Incas in the province of Paruro. Ph.D. diss., Department of Anthropology, University of Chicago.

Bauer, Brian, and Charles Stanish
 1990   Killke and Killke-related pottery from Cuzco, Peru, in the Field Museum of Natural History. *Fieldiana*, n.s. 15, publication 1419.

Betanzos, Juan de
1987   Suma y narración de los Incas [1551]. Transcription, notes, and
        prologue by Maria del Carmen Martin Rubio. Madrid: Ediciones
        Atlas.
Binford, Sally, and Lewis Binford
1968   New perspectives in archaeology. Chicago: Aldine Publishing.
Bingham, Hiram
1930   Machu Pichu: A citadel of the Incas. Memoirs of the National Geo-
        graphic Society. New Haven: Yale University Press.
Bird, Robert McK.
1970   Maize and its cultural and natural environment in the sierra of
        Huánuco, Peru. Ph.D. diss., Department of Anthropology, Univer-
        sity of California, Berkeley.
Bode, Maria E.
1967   A progress report on the analysis of Yacha pottery from the central
        highlands of Peru. Unpublished manuscript, Department of An-
        thropology, University of Wisconsin, Madison.
Buck, Fritz
1935   Cuzco-Tiahuanacu. Revista del Museo Nacional 4 (1): 111–114.
        Lima.
Cabello Balboa, Miguel
1951   Miscelánea Antártica: Una historia del Perú antiguo [1586]. Lima:
        Universidad Nacional Mayor de San Marcos, Facultad de Letras,
        Instituto de Etnología.
Cabrera, Amador de, and Antonio de Cháves
1965   Relación de la ciudad de Guamanga y sus terminos. Año de 1586.
        In Don Marcos Jiménez de la Espada, ed., Relaciones Geográficas de
        Indias (Peru), 183: 181–201. Biblioteca de Autores Españoles. Ma-
        drid: Ediciones Atlas.
Capoche, Luis
1959   Relación general de la villa imperial de Potosí, un capítulo inédito
        en la historia del nuevo mundo [1585]. Prologue and notes by
        Lewis Hanke. Biblioteca de Autores Españoles, 122: 9–221. Ma-
        drid: Ediciones Atlas.
Carabajal, Pedro de
1965   Descripción fecha de la provincia de Vilcas Guaman . . . [1586]. In
        Don Marcos Jiménez de la Espada, ed., Relaciones Geográficas de
        Indias (Perú), 183: 205–219. Biblioteca de Autores Españoles. Ma-
        drid: Ediciones Atlas.
Carlevato, Denise
1988   Late ceramics from Pucara, Peru: An indicator of changing site
        function. Expedition 30 (3): 39–45.

Castro R., Victoria, and Luis Eduardo Cornejo B.
1990   Estudios en el pukara de Turi, Norte de Chile. *Gaceta Arqueoló-gica Andina* 5 (17): 57–66. Lima: Instituto Andino de Estudios Arqueológicos.

Chapin, Heath MacBain
1961   *The Bandelier archaeological collection from Pelechuco and Charassani, Bolivia*. Posario: Imprenta de la Universidad Nacional del Litoral.

Checura, J.
1977   Fúnebria incaica en el Cerro Esmeralda. *Estudios Atacameños* 5: 125–141. San Pedro de Atacama.

Chiswell, Coreen
1984   A study of prehistoric Andean storage by means of phytolith analysis. Master's thesis, Department of Anthropology, Trent University, Peterborough, Ontario.

Cieza de León, Pedro
1984   *Crónica del Perú, primera parte* [1550]. Introduction by Franklin Pease G.Y. Note by Miguel Maticorena E. Lima: Pontificia Universidad Católica del Perú.
1985   *Crónica del Perú, segunda parte*. [1550–1552]. Edited by Francesca Cantù. Lima: Academia Nacional de la Historia, Pontificia Universidad Católica del Perú.
1986   *Crónica del Perú, primera parte* [1553]. 2d ed. Lima: Pontificia Universidad Católica del Perú.

Cobo, Bernabé
1890–95   *Historia del nuevo mundo* [1653]. 4 vols. Published for the first time with notes and other illustrations by Don Marcos Jiménez de la Espada. Andaluces, Sevilla: Sociedad de Bibliófilos.
1964   *Historia del nuevo mundo* [1653]. Biblioteca de Autores Españoles, 92: 5–275. Madrid: Ediciones Atlas.

Cock, Guillermo
Ms.   Etnia y etnicidad en Lucanas Andamarcas. Master's thesis, Department of Anthropology, Pontificia Universidad Católica del Perú, Lima.

Conrad, Geoffrey W., and Arthur Demarest
1984   *Religion and empire: The dynamics of Aztec and Inca Expansionism*. New York: Cambridge University Press.

Costin, Cathy Lynne, and Timothy Earle
1989   Status distinction and legitimation of power as reflected in changing settlement patterns of consumption in late prehispanic Peru. *American Antiquity* 54: 691–714.

Coupland, Gary
1979   A survey of prehistoric fortified sites in the north highlands of

Peru. Master's thesis, Department of Anthropology, Trent University, Peterborough, Ontario.

Crespo, Juan Carlos
1977   Los Collaguas en la visita de Alonso Fernández de Bonilla. In Franklin Pease, ed., *Collaguas I*, pp. 53–92. Lima: Pontificia Universidad Católica del Perú.

D'Altroy, Terence N.
1987   Introduction. *Ethnohistory* 34 (1): 1–13.

D'Altroy, Terence N., and Timothy K. Earle
1985   Staple finance, wealth finance, and storage in the Inka political economy. *Current Anthropology* 26 (2): 187–197.

D'Altroy, Terence, and Christine Hastorf
1984   The distribution and contents of Inca state storehouses in the Xauxa region of Peru. *American Antiquity* 49 (2): 334–349.

Dauelsberg, P.
1959   Contribución a la arqueología del valle de Azapa. *Museo Regional de Arica*. Boletín 3. Arica.
1983   Investigaciones arqueológicas en la sierra de Arica, sector Belén. *Chungara* 11: 63–83.
1985   Prospección del camino del inka sector Zapahuira-Lupica. Unpublished manuscript. Report of investigations UTA. Arica.

Dearborn, David S. P.
1986   Review of *Inkawasi: The new Cuzco*. *Archaeoastronomy* 9: 114–122.

Deetz, James
1988   History and archaeological theory: Walter Taylor revisited. *American Antiquity* 53 (1): 13–22.

Diez de San Miguel, Garci
1964   *Visita hecha a la provincia de Chucuito* [1567]. Lima: Casa de la Cultura del Perú.

Dillehay, Thomas
1976   Competition and cooperation in a pre-Hispanic multi-ethnic system in the central Andes. Ph.D. diss., Department of Anthropology, University of Texas, Austin.
1977   Tawantinsuyu integration of the Chillon Valley, Perú: A case of Inca geo-political mastery. *Journal of Field Archaeology* 4 (4): 397–405.

Dillehay, Thomas, and Patricia Netherly
1988   *La frontera del estado inca*. B.A.R. International Series 442. Oxford: British Archaeological Reports.

Duviols, Pierre
1967   Un inédito de Cristóbal de Albornoz: La instrucción para descubrir

todas las guacas del Pirú y sus camayos y haziendas. *Journal de la Société des Américanistes* 61: 7–39. Paris.

Dwyer, Edward

1971   The early Inca occupation of the valley of Cuzco, Perú. Ph.D. diss., Department of Anthropology, University of California, Berkeley.

Earle, Timothy, Terence D'Altroy, Christine Hastorf, Catherine Scott, Cathy Costin, Glenn Russell, and Elsie Sandefur

1987   *Archaeological field research in the upper Mantaro, Peru, 1982–1983: Investigation of Inka expansion and exchange.* Monograph 28, Institute of Archaeology, University of California, Los Angeles.

Earle, Timothy, Terence D'Altroy, Catherine LeBlanc, Christine Hastorf, and Terry Le Vine

1980   Changing settlement patterns in the upper Mantaro Valley, Peru. Preliminary report for the 1977, 1978, and 1979 seasons of the Upper Mantaro Archaeological Research Project. *Journal of New World Archaeology* 4 (1). Institute of Archaeology, University of California, Los Angeles.

Eisleb, Dieter, and Renata Strelow

1980   Altperuanischen Kulturen III. Tiahuanaco. *Veroffentlichungen des Museums für Völkerkunde Berlin*, Neue Folge 38. Abteilung Amerikanische Archäeologie V. Berlin.

Espinoza Soriano, Waldemar

1967a   El primer informe etnológico sobre Cajamarca. Año de 1540. *Revista Peruana de Cultura* 11–12: 5–41. Lima.

1967b   Los señorios étnicos de Chachapoyas y alianza hispano-chacha. Visitas, informaciones y memoriales de 1572–1574. *Revista Histórica* 307: 224–332. Lima.

1969   El memorial de charcas: "Cronica" inédita de 1582. *Cantuta* 4: 117–152. Huancayo: Universidad Nacional de Educación.

1970   Los mitmas Huayacuntus en Cajabamba y Andamarca, siglos XV y XVI. *Historia y Cultura* 4: 77–96. Lima.

1973   *La destrucción del imperio de los Incas.* Lima: Retablo de Papel Ediciones.

1974   Los señorios étnicos del valle de Condebamba y provincia de Cajabamba: Historia de las huarancas de Llucho y Mitmas, siglos XV–XX. *Anales Científicos de la Universidad del Centro del Perú* 3: 5–371. Huancayo.

Estete, Miguel de

1918   Noticia del Perú. In *El descubrimiento y la conquista del Perú*. Relación inédita de Miguel Estete. Introduction and notes by Carlos M. Larrea. *Boletín de la Sociedad Ecuadoriana Estudios Históricos* 1 (3): 300–350.

1947   La relación del viaje que hizo el Señor Capitán Hernando Pizarro por mandado del Señor Gobernador, su hermano, desde el pueblo de Caxamalca a Parcama, y de allí a Jauja [1533]. Biblioteca de Autores Españoles, 26: 338–343. Madrid.

Galdos Rodríguez, Guillermo
1986   Los yanaguaras de la Chimba de Arequipa. Revista del Archivo General de la Nación 9 (segunda epoca): 21–52. Huancayo.

Garcilaso de la Vega, El Inca
1966   Royal commentaries of the Incas and general history of Peru [1609]. 2 vols. Translated by H. V. Livermore. Austin: University of Texas Press.

Gasparini, Graziano, and Luis Margolies
1980   Inca architecture. Translated by Patricia J. Lyon. Bloomington: Indiana University Press.

Glave, Luis Miguel
1989   Un curacazgo andino y la sociedad campesina del siglo XVII: La historia de Bartolomé Tupa Hallicalla, curaca de Asillo. Allpanchis, 33, pp. 11–39. Cuzco: Instituto Pastoral Andina.

González Holguín, Diego
1952   Vocabulario de la lengua general de todo el Perú llamada lengua Quichua o del Inca. New ed., with prologue by Raul Porras Barrenechea. Lima: Imprenta Santa Maria.

Grosboll, Sue
1987   Ethnic boundaries within the Inca empire. In Reginald Auger, Margaret F. Glass, Scott MacEachern, and Peter H. McCartney, eds., Ethnicity in complex societies, pp. 115–125. Calgary: Archaeological Association of the University of Calgary, Alberta.
1988   An archaeological approach to the demography of prehispanic Andean communities. Ph.D. diss., Department of Anthropology, University of Wisconsin, Madison.

Guaman Poma de Ayala, Felipe
1936   Nueva corónica y buen gobierno [1615] (Codex peruvien illustre). Université de Paris, Travaux et Memoires de l'Institut d'Ethnologie XXIII. Paris: Institut d'Ethnologie.
1980a   El primer nueva corónica y buen gobierno [1615]. 3 vols. Critical ed. by John V. Murra y Rolena Adorno. Mexico City: Siglo Veintiuno.
1980b   Nueva corónica y buen gobierno [1615]. 2 vols. Transcription by Franklin Pease. Biblioteca Ayacucho, vols. 75–76. Caracas: Biblioteca Ayacucho.

Hampe Martínez, Teodoro
1979   Relación de los encomenderos y repartimientos del Perú en 1561. Historia y Cultura 12: 75–117. Lima: Museo Nacional de Historia.

Helmer, Marie
1955–56   "La visitación de los yndios Chupachos" inka encomendero, 1549. *Travaux de l'Institut Francais d'Etudes Andines* 5: 3–50. Paris-Lima.
Hemming, John
1970   *The conquest of the Incas.* London: Macmillan.
Hemming, John, and Edward Ranney
1982   *Monuments of the Incas.* Boston: Little, Brown.
Henderson, John S.
1987   Frontier at the crossroads. In Eugenia J. Robinson, ed., *Interaction on the southwest Mesoamerican frontier*, pp. 455–462. B.A.R. International Series 327. Oxford: British Archaeological Reports.
1992   Variations on a theme: A frontier view of Maya civilization. In E. Danien and R. J. Sharer, eds., *New World theories on the ancient Maya*, pp. 161–171. Philadelphia: University of Pennsylvania University Museum.
Hidalgo Lehuedé, Jorge
1972   *Culturas protohistóricas del norte de Chile: Testimonio de los cronistas.* Santiago: Editorial Universitaria.
1978   Revisita altos de Arica en 1750. *Documentos de Trabajo*, UNA, Arica.
1985   Ecological complementarity and tribute in Atacama 1683–1792. In Shozo Masuda, Izumi Shimada, and Craig Morris, eds., *Andean ecology and civilization: An interdisciplinary perspective on Andean complementarity*, pp 161–184. Tokyo: University of Tokyo Press.
Hyslop, John
1976   An archaeological investigation of the Lupaca kingdom and its origin. Ph.D. diss., Department of Anthropology, Columbia University, New York.
1984   *The Inka road system.* New York: Academic Press.
1985   *Inkawasi: The new Cuzco.* B.A.R. International Series 234. Oxford: British Archaeological Reports.
1990   *Inka settlement planning.* Austin: University of Texas Press.
Hyslop, John, and Mario Rivera
1984   The Inka road in the Atacama Desert. *Archaeology* 37 (6): 33–39.
Iribarren Charlin, Jorge
1972   Una mina de explotación incaica, El Salvador. *Actas del VI Congreso Arqueología Chilena*, Santiago.
Iribarren Charlin, Jorge, and Hans Bergholz
1971   El camino del Inka en un sector del Norte Chico. In Hans Niemeyer, ed., *Actas del VI Congreso de Arqueología Chilena*, pp. 229–265. Santiago. (Republished in 1972 with more illustrations in *Colección "11 de Julio,"* Compañía de Cobre Salvador, Potrerillos, Chile.)

Jiménez de la Espada, Don Marcos
1965   *Relaciones Geográficas de Indias (Perú)*. Real Academia Española, vol. 183. Madrid: Ediciones Atlas.

Julien, Catherine J.
1978   Inca administration in the Titicaca basin as reflected at the provincial capital of Hatunqolla. Ph.D. diss., Department of Anthropology, University of California, Berkeley.

1981   A late burial from Carro Azoguini, Puno. *Ñawpa Pacha* 19: 129–154. Berkeley.

1982   Inca decimal administration in the Lake Titicaca region. In George A. Collier, Renato I. Rosaldo, and John D. Wirth, eds., *The Inca and Aztec states, 1400–1800: Anthropology and history*, pp. 119–151. New York: Academic Press.

1983   *Hatunqolla: A view of Inca rule from the Lake Titicaca region*. Series Publications in Anthropology, vol. 15. Berkeley: University of California Press.

1985   Guano and resource control in sixteenth-century Arequipa. In Shozo Masuda, Izumi Shimada, and Craig Morris, eds., *Andean ecology and civilization: An interdisciplinary perspective on Andean ecological complementarity*, pp. 185–231. Tokyo: University of Tokyo Press.

1988a   How Inca decimal administration worked. *Ethnohistory* 35 (3): 257–297.

1988b   The Squire causeway at Lake Umayo. *Expedition* 30 (3): 46–55.

1991   Condesuyo: The political division of territory under Inca and Spanish rule. Bonn: Bonner Amerikanistische Studien 19.

Ms.   *Las tumbas de Sacsahuaman y el estilo Cuzco-Inca*.

Kendall, Ann F.
1974a   Architecture and planning at the Inca sites in the Cusichaca area. *Baessler-Archiv Beiträge zur Völkerkunde*, n. s., 22: 73–137. Berlin.

1974b   *Aspects of Inca architecture*. Translated by Patricia J. Lyon. Bloomington: Indiana University Press.

1976   Preliminary report on ceramic data and the pre-Inca architectural remains of the (Lower) Urubamba Valley, Cuzco. *Baessler-Archiv Beiträge zur Völkerkunde*, n. s., 24: 41–159. Berlin.

1978   Descripción e inventario de las formas arquitectónicas inca; patrones de distribución e inferencias cronológicas. *Revista del Museo Nacional* 42 (1976): 13–96. Lima.

1985   *Aspects of Inca architecture—description, function, and chronology*. 2 vols. B.A.R. International Series 242. Oxford: British Archaeological Reports.

Krzanowski, Andrzej
1986   The cultural chronology of the northern Andes of Peru (the Hua-machuco-Quiruvilca-Otuzco region). *Acta Archaeológica Carpathica* 25: 231–264. Warsaw.

La Lone, Mary, and Darrell La Lone
1987   The Inka state in the southern highlands: State administration and production enclaves. *Ethnohistory* 34 (1): 47–62.

Latcham, R.
1928   *Prehistoria chilena.* Santiago.

LePaige, Gustave
1972–73   Tres cementarios indígenos en San Pedro de Atacama y To-conao. In Hans Niemeyer, ed., *Actas del VI Congreso de Arqueología Chilena,* pp. 163–187. Santiago.
1977   Recientes descubrimientos arqueológicos en la zona de San Pedro de Atacama. *Estudios Atacameños* 5: 109. Antofagasta: Universidad del Norte.
1978   Vestigios arqueológicos incaicos en las cumbres de la zona ataca-meña. *Estudios Atacameños* 6: 36–52. Antofagasta: Universidad del Norte.

Le Vine, Terry
1987   Inka labor service at the regional level: The functional reality. *Ethnohistory* 34 (1): 14–46.

Llagostera, A.
1976   Hipótesis sobre la expansión incaica en la vertiente occidental de los Andes meridionales. *Anales Universidad del Norte* 10: 203–218. Antofagasta.

Loredo, Rafael
1942   *Alardes y Derramas.* Lima: Imprenta Gil.
1958   *Los repartos. Bocetos para la nueva historia del Perú.* Lima.

Lumbreras, Luis, and Hernan Amat
1968   Secuencia arqueológica del Altiplano occidental del Titicaca. *Actas y Memorias,* vol. 2. 37th International Congress of Americanists. Buenos Aires.

Lynch, Thomas
1978   Tambo incaico Catarpe-Este (informe de avance). *Estudios Ataca-meños* 5: 142–147. Antofagasta: Universidad del Norte.
1989   Regional interaction, transhumance, and verticality: Archaeological use of zonal complementarity in Peru and northern Chile. *Michigan Discussions in Anthropology* 8: 1–11. Ann Arbor: University of Michigan.
1990   Quaternary climate, environment, and the human occupation of the South-Central Andes. *Geoarchaeology* 5 (3): 199–228.

MacLean, Margaret G. H.
1986   Sacred land, sacred water: Inca landscape planning in the Cuzco
       area. Ph.D. diss., Department of Anthropology, University of Cali-
       fornia, Berkeley.
Magallanes, Manuel M.
1912   El camino del Inca. Revista Chilena de Historia y Geografía 2 (7):
       44–75. Sociedad Chilena de Historia y Geografía. Santiago: Im-
       prenta Universitaria.
Malpass, Michael
1987   Prehistoric agricultural terracing at Chijra in the Colca Valley,
       Perú: Preliminary report II. In William Denevan, Kent Mathewson,
       and Gregory Knapp, eds., Pre-Hispanic agricultural fields in the An-
       dean region, part i, pp. 45–66. B.A.R. International Series 359(i).
       Oxford: British Archaeological Reports.
Markham, Clements
1856   Cuzco: A journey to the ancient capital of Peru, with an account of the
       history, language, literature, and antiquities of the Incas. London.
Martinez Compañon, Obispo D. Baltasar Jaime
1978   La obra del Obispo Martinez Compañon sobre Trujillo del Perú en el
       siglo XVIII. 2 vols. Madrid: Ediciones Cultura Hispánica del Centro
       Iberamericano de Cooperación.
Matienzo, Juan de
1967   Gobierno del Perú [1567]. Edition and preliminary study by Gui-
       llermo Lohmann Villena. Travaux de l'Institut Français d'Etudes
       Andines, vol. 11. Paris-Lima.
Matos Mendieta, Ramiro
1972   Wakan y Wamalli: Estudio arqueológico de dos aldeas rurales. In
       Iñigo Ortíz de Zúñiga, Visita de la provincia de León de Huánuco en
       1562, vol. 2, pp. 367–383. Huánuco: Universidad Nacional Her-
       milio Valizán.
Maúrtua, Victor
1906   Juicio de límites entre el Perú y Bolivia, prueba Peruana presentada al
       gobierno de la República Argentina, vol. 1. Barcelona: Imprenta de
       Henrich y Comp.
Mayer, Enrique
1984   A tribute to the household: Domestic economy and the encomi-
       enda in colonial Peru. In Raymond T. Smith, ed., Kinship, ideology,
       and practice in Latin America, pp. 85–118. Chapel Hill: University
       of North Carolina Press.
McCown, Theodore D.
1945   Pre-Incaic Huamachuco: Survey and excavations in the region of
       Huamachuco and Cajabamba. University of California Publications in
       American Archaeology and Ethnology 39: 223–399. Berkeley.

Means, Phillip Ainsworth
1935   Notas polémicas: Cuzco-Tiahuanacu, su verdadera relación crono-
       lógica. *Revista del Museo Nacional* 4 (2): 206–208, II semestre.
       Lima.
Mejia Xesspe, M. Toribio
1955   Apéndice: Historia de la expedición arqueológica de 1937. In Julio
       C. Tello, *Valle de Casma, culturas Chavin, Santa o Huaylas, Yunga y
       Sub-Chimú*, pp. 319–337. Lima: Editorial San Marcos.
Mellafe, Rolando
1965   La significación histórica de los puentes en el virreinato Peruano
       del siglo XVI. *Historia y Cultura* 1 (1): 65–113. Lima: Museo Na-
       cional de Historia.
Menzel, Dorothy
1959   The Inca occupation of the South Coast of Peru. *Southwestern Jour-
       nal of Anthropology* 15 (2): 125–142.
1966   The pottery of Chincha. *Ñawpa Pacha* 4: 77–153. Berkeley.
1976   *Pottery style and society in ancient Peru: Art as a mirror of history in
       the Ica Valley, 1350–1570.* Berkeley: University of California Press.
Menzel, Dorothy, and John H. Rowe
1966   The role of Chincha in late pre-Spanish Peru. *Ñawpa Pacha* 4:
       63–76. Berkeley.
Middendorf, E. M.
1974   *Peru* [1895], vol. 3. Lima: Universidad Nacional Mayor de San
       Marcos.
Miranda, Cristóbal de
1925   Relación hecha por el Virrey D. Martin Enriquez de los oficios que
       se proveen la gobernación de los reinos y provincios de Perú,
       1583. Gobernantes de Peru, cartas y papeles, siglo XVI. *Documen-
       tos del Archivo de Indias*, publication directed by D. Roberto Le-
       viller, vol. 9, el Virrey Martin Enriquez, 1581–1583: 114–230.
       Madrid: Imprenta de Juan Pueyo.
Mogrovejo, Arzobispo Don Toribio Alfonso de
1920   Diario de la segunda visita pastoral que hizo de su arquidiocesis el
       Ilustrísimo Señor Don Toribio Alfonso de Mogrovejo Arzobispo de
       Los Reyes, entrega II. *Revista del Archivo Nacional* 1: 227–279.
       Lima.
Molina, Cristóbal de
1989   Relación de las fábulas y ritos de los Incas [1575]. C. de Molina,
       C. de Albornoz. In Henrique Urbano and Pierre Duviols, eds.,
       Fábulos y mitos de los incas, Historia 16, Crónicas de América 48:
       47–134. Madrid.
Monzón, Luis de
1965a Descripción de la tierra del repartimiento de Atunsora, encomen-

dado en Hernando Palomino, jurisdicción de la ciudad de Guamanga. Año de 1586. In Don Marcos Jiménez de la Espada, ed., *Relaciones Geográficas de Indias (Perú)*, 183: 220–225. Biblioteca de Autores Españoles. Madrid: Ediciones Atlas.

1965b Descripción de la tierra del repartimiento de los Rucanas Antamarcas de la corona real, jurisdicción de la ciudad de Guamanga. Año de 1586. In Don Marcos Jiménez de la Espada, ed., *Relaciones Geográficas de Indias (Perú)*, 183: 237–248. Biblioteca de Autores Españoles. Madrid: Ediciones Atlas

1965c Descripción de la tierra del repartimiento de San Francisco de Atunrucana y Laramati, encomendado en Don Pedro de Cordova, jurisdicción de la ciudad de Guamanga. Año de 1586. In Don Marcos Jiménez de la Espada, ed., *Relaciones Geográficas de Indias (Perú)*, 183: 226–236. Biblioteca de Autores Españoles. Madrid: Ediciones Atlas.

Morales, Adolfo de
1977 Repartimiento de tierras por el Inca Huayna Capac (Testimonio de un documento de 1556). Universidad Boliviana Mayor de San Simon, Departamento de Arqueología. Cochabamba.

Morris, Craig
1966 El *tampu real* de Tunsucancha. In *Cuadernos de Investigación, Antropología*, 1: 95–107. Huánuco: Universidad Nacional Hermilio Valdizán.

1967 Storage in Tawantinsuyu. Ph.D. diss., Department of Anthropology, University of Chicago, Chicago.

1982 The infrastructure of the Inka control in the Peruvian central highlands. In George A. Collier, Renato I. Rosaldo, and John D. Wirth, eds., *The Inca and Aztec states, 1400–1800: Archaeology and history*, pp. 153–172. New York: Academic Press.

1988a Progress and prospect in the archaeology of the Inca. In Richard W. Keatinge, ed., *Peruvian Prehistory*, pp. 233–256. New York: Cambridge University Press.

1988b Más allá de las fronteras de Chincha. In Thomas D. Dillehay and Patricia J. Netherly, eds., *La frontera del estado inca*, pp. 131–140. B.A.R. International Series 442. Oxford: British Archaeological Reports.

Morris, Craig, and Donald E. Thompson
1985 *Huánuco Pampa: An Inca city and its hinterland*. London: Thames and Hudson.

Mostny, Grete
1948 Ciudades atacameños. *Boletín del Museo Nacional de Historia Natural* 24: 125–211. Santiago.

Munizaga, Carlos
  1957   Descripción y análisis de la cerámica y otros artefactos de los valles
         de Lluta, Azapa y Vitor. *Arqueología chilena*. Santiago.
Murra, John V.
  1967   La vista de los Chupachus como fuente etnológica. In Iñigo Ortíz
         de Zúñiga, *Visita de la provincia de León de Huánuco en 1562*, 1:
         383–417. Huánuco: Universidad Nacional Hermilio Valdizán.
  1972   El "control vertical" de un maximo de pisos ecológicos en la eco-
         nomía de las sociedades Andinas. In Iñigo Ortíz de Zúñiga, *Visita
         de la provincia de León de Huánuco en 1562*, 2: 429–476. Huánuco:
         Universidad Nacional Hermilio Valdizán.
  1978   Los olleros del Inka: Hacia una historia y arqueología del Qolla-
         suyu. In Francisco Miró Quesada C., Franklin Pease G.Y., and Da-
         vid Sobrevilla A., eds., *Historia, problema y promesa, homenaje a
         Jorge Basadre*, pp. 415–423. Pontificia Universidad Católica del
         Perú. Lima: Fondo Editorial.
  1980   *The economic organization of the Inka state*. Research in Economic
         Anthropology, Supplement. Greenwich: JAI Press.
  1982   The *m'ita* obligations of ethnic groups to the Inca state. In George A.
         Collier, Renato I. Rosaldo, and John D. Wirth, eds., *The Inca and
         Aztec states, 1400–1800: Anthropology and history*, pp. 237–262.
         New York: Academic Press.
Murúa, Martín de
  1946   *Historia del origen y genealogía real de los reyes Incas del Perú*
         [c. 1605]. Introduction, notes, and edition by Constantino Bayle.
         Biblioteca "Missionalia Hispánica," vol. 2. Madrid: Instituto Santo
         Toribio de Mogrovejo.
  1962–64 *Historia general del Perú: Origen y descendencia de los Incas*
         [c. 1611–1615]. 2 vols. Colección Joyas Bibliográficas, Biblioteca
         Americana Vetus I, II. Madrid: Instituto Gonzalo Fernández de
         Oviedo.
Neira, Máximo
  1967   Informe preliminar de las investigaciones arqueológicas en el De-
         partamento de Puno. *Anales del Instituto de Estudios Socio-Economics*
         1. Puno: Universidad Técnica del Altiplano.
Netherly, Patricia
  1978   *Local level lords on the North Coast of Peru*. Ph.D. diss., Department
         of Anthropology, Cornell University, Ithaca, New York.
  1988a From event to process: The recovery of late Andean organiza-
         tional structure by means of Spanish colonial written records. In
         Richard W. Keatinge, ed., *Peruvian Prehistory*, pp. 257–275. New
         York: Cambridge University Press.

1988b   El reino Chimor y el Tawantinsuyu. In Thomas D. Dillehay and
         Patricia J. Netherly, eds., *La frontera del estado inca*, pp. 105–
         129. B.A.R. International Series 442. Oxford: British Archaeologi-
         cal Reports.
Niemeyer, Hans
1962   Tambo incaico en el valle de Collacagua. *Revisita Universitaria* 47:
         127–150. Santiago.
1981   Dos tipos de crisoles prehispánicos del Norte Chico, Chile. *Boletín
         del Museo Arqueológico* 17: 92–109. La Serena.
Niemeyer, Hans, M. Cervellino, and E. Muñoz
1983   Viña del Cerro, expresión metalúrgica Inca en el valle de Copiapó.
         Creces 4: 32–35. Santiago.
Niemeyer, Hans, and Mario Rivera
1983   El camino del Inca en el despoblado de Atacama. *Boletín de Prehis-
         toria de Chile* 9: 91–193. Santiago: Departamento de Ciencias So-
         ciológicas y Antropológicas, Universidad de Chile.
Niemeyer, Hans, and Virgilio Schiappacasse
1981   Aportes al conocimiento del período tardío del extremo norte de
         Chile. *Chungará* 7: 3–103. Arica.
1988   Patrones de asentamiento incaicos en el Norte Grande de Chile. In
         Thomas D. Dillehay and Patricia J. Netherly, eds., *La frontera del
         estado inca*, pp. 141–179. B.A.R. International Series 442. Oxford:
         British Archaeological Reports.
Niemeyer, Hans, Virgilio Schiappacasse, and I. Solimano
1971   Padrones de poblamiento en la Quebrada de Camarones (Prov.
         Tarapacá). VI Congreso Arqueología Chilena. Santiago.
Niles, Susan A.
1982   Style and function in Inca agricultural works near Cuzco. *Ñawpa
         Pacha* 20: 163–182. Berkeley.
1984   Architectural form and social function in Inca towns near Cuzco.
         In Ann Kendall, ed., *Current archaeological projects in the Central
         Andes: Some approaches and results*, pp. 205–223. B.A.R. Interna-
         tional Series 210. Oxford: British Archaeological Reports.
1987   *Callachaca: Style and status in an Inca community.* Iowa City: Uni-
         versity of Iowa Press.
1988   Looking for "lost" Inca palaces. *Expedition* 30 (3): 56–64.
In press Moya place or yours? Inca private ownership of pleasant places.
         Ñawpa Pacha.
1991   Of land, love, and ladies: Property rights in Inca royal families.
         Paper prepared for the 31st annual meeting of the Institute of
         Andean Studies, Berkeley.

Ortíz de Zúñiga, Iñigo
1967   *Visita de la provincia de León de Huánuco en 1562.* Vol. 1. *Visita de los cuatro waranqa de los Chupachu.* Documentos para la historia y etnología de Huánuco y la selva central. Huánuco: Universidad Nacional Hermilio Valdizán.
1972   *Visita de la provincia de León de Huánuco en 1562.* Vol. 2. *Visita de los Yacha y mitmaqkuna cuzqueños encomendados en Juan Sanchez Falcon.* Documentos para la historia y etnología de Huánuco y la selva central. Huánuco: Universidad Nacional Hermilio Valdizán.
Pachacuti Yamqui Salcamaygua, Juan de Santa Cruz
1879   Relación de antigüedades deste reyno del Piru. In Don Marcos Jiménez de la Espada, ed., *Tres relaciones de antigüedades peruanas,* pp. 231–328. Madrid: Ministerio de Fomento.
1968   *Relación de antigüedades deste reyno del Perú* [early 17th century]. In Don Marcos Jiménez de la Espada, ed., *Relaciones Geográficas de Indias (Perú),* 209: 279–319. Biblioteca de Autores Españoles. Madrid: Ediciones Atlas.
Palomino Flores, Salvador
1971   La dualidad en la organización socio-cultural de algunos pueblos del área Andina. *Revisita del Museo Nacional* 37: 231–260. Lima.
Paulsen, Alison
1976   Environment and empire: Climatic factors in prehistoric Andean culture change. *World Archaeology* 8: 112–132.
Pease, Franklin
1976–77 Etnohistoria Andina: Un estado de la cuestión. *Historia y cultura* 10: 207–228. Lima: Museo Nacional de Historia.
1982   The formation of Tawantinsuyu: Mechanisms of colonization and relationships with ethnic groups. In George A. Collier, Renato I. Rosaldo, and John D. Wirth, eds., *The Inca and Aztec states, 1400–1800: Anthropology and history,* pp. 173–198. New York: Academic Press.
1986   La noción de propiedad entre los Incas: Una aproximación. *Etnografía y Historia del Mundo Andino: Continuidad y Cambio,* pp. 3–34. Tokyo: University of Tokyo Press.
Piazza, F.
1981   Análisis descriptivo de una aldea incaica en el sector de Pampa Alto Ramirez. *Chungará* 7: 172–210. Arica.
Pizarro, Pedro
1978   *Relación del descubrimiento y conquista del Perú* [1571]. Edition and preliminary considerations by Guillermo Lohmann Villena. Lima: Pontificia Universidad Católica del Perú.

1986   Relación del descubrimiento y conquista de los reinos del Peru [1571].
        2d ed. Edited by Guillermo Lohmann Villena. Lima: Pontificia
        Universidad Católica del Perú.
Polo de Ondegardo, Juan
1872   Relación acerca del linaje de los Incas y como conquistaron y
        acerca del notable daño que resulta de no guardar á estos indios
        sus fueros [1571]. In Colección de documentos inéditos, relativos al
        descubrimiento, conquista, y organización de las antiguas posesiones es-
        pañoles de América y Oceanía, edited by Luis Torres de Mendoza,
        17: 1–177. Madrid.
1916   Relación de los fundamentos acerca del notable daño que resulta
        de o guardar a los indios ses fueros, junio 26 de 1571. Colección
        de libros y documentos referentes a la historia del Perú, biographical
        notes and concordances of the texts by Horacio H. Urtega, 3:
        45–188. Lima.
1940   Informe del licenciado Juan Polo de Ondegardo al licenciado Bri-
        viesca de Munatones sobre le perpeuidad de las encomiedas en el
        Perú [1561]. Revista Histórica 13: 125–196. Lima.
Raffino, R.
1981   Los Inkas del Kollasuyo. La Plata, Argentina: Editorial Ramos
        Americana.
Ramos Gavilán, Alonso
1976   Historia de nuestra Señora de Copacabana [1621]. 2d ed. Academia
        Boliviana de la Historia. La Paz: Cámara Nacional de Comercio,
        Cámara Nacional de Industria.
1988   Historia de nuestra Señora de Copacabana [1621]. Transcription,
        editor's notes, and indices by Ignacio Pardo Pastor. Lima: Ignacio
        Pardo Pastor.
Reinhard, Johan
1983   Las montañas sagradas: Un estudio etnoarqueológico de ruinas
        en las altas cumbres andinas. Cuadernos de Historia 3: 27–62.
        Santiago: Departamento de Ciencias Históricas, Universidad de
        Chile.
1985   Sacred mountains: An ethnoarchaeological study of high Andean
        ruins. Mountain Research and Development 5 (4): 299–317.
Reinhard, Johan, and Julio Sanhueza T.
1982   Expedición arqueológica al altiplano de Tarapacá y sus cumbres.
        Revista de la Corporación para el Desarollo de la Ciencia 2 (2):
        17–42. Santiago.
Reinhard, Johan, and G. Serracino
1980   Ruinas arqueológicas sobre la cima del volcán Paniri. Revista
        CIADAM 4. San Juan.

Repartimiento de Tierras por el Inca Huayna Capac
1977 *Repartimiento de tierras por el Inca Huayna Capac. (Testimonio de un Documento de 1556.)* Departamento de Arqueología, Museo Arqueológico. Universidad Boliviana Mayor de San Simon. Cochabamba.

Rivera, Mario
1977 Prehistoric chronology of northern Chile. Ph.D. diss., Department of Anthropology, University of Wisconsin, Madison.
1983 Patrones prehistóricos y contemporáneos del uso de la tierra en el valle de Azapa. *Diálogo Andino* 2: 9–21. Arica: Universidad Tarapacá.
1985a Alto Ramirez y Tiwanaku, un caso de interpretación simbólica a través de datos arqueológicos en el area de los valles occidentales, sur del Perú y norte de Chile. *Diálogo Andino* 4: 39–58. Arica Universidad Tarapacá.
1985b Prospección arqueológica en el valle de Codpa y Chaca. Unpublished manuscript. Proyecto UTA, Arica.

Rivera, Mario, and John Hyslop
1984 Algunas estrategias para el estudio del camino del Inca en la región de Santiago, Chile. *Cuadernos de Historia* 4: 109–128. Departamento de Ciencias Históricas, Universidad de Chile. Santiago.

Rostworowski de Diez Canseco, Maria
1962 Nuevos datos sobre tenencia de tierras reales. *Revista del Museo Nacional* 21: 130–194. Lima.
1963 Dos manuscritos inéditos con datos sobre Manco II, tierras personales de los Incas y mitimaes. *Nueva Crónica* 1: 223–239. Departamento de Historia, Facultad de Letras, Universidad Nacional Mayor de San Marcos. Lima.
1969–70 Los Ayarmaca. *Revista del Museo Nacional* 36: 58–101. Lima.
1970 El repartimiento de doña Beatriz Coya, en el valle de Yucay. *Historia y Cultura* 4: 153–268. Lima: Museo Nacional de Historia.
1977 *Etnía y sociedad: Costa perúana prehispánica.* Lima: Instituto de Estudios Peruanos.
1981 *Recursos naturales, renovables, y pesca, siglos XVI y XVII.* Lima: Instituto de Estudios Peruanos.
1988 *Conflicts over coca fields in XVIth century Peru.* Memoirs of the Museum of Anthropology, University of Michigan 21. Ann Arbor.
1989 Ordenanzas para el servicio de los tambos del Repartimiento de Huamachuco hecho por el licenciado González de Cuenca. *Revista Historica* 36. Lima. Biblioteca Nacional, Madrid Ms. 3035. Ordenanzas de la Hacienda Real en Indias. ff. 340–343.

Rowe, John H.
1943 Sitios históricos en la región de Pucara, Puno. *Revista del Instituto*

Arqueológico 6, nos. 10–11, semestres I and II (1942): 66–75. Cuzco.

1944　An introduction to the archaeology of Cuzco. Papers of the Peabody Museum of American Archaeology and Ethnology, Harvard University, vol. 27, no. 2. Cambridge, Mass.: Peabody Museum.

1945　Absolute chronology in the Andean area. *American Antiquity* 10 (3): 265–284.

1946　Inca culture at the time of the Spanish conquest. In Julian H. Steward, ed., *Handbook of South American Indians*, 2: 183–330. Washington, D.C.: Bureau of American Ethnology Bulletin 143.

1967　What kind of a settlement was Inca Cuzco? *Ñawpa Pacha* 5: 59–76. Berkeley.

1979　An account of the shrines of ancient Cuzco. *Ñawpa Pacha* 17: 1–80. Berkeley.

1982　Inca policies and institutions relating to the cultural unification of the empire. In George A. Collier, Renato I. Rosaldo, and John D. Wirth, eds., *The Inca and Aztec states, 1400–1800: Anthropology and history*, pp. 93–118. New York: Academic Press.

1985a　La constitución inca del Cuzco. *Histórica* 9 (1): 35–73. Lima.

1985b　Probanza de los incas nietos de conquistadores. *Histórica* 9 (2): 193–245. Lima.

1987　Machu Pijchu a la luz de los documentos del siglo XVI. *Kuntur* 4 (marzo–abril): 12–20. Lima.

1990　Machu Picchu a la luz de documentos de siglo XVI. *Histórica* 14 (1): 139–154. Lima.

Rudecoff, Christine A.
1982　The Higueras-Huallaga archaeological survey. Paper submitted to Sigma Xi Scientific Research Society of North America.

Ruiz Estrada, Arturo
1973　Las ruinas de Sillustani. Ph.D. diss., Programa de Antropología, Universidad Nacional Mayor de San Marcos, Lima.

Ruppert, Hans
1984　Zur Verbreitung und Herkunft von Türkis und Sodalith in Präkolombischen Kulturen der Kordilleren. *Baessler-Archiv* (neue folge) 30: 69–124. Berlin.

Ryden, Stig
1947　*Archaeological researches in the highlands of Bolivia.* Goteborg, Sweden: Elanders Boktryckeri Aktiebolag.

Saignes, Thierry
1983　Quiénes son los Kallawaya? Nota sobre un enigma etnohistórico. *Revisita Andina* 1 (2): 357–384. Lima.

Salomon, Frank
1986   *Native lords of Quito in the age of the Incas.* New York: Cambridge University Press.
1987   A north Andean status trader complex under Inka rule. *Ethnohistory* 34 (1): 63–77.
1988   Frontera aborigen y dualismo Inca en el Ecuador prehispánico: pistas onomásticas. In Thomas D. Dillehay and Patricia J. Netherly, eds., *La frontera del estado inca,* pp. 59–85. B.A.R. International Series 442. Oxford: British Archaeological Reports.
Sandweiss, Daniel
1989   The fishermen of Chincha, Peru: An archaeological investigation of late prehispanic coastal specialization. Ph.D. diss., Department of Anthropology, Cornell University, Ithaca, N.Y.
Sanhueza, J.
1980   Revisión de un entierro incaico en la cordillera de la costa: Cerro Esmeralda. *Revisita CIADAM* 4: 9–12. San Juan.
San Pedro, Fray Juan de
1992 [1560]   Crónica Agustina de Huamachuco. In *La Persecución del Demonio: Crónica de los Primeros Agustinos en el Norte del Perú (1560).* Manuscrito del Archivo de Indias. Transcrito por Eric E. Deeds, Introducción por Teresa van Ronzelen, Estudios Preliminares por Luis Millones, John R. Topic, y José L. González. Algazara y C.A.M.E.I. Málaga y México.
Santoro, Calogero
1983   Camino del Inca en la sierra de Arica. *Chungará* 10: 47–55. Arica.
Santoro, Calogero, and I. Muñoz
1981   Patrón habitacional incaico en el área de Pampa Alto Ramírez. *Chungará* 10: 47–55. Arica.
Sarmiento de Gamboa, Pedro
1906   Geschichte des Inkareiches von Pedro Sarmiento de Gamboa [1572]. Edited by Richard Pietschmann. *Abhandlungen der Koniglichen Gesellschaft der Wissenschaften zu Gottlingen, Philologisch-Historische Klasse,* neue folge, band VI, no. 4. Weidmannsche Buchhandlung, Berlin.
1960   *Historia de los Incas* [1572]. In Don Marcos Jiménez de la Espada, ed., *Relaciones Geográficas de Indias (Perú),* 135: 195–279. Biblioteca de Autores Españoles. Madrid: Ediciones Atlas.
Sawyer, Alan
1981   Squier's "palace of Ollanta" revisited. *Ñawpa Pacha* 18 (1980): 63–72.

Schmidt, Max
1929   Kunst und Kultur von Peru. Berlin: Propyläen-Verlag.
Schreiber, Katharina J.
1984   Prehistoric roads in the Carahuarazo valley. In Ann Kendall, ed.,
       Current anthropological projects in the central Andes: Some approaches
       and results, pp. 75–94. B.A.R. International Series 210. Oxford:
       British Archaeological Reports.
1987   Conquest and consolidation: A comparison of the Wari and Inka
       occupations of a highland Peruvian valley. American Antiquity 52
       (2): 266–284.
1991   The association between roads and polities: Evidence for Wari
       roads in Peru. In Charles D. Trimbold, ed., Ancient Road Networks
       and Settlement Hierarchies in the New World, pp. 243–252. Cam-
       bridge: Cambridge University Press.
1992   Wari imperialism in Middle Horizon Peru. Anthropological Papers
       No. 87, Museum of Anthropology, University of Michigan. Ann
       Arbor.
Shimada, Izumi
1985   Introduction. In Shozo Masuda, Izumi Shimada, and Craig Morris,
       eds., Andean ecology and civilization: An interdisciplinary perspective
       on Andean ecological complementarity, pp. xi–xxxii. Tokyo: Univer-
       sity of Tokyo Press.
Silva Galdames, Osvaldo
1977   Consideraciones acerca del período inca en la cuenca de Santiago
       (Chile Central). Boletín del Museo Arqueológico 16: 211–243. La
       Serena.
1983   Detuvo la batalla del Maule la expansión Inca hacia el Sur de
       Chile? Cuadernos de Historia 3: 7–25. Santiago.
1985a Informe de avance de las investigaciones en el centro ceremonial
       de Cerro Verde (Talikuna 4), provincia El Loa. Unpublished manu-
       script. Universidad de Chile.
1985b La expansión incaica en Chile: problemas y reflexiones. IX Con-
       greso Arqueología Chilena 1: 320–344. La Serena.
Silverblatt, Irene
1987   Moon, sun, and witches: Gender ideologies and class in Inca and colo-
       nial Peru. Princeton: Princeton University Press.
Smith, Raymond T., ed.
1984   Kinship, ideology, and practice in Latin America. Chapel Hill: Univer-
       sity of North Carolina Press.
Squier, E. George
1877   Peru: Incidents of travel and exploration in the land of the Incas. New
       York: Henry Holt.

Stanish, Charles
1992 *Ancient Andean political economy.* Austin: University of Texas Press.
Stark, Barbara L.
1985 Archaeological identification of pottery production locations: Ethnoarchaeological and archaeological data in Mesoamerica. In Ben A. Nelson, ed., *Decoding Prehistoric Ceramics*, pp. 158–194. Carbondale and Edwardsville: Southern Illinois University Press.
Stehberg, Rubén, and Nazareno Carvajal
1988a Red vial incaica en los términos meridionales del imperio: Tramo valle del Limar—valle del Maipo. In Thomas Dillehay and Patricia Netherly, eds., *La frontera del estado inca*, pp. 181–214, B.A.R. International Series 442. Oxford: British Archaeological Reports.
1988b Road system of the Incas in the southern part of their Tawantinsuyu empire. *National Geographic Research* 4 (1): 74–97. Washington, D.C.: National Geographic Society.
Thatcher, John P.
1972 Continuity and change in the ceramics of Huamachuco, north highlands, Peru. Ph.D. diss., Department of Anthropology, University of Pennsylvania, Philadelphia.
Thompson, Donald E.
1967 Investigaciones arqueológicos en las aldeas Chupachu de Ichu y Auquimarca. In Iñigo Ortíz de Zúñiga, *Visita de la provincia de León de Huánuco en 1562*, 1: 359–362. Huánuco: Universidad Nacional Hermilio Valdizán.
1972 Peasant Inca villages in the Huánuco region. *Verhandlugen des XXXVIII Internationales Amerikanistenkongresses* (1968) 4: 61–66. Stuttgart–München.
Thompson, Donald E., and John V. Murra
1966 Puentes incaicos en la región de Huánuco Pampa. *Cuadernos de Investigacion, Antropología*, no. 1: 79–94. Huánuco: Universidad National Hermilio Valdizán.
Thompson, L. G., E. Mosley-Thompson, J. F. Bolzan, and B. R. Koci
1985 A 1500-year record of tropical precipitation in ice cores from the Quelccaya ice cap, Peru. *Science* 229: 971–973.
Tierras de Sorama
1985 Expediente sobre las tierras de la quebrada de Sorama [1672]. Corregimiento. Causas Ordinarias. Legajo 18, 1671–73. Unpublished manuscript. Partial transcription by John H. Rowe. Archivo Departamental de Cuzco.
Topic, John R., and Coreen E. Chiswell
1992 Inka storage in Huamachuco. In Terry Y. Le Vine, ed., *Inka storage systems*, pp. 206–233. Norman: University of Oklahoma Press.

Topic, Theresa Lange, and John R. Topic
  1987   Huamachuco Archaeological Project: Preliminary report on the
         1986 field season. *Trent University Occasional Papers in Anthropol-
         ogy*, no. 4. Peterborough, Ontario.
Trimborn, Hermann
  1923–25   Der Kollektivismus der Inkas in Peru. *Anthropos* 18–19: 978–
            1001; 20: 579–606.
Troll, Carl
  1968   *Geo-ecology of the mountainous regions of the tropical Americas.* Bonn:
         Ferd. Dummler Verlag.
Tschopik, Marion H.
  1946   *Some notes on the archaeology of the Department of Puno, Peru.* Pa-
         pers of the Peabody Museum of American Archaeology and Eth-
         nology, Harvard University, vol. 27, no. 3. Cambridge, Mass.:
         Peabody Museum.
  N.d.   Unpublished field notes from the excavations of Inca Uyu.
Uhle, Max
  1900   Letter to Phoebe Hearst (July 17). Typewritten transcript in Uhle
         Catalogue, vol. 5, pp. 98–142. Lowie Museum, University of Cali-
         fornia, Berkeley.
  1923   *Las ruinas de Tumebamba.* Quito: Imprenta Julio Saenz Rebollendo.
  1924   Explorations at Chincha. *University of California Publications in Ar-
         chaeology and Ethnology* 21 (2): 55–94.
Ulloa, Luis
  1909   Visita general de los yndios del Cuzco, Año de 1571. *Revista Histó-
         rica* 13: 332–347. Lima.
Ulloa Mogollón, Juan de
  1965   Relación de la provincia de los Collaguas [1586]. In Don Marcos
         Jiménez de la Espada, ed., *Relaciones Geográficas de Indias (Perú)*,
         183: 326–333. Biblioteca de Autores Españoles. Madrid: Edi-
         ciones Atlas.
Vaca de Castro, Cristóbal
  1908   Ordenanzas de tambos, distancias de unos a otros, modo de cargar
         los indios y obligaciones de las justicias respectivas hechas en la
         ciudad del Cuzco en 31 de Mayo de 1543. *Revista Histórica* 3:
         427–492. Lima: Instituto Histórico del Perú.
Valcárcel, L.
  1934–35   Sajsawaman redescubierto (3 parts). *Revista del Museo Nacional*
            2(1): 3–36; 2(2): 211–240; 4(1): 5–24.
  1935   Los trabajos arqueológicos en el Departamento de Cuzco. *Revista
         del Museo Nacional* 4(2): 163–208. Lima.
Vansina, Jan
  1985   *Oral tradition as history.* Madison: University of Wisconsin Press.

Vázquez de Espinosa, Antonio
1948   Compendio y descripción de las indias occidentales [c. 1629].
        Smithsonian Miscellaneous Collections, vol. 108. Washington, D.C.:
        Smithsonian Institution.
Villanueva Urteaga, Horacio
1971a   Documentos sobre Yucay, siglo XVI. *Revista del Archivo Histórico
        del Cuzco* 13 (1970): 1–148. Cuzco.
1971b   Información ad perpetuam dada en 13 de enero de 1567 ante la
        real justicia de la ciudad del Cuzco. Reino del Perú, a pedimento
        de la muy ilustre señora Doña Maria Manrique Coya, vecina de
        dicha ciudad. *Revista del Archivo Histórico del Cuzco* 13 (1970):
        149–184. Cuzco.
Villanueva Urteaga, Horacio, and Jeanette Sherbondy
1979   *Cuzco: Aguas y poder*. Archivos de Historia Rural Andina 1. Cuzco:
        Centro de Estudios Rurales Andinos "Bartolomé de las Casas."
Vivar, Jerónimo de
1966   *Crónica y relación copiosa y verdadera de los reinos de Chile* [1558].
        Paleographic transcription by Irving A. Leonard. Santiago: Fondo
        Histórico y Bibliográfico José Toribio Medina.
1988   Crónica de los reinos de Chile [1558]. Edition by Angel Barral
        Gomez. *Historia* 16. Madrid.
von Hagen, Victor W., ed.
1959   *The Incas of Pedro de Cieza de León* [1550–1553]. Translated by
        Harriet de Onis. Norman: University of Oklahoma Press.
Wachtel, Nathan
1981   Les *mitimas* de la vallée de Cochabamba: La Politique de colonisa-
        tion de Huayna Capac. *Journal de la Société des Américanistes* 66
        (1980–81): 297–324. Paris.
1982   The *mitimas* of the Cochabamba Valley: The colonization policy of
        Huayna Capac. In George A. Collier, Renato I. Rosaldo, and
        John D. Wirth, eds., *The Inca and Aztec states, 1400–1800: Anthro-
        pology and history*, pp. 199–235. New York: Academic Press.
Watson, Patty Jo, Steven LeBlanc, and Charles Redman
1971   *Explanation in archaeology: An explicitly scientific approach*. New
        York: Columbia University Press.
Weber, David J.
1983   A grammar of Huallaga (Huánuco) Quechua. Ph.D. diss., Depart-
        ment of Anthropology, University of California, Los Angeles.
Wiener, Charles
1880   *Perou et Bolivie: Recit de voyage*. Paris: Hachette.
Xérez, Francisco de
1917   Verdadera relación de la conquista del Perú y provincia de Cuzco
        llamada la Nueva-Castilla. In H. H. Urteaga and C. A. Romero,

eds., *Colección de libros y documentos referentes a la historia del Perú*, 1st ser., 5: 1–121.

Zuidema, R. Tom

1964   *The ceque system of Cuzco: The social organization of the capital of the Inca.* International Archives of Ethnography. Supplement to vol. 50. Leiden: E. J. Brill.

1990   *Inca civilization in Cuzco.* Austin: University of Texas Press.

INDEX

Albornoz, Cristóbal de, 39
Andamarca Lucanas. *See* Province, Andamarca Lucanas
Altiplano. *See* Lake Titicaca region
Archaeology, 2–5, 8, 11–12, 17, 130, 177–181, 187, 199, 223, 225, 227–230, 234–236, 244; Andamarca Lucanas, 77–78, 80, 87, 91–112, 115–116; Chile, 218; Chupachos, *see* Province, Chupachos; Cuzco, 4, 8; Huamachuco, 18, 30, 40–41, 214; Huánuco, 44–45, 47, 53–60, 64, 66–67, 69–75, 210–211; Lake Titicaca region, 4, 190–199; limitations of, 8–9; Upper Mantaro, 4. *See also* Inca, archaeology
Architecture, domestic, 55–60, 92, 102, 216, 237; Late Horizon, 34–36, 45, 47, 54, 55–62, 65–66, 68–69, 71, 74, 91–92, 237. *See also* Inca, architecture
Atahuallpa, 19, 102, 150, 163
Ayllu, 86, 90–91

Betanzos, Juan de, 19, 30, 146, 150–151, 159, 175, 200, 219–220

Cabello Balboa, Miguel, 31, 146, 150
Carhuarazo Valley. *See* Province, Andamarca Lucanas
Catarpe, 7, 117–134, 237–238
Ceramics, Andamarca Lucanas sequence, 80–82; *aryballos*, 10, 16, 25, 34–35, 45, 60, 133, 191, 196, 236–237; Huamachuco sequence, 41–42, 237; Killke, 196; Lake Titicaca region, 190–198; Late Horizon, 17, 33–36, 42, 54, 58, 60–63, 66, 68–71, 74, 77, 91, 101, 237;

Late Intermediate Period, 17, 33, 42, 47, 80; Middle Horizon, 42; pastes, 17, 33–37, 58, 60, 237; Tiahuanaco, 195–196, 232–233. *See also* Inca, ceramics
Chaupi yunga, 17, 22, 32, 38, 40, 43, 212, 235
Chile. *See* Province, Chile
Chucuito, 4–5
Chullpas, 103, 107, 194
Chupachos. *See* Province, Chupachos
Chupachu, x, 49–51, 53–56, 58–62, 64–75, 209–210
Cieza de León, Pedro, 3, 5, 18, 84, 178, 186, 202, 204–205, 213–214, 225, 232
Cobo, Bernabe, 3, 85–86, 97, 146, 150, 184, 243
Colcas. *See* Inca
Copacabana, 186, 188, 196–197, 224, 233
Corregimiento, 181–182, 199, 204, 211–212, 215, 218–220, 224
Cuzco, 4, 8–9, 51, 53–54, 60–61, 97, 149–151, 153–155, 157, 159, 166, 169, 171–172, 184, 186–189, 192, 194, 200, 209, 213, 219–222, 225, 232–233, 238. *See also* Province, Cuzco

D'Altroy, Terence, 3–4

Encomienda, 186, 199, 201–202, 204, 207–208, 211–212, 222, 231–233
Espinoza Soriano, Waldemar, 19, 36–38, 42
Estete, Miguel de, 18, 31–32
Ethnohistory, 2–8, 11–12, 17, 177–178, 180, 188, 198, 200, 210, 215, 223, 225, 228, 234–236, 242,

Ethnohistory, *continued*
244; Altiplano, 4; Andamarca Lucanas, 7, 77–78, 82–87, 91,
111–112, 114, 116, 199–203;
Chile, 117, 215–219; Chupachos,
4–5, 203–211, 227; Cuzco, 146,
154–155, 161, 219–223; Huamachuco, 7, 18–22, 30, 37, 40–41,
211–215; Huánuco, (*see also* Chupachos), 44, 47–55, 60, 66, 70–
72, 74–75; Huánuco Pampa, 204;
Lake Titicaca region, 181–190,
197; limitations of, 6–7, 178–179,
181, 204, 218–219. *See also* Inca,
ethnohistory

Garcilaso de la Vega, Inca, 19, 40
González de Cuenca *Ordenanza*, 19,
32, 36–39, 42–43
Guaman Poma de Ayala, Felipe, 3, 19,
31–32, 86, 89–90, 166, 221,
223–224

Hatuncolla, 154, 190, 225
Huacas. See Inca, *huacas*
Huamachuco. *See* Province,
Huamachuco
Huánuco. *See* Province, Chupachos
Huánuco Pampa, 10, 12, 40, 47, 51,
54–55, 58, 60–62, 71, 108, 154,
169, 204, 213–215, 222,
225–226, 233, 237, 243
Huarangas. See Inca, *huarangas*
Huascar, 14, 147, 150, 157, 163–164,
166, 171, 209–210
Huayna Capac, 19, 149–151, 153,
157, 159, 161, 168–171, 175,
184–185, 187–188, 200, 205,
210, 213, 216–217, 237–238
Hyslop, John, 5, 10–11, 30, 126, 128,
130–131, 133–135, 155

Inca, agricultural systems, 11, 114; archaeology, 2–4, 236; architecture,
9–12, 25, 44, 54–56, 58–63,
72–75, 92–112, 117–118,
126–128, 131–137, 145–146,
154–155, 157, 159, 161, 163, 166,
168, 170–173, 176, 219, 222–
223, 227, 236–238, 242–243;
bridges, 11, 82, 112, 115, 200, 227;
camayos, 205–206, 210, 215,
229–230, 237; centers, 22–24, 33,
44, 47–48, 75, 90–91, 108, 114,
116–118, 122, 127–129, 163,
169, 172–174, 182, 187–189,
199–200, 204, 208, 211, 213–
218, 221–222, 224–227, 230,
238–243; ceramics, 9–12, 17,
24–25, 33–36, 54–55, 58–62,
71–75, 77, 82, 91, 111, 117–118,
133, 135, 137, 190–198, 222, 226,
228–229, 236–237, ceramic production, 189, 191, 194, 198, 203,
205–206, 211, 213, 229–230;
chasquihuasis, 121, 127, 130, 133,
136; cloth, 115–116, 207, 212,
219–220; *colcas*, 24, 26–27, 30,
62, 77, 104–110, 114–115, 136,
215, 236, 238; control, 8, 17, 11,
38, 44–45, 47, 51–54, 60, 64,
69–70, 72–75, 77, 114–115, 129,
152, 179, 198, 202–204, 213, 215,
226–229, 235, 237, 239–240,
242, 244; decimal system, 44,
49–50, 71, 188, 205–206;
economy, 3–4, 40, 149, 154, 184,
187, 202, 206–207, 211, 214,
218–220, 225–226, 230–231,
240–242; estates, 145–147,
149–155, 157, 159, 161, 163–
164, 166, 168–170, 172–173,
176, 184–186, 190, 198–199,
209, 220–222, 226–227, 233; ethnohistory, 2–5; *hanan*, 131, 169;
houses, 9, 45, 166, 168–169; *huacas*, 39, 97, 222; *huarangas*, 19,
40, 44, 50–55, 60–61, 69, 71–73,
75, 185, 203, 205, 207–210,
212–213, 215, 224; *hurin*, 131–
132, 169; *kallankas*, ix, 9–11, 25,
126, 131–132, 214; *kanchas*, ix,

9–11, 126–128, 130–131, 135, 168–169, 237–238; material culture, 3, 8–11, 45, 58, 64, 74, 188, 215, 236; *mitimas*, 17, 19, 22, 34, 36–40, 42–43, 53, 55–56, 60–61, 69, 72–73, 75, 77, 87, 90–91, 111, 114–116, 152–153, 170–171, 184–187, 204–205, 207, 210–213, 215, 224, 228–229, 231, 236, 239, 241–242; mummies, 149, 153–154, 175; niches, 9, 54, 61, 94–97, 105, 161, 237; *pachacas*, 50–51, 56, 205, 209, 213, 238; plazas, 24–25, 36, 126, 130–131, 137, 188, 200, 205, 214, 238; prestige categories, 146, 155, 172–174, 243; provincial boundaries, 181–182, 184, 186–189, 199, 201, 204, 207–208, 220, 223–224; religion, 3, 149–150, 175, 188–189, 218; retreats (or hunting lodges), 102, 113, 116, 161, 168; roads, 5, 7, 11, 17, 19, 24, 30–32, 36, 38, 40, 52, 77, 88, 91, 102, 104, 109, 111, 113–119, 123, 127, 130–131, 134, 136, 138, 140, 146, 179, 191, 200–203, 215, 218, 226–227, 232, 236, 238–241; settlement planning, 5, 9–10, 130–131, 133, 135–136, 154, 164, 166, 168–169, 236; shrines (or sanctuaries), 52, 97, 101–102, 113, 126, 136, 163, 175, 186, 188, 190, 197–198, 224, 226–227; sociopolitical structure, 3, 51–52, 54–55, 64, 71, 74, 87–88, 113, 150, 154, 182, 184, 188–189, 200, 205, 210–213, 217, 221–222, 225, 227, 229, 235, 238, 240–242; *tambos*, 7, 17–19, 31–34, 36, 48, 52, 77, 82, 88, 102, 104, 108, 114, 116–119, 122, 127–128, 130–131, 133–138, 168, 182, 200, 206, 208, 214–215, 218, 227, 231, 239; terraces, 11, 26, 40, 56, 104, 106–111, 114, 116, 146, 149, 161,

203, 227, 235–236, 239; *yanaconas*, 77, 88, 114, 149, 152, 168–169, 185, 209–210
Island of Titicaca, 170–171, 191, 196, 198

Kendall, Ann, 4, 155

Lake Titicaca region, 1, 3–4, 179–180, 182, 185–187, 189, 197–198, 209, 218, 224, 227, 233. *See also* Archaeology, Lake Titicaca region; Ethnohistory, Lake Titicaca region; Province, Lake Titicaca region; Island of Titicaca
Late Horizon, sites, 32–35, 45, 55–56, 61–62, 65–68, 80. *See also* Architecture, Late Horizon; Ceramics, Late Horizon; Inca
Late Intermediate Period, sites, 32–33, 35, 40–41, 55, 73, 80. *See also* Architecture

Marcahuamachuco, 22, 31, 35–36, 40–41
McCown, Theodore D., 18, 23–25
Menzel, Dorothy, 3, 171, 229
Mitimas. See Inca, *mitimas*
Monzón, Luis de, 86, 89
Murra, John, 3, 49, 51, 55, 72, 115
Murúa, Martin de, 146, 150

Netherly, Patricia, 4, 38
Niemeyer, Hans, 122, 126, 128, 135
Niles, Susan, 4, 175

Orden sobre el servicio de los tambos del Repartimiento de Guamachuco. See González de Cuenca *Ordenanza*
Ortíz de Zúñiga, Iñigo, 49, 51, 53, 55, 70, 72–74

Pachacas. See Inca, *pachacas*
Pachacuti, 150–151, 155, 157, 159, 163, 171, 198, 200, 219–221, 237, 242–243

Polo de Ondegardo, Juan, 3, 223
Pottery. See Ceramics; Inca, ceramics
Province, 7, 8, 9, 12; Andamarca Lucanas, Ch. 4, 7, 199–203, 226–
227, 237, 239, 240, 242–243;
Chile, Ch. 5, 215–219, 239–240;
Chupachos, Ch. 3, x, 4–5, 7, 12,
203–211, 224, 226–227, 230–
231, 233, 235, 237–243; Cuzco,
Ch. 6, 219–223, 243 (see also
Cuzco); Huamachuco, Ch. 2,
211–215, 227, 229, 237, 240–
243; Huamachuco, provincial capital
of, 22–26, 40; Lake Titicaca region,
181–199, 237–238, 242; Vilcashuamán, see Andamarca Lucanas.
See also Archaeology; Ethnohistory

Quero, 49–50, 53–56, 58, 60–61,
64–69, 71, 73–74, 209–210

Reducción, 31, 36–37, 42, 86, 101,
113, 199, 212, 215, 232
Roads, pre-Inca, 30–31, 40, 111, 140,
202, 241. See also Inca, roads
Rostworowski de Diez Canseco, Maria,
4, 19, 175
Rowe, John H., 3–6, 8–9

San Pedro, Juan de, 19, 39
Sarmiento de Gamboa, Pedro, 5, 146,
150, 213, 217, 220–221
Schiappacasse, Virgilio, 122, 126
Shrines, 31, 35. See also Inca, shrines

Tahuantinsuyo, 1, 5, 152, 244
Tambos. See Inca, tambos
Thatcher, John P., 18, 23, 41–42
Thompson, Donald E., 44, 55
Tiahuanaco, 157, 186, 195–196, 198,
232–233
Topa Inca, 149, 151–152, 157, 166,
168–171, 184, 198, 205, 209, 213,
216–217, 221–222, 232–233,
238, 243
Tschopik, Marion H., 3, 191, 194

Uhle, Max, 18, 22, 25

Vázquez de Espinoza, Antonio, 202
Vilcashuamán, 86, 90, 111, 188,
200–204, 213, 219, 221, 225, 243.
See also Province, Andamarca
Lucanas
Viracocha, 147, 155, 157
Viracochapampa, 22, 33
Visitas, 4–5, 47, 49, 52–55, 61, 65,
69, 71, 74, 182, 205, 224

Wamali, 49, 65–67

Yacha, 49, 53–54, 65–66, 68–69,
209–210
Yaros, 49, 65–66, 68, 206–208, 224

Zuidema, R. Thomas, 3, 174